DIGITAL
ABORIGINAL

DIGITAL
ABORIGINAL

THE
DIRECTION OF
BUSINESS NOW:
INSTINCTIVE,
NOMADIC, AND
EVER-CHANGING

MIKELA TARLOW
WITH
PHILIP TARLOW

WARNER BOOKS

An AOL Time Warner Company

WARNER BOOKS, INC., 1271 AVENUE OF THE AMERICAS, NEW YORK, NY 10020

VISIT OUR WEB SITE AT WWW.TWBOOKMARK.COM.

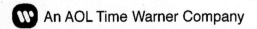 An AOL Time Warner Company

PRINTED IN THE UNITED STATES OF AMERICA

FIRST PRINTING: APRIL 2002

10 9 8 7 6 5 4 3 2 1

LIBRARY OF CONGRESS CATALOGING-IN-PUBLICATION DATA
Tarlow, Mikela.
    Digital aboriginal / the direction of business now: instinctive, nomadic, and
    ever-changing / Mikela Tarlow with Philip Tarlow
    p.cm
    ISBN 0-446-52825-0
    1. Industrial management--Data processing. 2. Technological
innovation--Management. I. Tarlow, Philip. II. Title.

HD30.2 .T37 2002
658.5'14--dc21

                                                    200104660

Book Design by Mada Design, Inc./NYC

CONTENTS

The first half of each chapter offers a discussion of the topic. The second half focuses on application and how to take these ideas into practice.

In the beginning was the One.
The One became two.
The two became ten thousand things.

Ten thousand things became two,
the whole world represented in binary
form by zeros and ones.

Binary landscapes will once again connect
us to all things, linking us through time
and space to one another.

Thus two will once again become one.

PREFACE

We are witnessing the birth of a new generation, described not so much by their age, as by their actions in the world. They are using the freedoms of the new economy to develop a set of behavioral strategies: Digital Aboriginal.

This new generation is driven, yet they rarely plan. They function equally well in the accelerated Net time of the high-tech world and in the empty spaces that tend to provoke synchronicities. Although brilliant strategists, they often chart their courses based on pure instinct. They are highly individualized, yet depend on deeply tribal ways of birthing ideas. In the guise of looking for killer applications and the next technical edge, they are leading a revolution. They are operating from clear and coherent models of success and leadership, which are the heart of this book.

They are forging new business scenarios based on their insatiable creative spirit. They are driving new values in the workplace from their relentless commitment to reshape the future with greater meaning.

These emerging behaviors are changing the shape of business as much or more than all the underlying technology that triggered them. So much focus is placed on the technical side of the equation, it is easy to lose sight of the fact that it is people who are driving the future of business.

In the current economy there is almost no lag time between a dream and its implementation, a purchase and its fulfillment, a change in the market and a corresponding response. At first this kind of acceleration feels like a need to move faster and integrate unfathomable amounts of information. But once you are doing business at the speed of thought, it no longer feels like speed. It describes a new dimension, rather than a response time. It's a new domain of knowledge, not just a faster version of what already exists. Radical acceleration frees you to track information in a far different way.

I will gradually introduce a broad cast of characters from a wide variety of occupational fields who are actively using strategies that often fall outside the familiar habits of highly effective people. In fact, they are going against the well-known dictums we've been told are critical for success. They don't begin with the end in mind; instead, they actively deconstruct any preconceptions of how things should unfold. Rather than set priorities, they will deliberately destabilize their surroundings so new directions can peek through. They've gone way past blurring the lines between home and work; they are blurring the lines between almost everything. They don't just think outside the box; it's their permanent address.

Of course, this has always been the way of adventurers, pioneers and revolutionaries. Great leaders never let the rules stop them; this is how they are wired. But what is most startling about our current conditions is that now we all have to operate this way, merely to survive. When I speak about this new breed of digital aboriginals who are changing the face of business, *I am talking about you.* I am talking about a set of behaviors that have already begun to bubble up in your own psyche. My hope is that making these emergent faculties more explicit will accelerate your journey into this far more creative, dynamic way of living and working.

I tell this story not as an expert on the technical side of what lies ahead. I write from the perspective of an anthropologist observing one of the most dramatic shifts in the organization of our social universe that has ever occurred. I write from the vantage point of someone striving to understand the creative and emotional challenges being triggered by this new economic world. But precisely because of my outsider perspective, my words should evoke some fresh ideas for doing business and charting your career in this radical new environment. I offer a road map for the evolutionary challenges we are all about to encounter.

IN THE BEGINNING

My own experience with these ideas began almost a decade ago through a very personal and quite unexpected experience at the Museum of Modern Art in New York City.

I have always loved indigenous art. Whenever I visit a museum, normally I head straight for this section. It never ceases to amaze me how this ancient work holds up under the test of time. It stays fresh and strikingly contemporary despite the fact that these relics may be tens of thousands of years old. Great artists like Picasso have even copied motifs from ancient masks and passed them off as their own, clearly recognizing how edgy these primal images could be.

Of all the indigenous art I know, I particularly love the Australian aboriginal paintings of songlines. Their seemingly random dots and wavy lines do not represent anything you've ever seen, and yet somehow they seem strangely familiar. These unusual patterns were first drawn in sand, long before they became more permanent images. A particular wavy abstract pattern may represent an emu, a large native Australian bird, walking to a watering hole. Other seemingly unintelligible rhythms of dots and lines may reveal the path the tribe would take to a nearby hill.

The images are not literal, yet they stir some deep primal memory and make sense even though you don't exactly know why. Like a dream you just barely recall—you know what the images mean, even if you can't quite explain them. They convey a familiarity that is hard to place.

For years I tried to imagine the extraordinary visual experience that would trigger such unique pictographs. I would envision what it might be like to live nomadically, crossing new terrain every day. *With no theories in my head and no plans for tomorrow, maybe I too would be able to look out on the world and no longer see such fixed images.*

But what did these early inhabitants really see when they looked out on the vast landscape they called their home? Did they truly perceive information differently? Or were their brains just wired differently, so data was processed in patterns now unfamiliar to the Western mind. Why did they translate the very same physical objects that you and I see as solid into what appear as pure radiating fields of energy?

Then one day, I walked into the Museum of Modern Art and turned to the right where the new shows are often hung. There in front of me were six to eight large canvases replicating the patterns of computer boards. The brightly contrasting colors and channels of the circuits wove beautiful and dramatic patterns. They were abstract and yet the designs were purposeful. Although they were presented as works of art, these patterns allowed real events to take place.

In a sudden flash of recognition, I realized I had seen images like these in only one other place— *the aboriginal songlines.* The channels of these circuit boards were not unlike the wavy abstract lines that these ancient visionaries might have used to indicate a watering hole. The stark colors of both the songlines and the circuits were curiously comparable; both defied the gentle gradations one sees in most art. Both images were at once abstract and yet clearly representational of how energy and matter might interact.

It was in that exact moment that the phrase *digital aboriginal* first entered my mind. An avalanche of thoughts spilled over me that became the conception of this book. Many years before I ever committed to put words on paper, I began to contemplate this marriage of the ancient and the new. I found the juxtaposition of these two echoing and parallel realities, joined just outside of space and time, endlessly provocative.

> *How could these ancient people have articulated patterns that would stretch through countless generations and forge their way straight into our present moment?*
>
> *Why would the most cutting edge of modern technology rest on visual images that were first drawn at the dawn of human history?*

This could not be an accident. Obviously these ancient observers sensed a picture of reality so profound and advanced that we have only just recently arrived at their doorstep.

A TIMELESS DAWN AND YOU ARE THERE

The aborigines' strikingly prescient view of the world says that all things are connected. Every relationship influences every other relationship. You cannot separate one event from any other; they can exist only as a continuum.

Further, the *within-ness* of all things is connected. This allows information from everywhere to freely flow between any two points, building a fabric of connectedness that can be accessed from anywhere.

Every time a layer of appearance is taken away, a deeper order lies beneath. What may at first appear as solid inevitably turns toward the invisible. Matter irresistibly turns to energy. If you look beneath that which seems stable, you will always find the intangible peeking through.

Thus, reality is not a fixed proposition. It is fluid and moving, continually shaped by the beliefs you have about it. We ourselves organize this unbounded field of possibility into the shapes we desire and can reorganize everything once again merely by shifting our beliefs.

Now try reading through the above description once again and it could just as easily be a description of the new economy. The same principles apply.

As I began a deeper investigation into this ancient mirror of our ultra-high-tech world, I realized that these aboriginal paintings also echoed the appearance of mathematically generated fractals, the underlying equations that seem to describe the growth of all living forms. They were also reminiscent of photos I had seen of subatomic elements racing through a particle accelerator. On film, these particles leave only a spray of patterns to suggest their illusive, indeterminate shape.

Modern science, as well as many leading thinkers in the social sciences, is beginning to look to far more indeterminate and holographic models of reality to explain how systems are organized. Obviously, these early observers looked beyond the world of appearances to see a more profound order that lies enfolded within our obvious reality. They saw how physical matter conducts energy in the same way a microchip conducts bits of information. *Without benefit of advanced electronic microscopes or complex mathematical formulas, these ancient observers saw through the veil of matter.*

The new economy is leading all of us to look out and experience the very same view of reality that these early observers saw. You don't have to read a book to get it. Just participating in popular culture or having to adapt to the crazy new rules of *business unusual* provokes very similar realizations to those of the ancient shamans, cutting-edge scientific theorists and emerging digital mystics. It is not a conceptual realization; it is a lived experience that gets triggered merely by becoming involved in this new terrain. You don't have to learn how to *think different:* you do it because the sensory experience of the electronic world naturally provokes it.

You innocently download your e-mail, look in on your company's Intranet, participate in an on-line chat, research some information and suddenly your nervous system is no longer the same. Merely by touching the electronic world, you have entered into a universe that your ordinary mind may not have even considered, and the traces of this contact cannot be erased.

You probably did not have e-mail until well after 1993. Even cell phones weren't widespread until just about that time. Yet it probably feels like you've always lived this way. This is because you have effortlessly slipped into Net time, where one year now feels like seven.

Our passion for heightened connectivity and faster response has led all of us to a place where our rational ways of defining the world are now insufficient. Without skipping a beat, we have already begun to speak the language of intangible forces. Once familiar business models are collapsing in on themselves, and in their places far more dynamic, nonlinear ways of knowing are naturally emerging. Street heat is making every organization boil, forcing all of us to deconstruct our notions of what is really important. And merely because we have begun to play around in this emerging electronic universe, whether we consciously realize it or not, we are also looking out at the very same timeless, fluid, morphing world that was first seen at the dawn of human history.

This is why I have turned my eyes to the aboriginal world. The very same skills that they used to negotiate their magical, networked, multidimensional world are what we now need to negotiate ours. We may have the theories, but these ancient nomads had the behaviors worked out.

SHEDDING AN OLD SKIN

Although we are all beginning to use far more instinctual paths for doing business, we are still dwellers between two worlds. We are still saddled with antiquated conceptual images of what drives success that we have not entirely let go, mostly because we are not clear what will stand in its place. We have not yet been given a new language to replace the one we now speak.

For example, developing a mission statement is extremely useful in a stable environment, but has far less relevance in an industry where the rug is being pulled out from under you. Business plans are great for focusing your thoughts, but they don't prepare you for the random events that are far more likely to shape what lies ahead. Normal commission structures were once considered motivating. Now many find that they cause people to focus on short-term goals and neglect the deeper client relationships that are so necessary in this new economic climate. *Actions that made sense even ten years ago are often shortsighted in today's supercharged atmosphere.*

Much of the standard business literature still relies on the idea that we need to define our goals, set priorities, develop our strategies, manage the outcomes and evaluate our impacts. I can assure you that if you operate in this way, someone has already beaten you to the finish line. *You cannot plan fast enough.* We need behaviors that are far more bold and attuned to the unique nature of our time.

In the pages ahead, you will discover that the new economy requires a body of knowledge that I have likened to the aboriginal way. It is more instinctual, collaborative and intimately resonant with the surrounding environment. As I describe these new laws of success, I am not suggesting something you need to study and learn.

- These are behaviors you are probably already using, but perhaps did not realize.
- These are skills you value, but perhaps have kept hidden in the closet because the standard literature on success had not yet certified these choices as socially acceptable.
- You will discover leadership strategies that build on intrinsic abilities that you have perhaps dismissed as trivial, because they came to you so naturally.

- You will discover paths for creativity that you have probably used frequently, but because they were so effortless, you did not appreciate their true power and significance.

You will discover a series of cognitive and behavioral maps for organizing these emergent capacities into practical paths for solving real-life business challenges. Merely having new language for what you are naturally beginning to do anyway will accelerate your creative process and provoke heightened acts of courage.

As usual, pop culture is well ahead of mainstream business theory when it comes to understanding the new rules of the game.

In the hit movie The Matrix, *the two heroes, dressed in black, are suddenly transported onto a stark white screen. Neo, in the role of the student, has just gone through a mind-altering experience that has erased his memories of reality. Because he chose the red pill and the path of courage, his past and everything he believes has just been shattered.*

Against the backdrop of this dazzling white ground, Morpheus, the teacher figure, explains that the world Neo has always known, that is so filled with familiar people and things, is really just a blank screen. A matrix.

Nothing is real except the programs you feed in. Everything is an illusion created by the software you use. Images can be shaped any way you desire.

This is a very accurate image of our current cultural and economic landscape. We are in the midst of a powerful shattering of our beliefs about what is important, the nature of loyalty, what the rules are, etc. As the traditional boundaries defining economic activity are fractured and dismantled, there is no longer a fixed order. The more anything goes, the more we are functioning with a blank screen. We can feed in whatever programs we choose. We have never been freer to design our career paths however we desire. We have never had more options for how we construct our organizations. Access to creative expression has never been more available. The landscape is endless, the features undefined, the paths can go anywhere. *And that is much of the problem.*

To take advantage of a blank screen, you must be more awake, creative and self-aware. It forces you to look more deeply at yourself because there are fewer outside forces determining your choices. Freedom is there for the taking. Unencumbered vision is critical. Bold risks are the path. *And that is also the beauty of this new world.*

ACKNOWLEDGMENTS

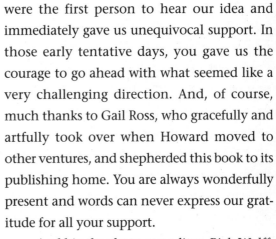

We must begin by acknowledging our agent, Howard Yoon. You were the first person to hear our idea and immediately gave us unequivocal support. In those early tentative days, you gave us the courage to go ahead with what seemed like a very challenging direction. And, of course, much thanks to Gail Ross, who gracefully and artfully took over when Howard moved to other ventures, and shepherded this book to its publishing home. You are always wonderfully present and words can never express our gratitude for all your support.

And big thanks to our editor, Rick Wolff. The minute we first walked through your door, we felt your contagious enthusiasm. We have felt that level of support unwaveringly throughout this project and it made us want to give all we could. Your ideas for refining the direction of many chapters were right on the money and gave us much-needed perspective. And of course we must thank all the people at Warner who helped bring things to final form and give this book a presence in the world.

This book is also the result of the many

folks who have worked with us in our seminars over the course of all these years. Your willingness to spend time at the edge of chaos consistently gave us the freedom we needed to take chances. It's encouraging to know that once you peel back the layers of business as usual, you so often find bold adventurers and wild creatives. It would take too long to point out all the individuals we'd like to thank by name, and some would surely be overlooked; thus we limit ourselves to giving special thanks to Phyllis Salina and Windy Wilson for an evolving working relationship and friendship that has no bounds.

Of course, our friends and family are a constant source of inspiration. We love you all and have something we could say to each and every one of you. We will limit ourselves to thanking Roy Tarlow, as a fellow writer in the family whose commitment to learning and sharing, which is unwavering even at the age of ninety, inspires us to follow in his path. And we want to share our gratitude for the other end of the age spectrum. To Tracy; you have already given to us in so many wonderful ways.

Finally, and most important, we would like to dedicate this book to Jimmy, Lee, and Leah of the Pitjantjatjara people and all the wise indigenous elders all over the world who are fighting to keep ancient wisdom alive.

DIGITAL
ABORIGINAL

One of my favorite Chinese poems tells of a wandering monk.
He travels light, his only possession a water jar.

Every night the monk walks to the river's edge to get a drink.

One particular evening on his way back from the river he trips.
His sole possession, the water jug, is smashed in a thousand pieces.
The monk is also shattered; he is left with nothing.

For a moment, the spilled water briefly collects on the ground.
In the reflection of the spilled water he sees the moon.

In that moment he is enlightened.

It was not until his last attachment was released
that he finally understood the nature of illusion
and the profound creativity of unencumbered choice.

WHO OWNS THE WIND?

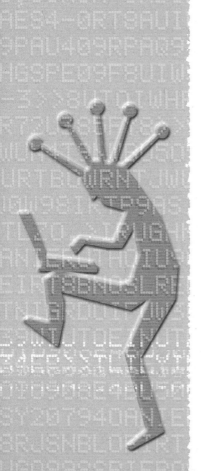

Those who have gardens cherish their time with the earth. They will tell you it brings them back to a more centered and simple way of being. While this may be true, there is a far more primal experience that few Westerners have ever even imagined.

One summer a few years ago, an interesting man came to our small town, high in the mountains of Colorado. This traveler had spent many years living in the outback of Australia with an aboriginal tribe. He came to know them and be trusted. He told us that the aboriginal elders counseled their people to avoid the seduction of agriculture. For the average Westerner, working in a garden is a wonderful return to the earth, but to these wise elders, planting is the beginning of the end.

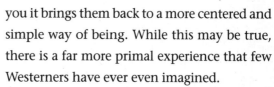

Suddenly, instead of following the weather, you want the weather to be different. And it is now easier to put things in straight lines. And because you have planted, you need fences. And since you have planted, you can accumulate possessions. And once your tribe is bound to a fixed address, forms

1

of hierarchy emerge that were not possible when it had to stay on the move. Because you have put down roots, for the first time you must consider defending your territory. Thus, convenient as it is, planting is the beginning of control.

Merely because you put a small seed in the ground, you are now invested in a whole system of maintenance that requires you to stay put. You are no longer free to follow what calls. So the aboriginal elders wisely teach their people to avoid agriculture. The aboriginal spirit requires the freedom to follow the wind.

The ancient nomad carries little on his back so he can travel at a moment's notice. He senses a pulse that tells him of the weather long before there are any detectable shifts in the wind. There are no straight lines or obvious paths in his world.

His profound sensitivity is possible only because he does not have to wait for seeds he has planted. His perceptions can be long and deep, since he has no territory that he must defend. His mind is quiet, since he is not attached to outcomes. Because he does not have to plan, his spirit is free.

This is a perfect metaphor for the transition we all now face. Many of our values are based not only on the fading assumptions of the industrial era, but on a lingering agricultural mind-set—that territories can be defended; amassed assets make you powerful and control protects what you have.[1]

The digital landscape is a nomadic world. Access is hindered for those who insist on traveling with heavy baggage. You will soon understand why it makes ownership a very difficult thing to pin down.

Most of us long for the opportunity to bring forth a vision we have held deep inside—plant an idea and stay with it until it bears fruit. It's hard to let go of this sweet dream of our seeds bearing harvest. But in fact, the way of the gardener is only a rest stop along our return path to a more dynamic creative state. To return to the aboriginal mind we must give up any desire to control what lies ahead. We can no longer waste energy on wanting the weather to be different.

Idea creation is no longer a question of finding a deep personal vision you dream of bringing forth. Idea creation is now a far more nomadic process that rests on seeing an opportunity in the moment and seizing it, long before you even know where the trail will lead. It is far more about being awake and alert, flexible and sensitive, than it is about being forceful and commanding. *The well-worn advice of searching your soul for something you love to do may no longer be quite as relevant. It comes from a gardening mentality, and the new economy is the domain of hunters and gatherers.*

WHEN MATTER TURNS TO ENERGY

John Perry Barlow, former lyricist for the Grateful Dead, founder of the Electronic Frontier Foundation and leading pioneer in the digital field, wrote a wonderful article titled "Selling Wine without Bottles." [2] Copyright has been relatively easy up to this point because *information* such as music, writing or film was transported through atoms in the form of a CD, bound book or videotape. The physical form was controllable, therefore the ideas held within had the semblance of defensible copyright.

We believed we were copyrighting ideas when in truth we were mostly controlling the atoms upon which they were imprinted. This reality came home to roost when the technology of MP3 came along and allowed music to be downloaded directly to our homes via computer. With similar forms of somewhat uncontrollable dissemination now in place for every form of personal expression—software, publishing, video, photography, books, games, etc.—it puts all of us in the challenging position of selling wine without a bottle.

The short-term solution has been to impose a set of copyright laws on a system that defies these kind of controls. Some cheer whenever a new piece of legislation or technical development arises that seems to defend the parameters of intellectual property. While temporarily this may have impact, Barlow's belief is that in the long term, it just won't work.

It is a rare individual who does not have any pirated software on his or her computer. Content providers cry that their images and text are often sent freely traveling through cyberspace without footnote or payment. Even with tightened security and more protective international trade laws, Microsoft estimates that 40 percent of the copies of Windows 2000 in circulation internationally will be illegal. And though Microsoft and others have moved toward versions of their software that can be accessed only on-line, and toward monitoring unregulated copies more closely, it's still probably only a question of time before that moat is also crossed. Video files have been encrypted using a system called CSS. In 1999, hackers cracked the code and a program called deCSS began circulating. The industry had to resort to lawyers, asking sites that offered this program to cease and desist. In short order, encryption for Microsoft's eBook and Adobe's reader were also broken. Even with Digital Rights Management (DRM), a more recent form of encryption, a natural civil disobedience is still bound to continue to occur under the banner "information just wants to be free," as some portion of the public disseminates to their heart's content.

In her book *Digital Copyright,* Jessica Litman offers a review of the history and problems involved in this domain. From even a far more conservative and legalistic perspective than the information-want-to-be-free crowd, she writes:

> The more burdensome the law makes it to obey its proscriptions, and the more draconian the penalties for failing, the more distasteful it will be to enforce . . . Laws that people don't obey and that governments don't enforce are not much use to the interests that persuaded Congress to enact them.

Later she says:

> Even if copyright stakeholders refuse to give the public a seat at the table, they may discover that they need to behave as if they had.[3]

Napster became the early mythical symbol for everything that is right or wrong with this new world, depending on your perspective. Napster and a host of Napster-like companies offered a way for consumers to upload music or other media they already had in their possession to a central database where it could then be downloaded by others. The premise was that the physical CD was purchased, therefore transmitting this data to an on-line friend was a simple act of sharing. If the atoms are owned, the information should follow.

"Nonsense," said the record companies. Slapped with lawsuits by every major record label, Napster was among the first to test the limits of this new ideology: ownership of the physical property on which information is imprinted versus ownership of information.

The dilution of Napster's ability to function led to dozens of new sites based on a software model of peer-to-peer exchange of music, video, software, books, etc. The most popular of these programs, Morpheus or Audio Galaxy Satellite, require no central server and are almost impossible to shut down. In this post-Napster world we have entered, no matter what the name of the particular company is that is currently tangling with the courts, the core argument remains the same: *Should we, can we, will we be able to hold on to our ownership of information once the digital world is in full force?*

You may think this is a simple case of technology moving faster than the law, but it is far deeper than legal wrangling. Information has been detached from the physical plane. It is beginning to live in the realm of pure energy, which requires a radically different relationship. The entertainment industry is still banking on DRM, which will allow every download to be counted. However, it still leaves many important questions unanswered.

You might also think that this discussion is just about intellectual property rights, and perhaps not directly relevant to your industry. But the moment a chip is placed in your product or anywhere in your system, you are affected by all the same forces influencing intellectual property. As Patricia Seybold points out in *The Customer Revolution,* musicians and their end customers share an ecosystem that is similar to those of other industries. So what is happening for the entertainment industry is bound to be coming to a neighborhood near you very soon. ***The music industry is merely the canary in the coal mine; what happens to them is a harbinger for others.***

Every major label now has an agreement with an on-line distribution site like Yahoo! using systems like RioPort or RealPlayer. Even Napster has secured these licensing rights. These approved sites license the song from the label and charge for each download. This answers part of the Napster equation, but avoids a lot of very important concerns that were bound up in the social side of the equation.

Most solutions have focused on the role of the customer in this issue. The users of MP3 technologies were not just excited about the *freeness* of the music. They wanted the ability to make their own mixes, catalog their own songs, take some songs and not others or to sample the material to use for other purposes like adding to their cell phone rings. The labels are now focused on giving the customers what they want while still exacting a payment, but little changes for the musician.

Due to accounting systems that favor the labels, the majority of musicians never see any money beyond their initial advance anyway. As far as many musicians are concerned, their music *is* free. Many of them loved Napster. Some saw their visibility and concert attendance soar. Less than one hundred music groups make the lion's share of the money. Similar ratios reign in film, TV, publishing, games and software. This leaves a huge underrepresented but now very empowered population with access to communication at a level never before possible. That's a lot of artistic energy itching for an outlet. These media-savvy creatives are clamoring for a more decentralized entertainment industry and they are taking concrete steps to make it happen. They are flocking to on-line venues such as Riffage and iCast, which bring smaller audiences direct to the artist. *The people to really watch in this scenario are the artists.*

Every revolution in history has occurred for the very same reasons: Too many people feel left out of the system and they have very little to lose by changing it. This is the spirit that Napster represented, which is still mostly ignored by the industry titans. In the past, as long as the record companies could give the buyers what they wanted, although technically and organizationally challenging, they could feel their job was done. But domination is now a very unreliable strategy. Every player in any economic ecosystem has newfound access to power. *Whenever social exchange is transformed, whenever people have the means to come together in radically new ways, then the rules defining economic exchange are also altered.*

You can build bigger fences around your property, but you can't legislate the social equation. Once you introduce the possibility of finding a mortgage, choosing insurance, getting groceries or buying a car on-line, you decimate a system of middlemen and retailers that used to control the exchange. You are participating in the dismantling of a once well-established system of delivery. New classes of digital middlemen arise, who connect customers with products and services in ways that often add information about pricing, quality, timing, etc. And in doing so, they create a far more savvy, self-directed and demanding consumer, who in turn forces the supplier to respond at an ever-higher level. Down the line, once the *software* for conducting auctions, comparing prices, creating chat rooms, sharing data or collaborating on projects is made more readily available, consumers may discover they don't even need digital middlemen. They may begin to self-organize their own buying clubs, political lobbies, creative communities and information exchanges.

Suddenly the social equation becomes more significant than the legal one. Ownership is far less a technical issue than a creative one. Copyright, intellectual property and power become subservient to the social exchange that now exists between artists and their audience, between buyers and their suppliers.

Information is no longer a noun, something we can own, store and accumulate. Information has become a verb, acting upon any system it touches. Information is now a verb, full of sound, rhythm and cultural nuance.

This is a very critical point. This is why the entertainment industry will eventually be forced to consider new models for how its products are sold, how much it charges, how it interfaces with the public, how it interfaces with artists, how truthfully it supports the creative spirit, etc. There are no bad guys in this scenario—not the profit-driven industry titans, nor the free-spirited artists or the unruly customers. The creative challenge is that none of these players have ever had to deal with true social parity.

If you read the business magazines, you see the same stories over and over, told by free agents, small companies and multinationals alike. They tell of having to share some closely held knowledge in order to share costs, save money, serve a client or develop a new market. They tell of having to share their product with another entity in order to develop a new level of service. They also discover that the transparency that is required when two enterprises come together to develop a shared effort, leaves both parties just a little vulnerable. In other words they have to trust one another just a little bit more than they are used to.

We are no longer walking on solid ground; the path ahead can be instantly transformed with a swipe of a programmer's hand. *We have entered a very unstable world where information in the form of pure energy can easily fly out the door and morph into a thousand variations of the product or service we used to think we owned.*

Lawyers persist with models that regulate information in ways similar to how we track physical products. Encryption is often a cat-and-mouse game, where one side or the other wins for a while, until the next hacker does what all the high-paid experts said was impossible. Further, many legal efforts to pursue information violators step on the privacy of ordinary citizens or the right of free speech and are therefore very challenging to even consider. Most important, if the participants on both sides of the equation—the buyer and the seller—want a new form of exchange, no matter how much power the middleman appears to have right now, the intermediary will be forced to adapt.

While some musicians joined the early Napster lawsuits, many others, like hit singer/songwriters Alanis Morrisette, an early investor in MP3.com, and Don Henley, testified before congress offering support and even desire for a Napster-like world. Many leading musicians have purposely leaked their material to free sites. An interesting fact that the press rarely pointed out in their Napster coverage is that most musicians make more money from concerts than CDs. The record labels and much of the studio infrastructure profit from CD sales, but the majority of less visible musicians make their money from concerts. All one needs to do is follow the money. These musicians profit more when free downloads drum up business for their income-generating concerts.

Even more important, the early public debate hardly mentioned peer-to-peer distribution. Napster took all the heat because they had eighty million users. Freenet- and Gnutella-type sites offer software that allow people to exchange data one to one. There is no centralized entity to sue, shut down or take to court. At first, these types of sites were not very popular; they were cumbersome to use and as long as Napster was around there was a better alternative. In just the first week after Napster was shut down, nearly six million had flocked to the dozens of sites that made peer-to-peer software more user-friendly and kept the music free. Believe me: There is someone in a garage somewhere, right now, making even more serious improvement to what is available today. Adapting to freer distribution is a critical feature of the new economic environment.

Many programmers feel that over the long term, traditional copyright models just won't work. They move through this territory every day and instinctively feel the mind-set it requires. When Adobe went to prosecute the first violator of the DRM act, their customers organized a product boycott and Adobe relented. The industry hopes DRM will be a bigger fortress, but many want a larger playground.

There is only one reason these post-Napster-type sites have not completely toppled the applecart already: *limited bandwidth.* Without high-speed lines it still takes a long time to download a song, and quality suffers. Many still check a song out on-line, and if they like it, they buy it.

Some studies even showed that Napster contributed to the music industry's extraordinary profits during that period. Free downloads are troubling in the long term, but not bad in the short run. Once bandwidth is more available, and yes, cheap, the social equation will become even more inventive and hard to control.

DISCONTINUITY IS THE NEW NAME OF THE GAME

As you probably know, Moore's Law predicted the doubling of chip speed every eighteen months. With new developments such as ultraviolet light inscription, the use of organic molecules for data processing and our brand-new ability to stop a light beam in the laboratory with applications for data transmission, the acceleration of computing capacity seems assured for a very long time. The commercial impact is that it rapidly brings data-intensive services, such as language translation or voice recognition, into a range that is cost-effective for the average consumer. With every new doubling of chip capacity, applications explode and creative opportunities abound.

According to George Gilder, bandwidth will explode even faster, doubling every six months. Gilder claims it will trigger a revolution that will make the one we have just encountered seem like child's play. He opens his provocative treatise *Telecosm* with the following vision:

> After a global run of thirty years, the PC revolution has stiffened into an establishment. So swiftly and subliminally did this silicon tide pass through the economy that, like many experts, you might have missed some of the motion until it stopped.... The computer era is falling before the one technological force that could surpass the computer's ability to process and create information. That is communication, which is more essential to our humanity than computing is. Communication is the way we weave together a personality, a family, a business, a nation and a world.[4]

The explosion of bandwidth will turn many of our current values upside down. Suddenly bandwidth will become cheap and silicon will be the costly end of the equation. When bandwidth was expensive and rare, we needed to build bigger, faster machines that could do more and more. When bandwidth becomes cheap and easy, we will switch from pumping up our silicon-based products to moving around the capacity we need.

This is why many forecast that personal computers as we now know them will probably cease to exist. We will access only whatever memory, data or software that is necessary for the particular task at hand. Whether it is the new set-top boxes for our TVs that are being touted by Microsoft and others, or some other wireless device, we will no longer purchase fixed capabilities; we will subscribe and pay for the functions we need, when we need them. This opens the door to a host of current products becoming far more transient. In Asia and parts of Europe, where wireless has taken off, they may bypass the PC stage altogether.

On another front, one hundred thousand people signed up with the Search for Extraterrestrial Intelligence (SETI) Institute, contributing their personal computing capacity for this collaborative project. Thirty thousand also signed up to help NASA's Mars Project and thirty-five thousand man the Open Directory Project, ushering in a new form of cyber volunteerism. Distributed computing is a fascinating development that is being used for scientific research in a number of areas, including pharmaceutical studies. Computers are linked and their capabilities aggregated, shifted and exchanged. It diminishes the need for an organization to own large computing capacity for a particular project, since with the right software they can tap into a resource that is freely available.

In the same way that the record labels must consider what they are, if not the CDs they sell, what is Dell, Apple or Gateway if not the plastic box you take home from the store? What is Palm, Handspring or Psion, if not the snazzy device you hold in your hand? What happens when more and more industries realize they will soon be selling *verbs* and not just all those *nouns* that they pack in a box. Encyclopedia Britannica is a prime example of product dissolving into service. What was once a line of expensive hardback books now exists only as a service where for $89.95 a year you have access to their continuously evolving research base.

Another example is Anderson Windows, who developed a piece of software so that high-end architects could easily order customized windows straight from the computer renderings of a building. Because the ordering process became so easy, their windows were ordered more frequently. Anderson's future now rests more on marketing and expanding the capabilities of its software than on developing the features of their product.

Similarly, almost every product is well on its way to becoming smart, thus dependent on the communication partnerships it can forge. So a car is no longer just a vehicle for transport; it is your mobile work station. It connects you with subscription radio and is fully wired so service, repairs, oil levels and tire tread are monitored and communicated to you. A working vehicle must offer a global positioning device for navigation and safety, and also help if you want to know where the closest Gap is and if it's open at this hour. Like so many other industries, much of the innovation efforts in auto manufacturing are focused on developing new uses for chips and developing the alliances that will allow connection to bigger, better services. This we have come to accept.

In the unlimited bandwidth scenario, smart products are no longer the brains behind transactions, they are just the mouthpieces. This means that soon the automakers won't have to develop individual vehicle brains; they will just wire every element and the driver will choose what he/or she wants and when. You don't need global positioning all the time; you can choose it only when you take a long trip out of town. Of course the price goes down with frequency of use or when several services are bundled.

As a result of thinking of products as solid objects, our notions of service are still very fractured. The subscription-radio people work in different offices than the global-positioning folks and pursue separate and competing relationships with the auto industry, because, after all, how much more expense will the customer be willing to absorb in order to have a smart car?

But once we move from a focus on building the car's brain, to letting the car owner download whatever he or she wants, when he or she needs it, these now divergent services have the freedom to become far more integrated. Companies like OnStar have already begun to think this way, considering directions outside their traditional scope of service.

Further, in the new era of *Telecosm*, 3-D communication, complete with special effects, musical accompaniment and a full spectrum of hyperlinks, will become widely accessible. If you think information is hard to bottle, communication is even harder to pin down. This next wave of technological magic coming down the pike will only highlight the need for Barlow's wise suggestion: *a shift in consciousness.*

With ample bandwidth, live concerts, theatrical events, conferences or intimate songwriting sessions can be easily Webcammed to subscribers. The subscribers can act as a virtual audience expressing their responses to you. Several musicians can jam live on-line and whoever wants to can attend. As long as these capabilities remain expensive, industry titans will dominate. But if, as Gilder predicts, this capacity gets cheap, then the bandwidth for sharing live events will be widely accessible. What happens when the artist, the audience and the creative process become more relevant than a particular set of songs? Suddenly entertainment begins to look like a service contract between the buyer and seller, the artist and his or her audience.

In an interesting collection of articles titled *Digital Archetypes,* Laura Fillmore makes a similar point.

> One may not want to pay $5 for an on-line, finite, static text of James Michener's *Chesapeake,* but one might pay considerably more if one could follow the electronically generated thought path resulting from the course taught by the author himself . . . where one could navigate the links students make in their critical thinking about the novel, navigate and link to real documents, graphics, video, sounds, experiences, and the author himself—all in real time.[5]

Further, what happens when the creative exchange between two or more groups, representing two or more different companies, perhaps even from different industries, becomes the heart of the innovation process? *Who owns the idea? Is the idea the moment of conception or is it all the negotiation that makes it real?*

This is what has led consultants like Stan Davis and Christopher Meyer to say in their book *Blur* that products will become negotiated events between two or more participants in a process. When relationship is the basis of exchange, products are no longer center stage and they become elements in a much larger creative dialogue. Suddenly the product is subservient to the conversation that surrounds it and intellectual property rights become very fuzzy.

Peter Gabriel, hit musician and founder of World of Music, Arts and Dance (WOMAD) and Real World, foresees this interactive environment also forging a new role for the artist. Keep in mind as you read the following quote that the term *artist* can also refer to a very broad spectrum of creative roles, from product development to marketing to management, and not just the traditionally narrow definition of an artist.

Traditionally the artist has been the final arbitrator of his work. He delivered it and it stood on its own. In the interactive world, artists will be the suppliers of information and collage material, which people can either accept as is, or manipulate to create their own art. It's part of the shift from skill-based work to decision-making and editing work—where the choice becomes as important as the actual piece of work. That's what's so exciting—the fluidity and flexibility of technology is a good complement to the human artistic spirit.[6]

We hold the idea of authorship so dear, forgetting that authorship as a property right did not exist until the printing press was invented. It was not until thoughts could be contained on paper, and that paper could be regulated, that copyright first came on the scene. Until then, stories, music, theater, and artistic images were all public domain. Each new generation *sampled* the content of the generation before, and used it to evolve the next layer of creative material. In this early system of free exchange, artists did make a living and some would always rise to the top. But their visibility rested far more on the quality of their work and a natural word of mouth than a system designed to hype and unnaturally promote a select few. This is a point I will discuss more fully in the next chapter.

Further, it is upon this notion of fixed authorship that we have constructed so many of our organizational values. Ideas such as *someone must be accountable* and *the buck stops here,* rest on the assumption that someone has ownership of a final result. You can begin to see how the changing role of the artist and audience will also forge new roles for managers and leaders. When the notion of authorship becomes more fluid, the underlying assumptions behind many of our organizational values also become more malleable. In an economy driven by communication, the quality of discourse is often more important than what you think you own. As you will see in the next chapter, this is why tightly knit on-line communities will have so much power to drive markets and define how they interface with the author of a product service.

It sends shivers down everyone's spines to even consider this possibility, but like the mighty dinosaurs that once ruled the earth, the concept of fixed authorship as we now know it may be reaching the end of its rather brief life span. This will occur not so much because we *can't* control dissemination, but because we won't want to. The hyperlinked document, thus the hyperlinked company, and eventually the hyperlinked culture will change the very rules of storytelling.

In physics there is a state called superfluidity, where fluids are cooled down far below normal conditions. Once this critical temperature is reached, almost nothing acts the way it did before. Entirely different laws of physics seem to be set in motion merely because the very same elements are being subjected to a different context. It is a perfect metaphor for this ownership issue. What made sense in the world of stable products and clear avenues of dissemination, makes far less sense in a superfluid digital landscape. ***People keep taking sides based on what they think is right and wrong, but that is not where this decision lives. It is not a moral question; it is a creative issue.***

Barlow is definitely one of the ringleaders of the information-just-wants-to-be-free crowd, and most would not go as far out as he does in terms of the actual solutions he offers. But he is right on the money when he says that unless there is a *shift in consciousness* to accommodate this unstoppable reality, we are destined to enter a future riddled with litigation, controls and ultimately systemic failure. It is *not* new sets of rules that will define this world, but new mind-sets.

THERE IS A BIG OLD HAIRY ELEPHANT IN THE LIVING ROOM

In psychological jargon, the *elephant in the living room* is the behavior that is running the whole family that no one acknowledges or talks about, like the father who gambles or the mother who drinks. The family never discusses the fact that the mother is drinking; rather, they spend their time analyzing why one of the children got a bad grade or why some neighbor did something stupid. The whole family is organized to avoid, deny and ignore this behavior, because to address it would require looking at the deepest layers of what is really going on and potentially making some hard choices.

In many ways, ownership is the elephant in the living room when it comes to thinking about our current economy. Much of the coming economic transformation will ride on a redefinition of our images of creative territories; whether it is really possible to hold on to products in the way we once did, and ultimately whether it actually serves us to focus our attention in that way. No one *really* wants to talk about this topic because it threatens the heart of many assumptions we now hold dear and potentially necessitates some hard choices.

Everyone dances around the edges. We discuss Napster's bad behavior or talk about the predatory behavior of digital companies. We talk about the rights of artists and needs of businesses. We bemoan the collapse of the gatekeepers we have come to know. We *psychologize* about the youthful rebelliousness of unruly hackers and hope they will grow up some day to act responsibly like the rest of us. Sometimes we even comfort ourselves by saying that there really is no new economy; the good old fashioned rules of business are still what drive profit. Few talk about this elephant directly because to really explore this topic would challenge the very core of the capitalist dream.

In his extraordinary book *Weaving the Web,* Tim Berners-Lee profiles the early days that allowed this woven wonder to come into existence. It is a very important piece of history that explains a lot of what we are currently witnessing. Much of what we see would not have been possible if the key players had insisted on intellectual property rights. He explains:

> Software patents are new. The internet ethos of the seventies and eighties was one of sharing for the common good. It would have been unthinkable for a player to ask fees just for implementing a standard protocol such as http. Now things are changing. Large companies stockpile patents as a threat of retaliation against suits from their peers. Small companies may be terrified to enter the business.
>
> ...The lure of getting a cut of some fundamental part of the new infrastructure is strong. Some companies (or individuals) make a living only by making up patents and suing larger companies, making themselves immune to retaliation by not actually making any products at all.
>
> ...The threshold of innovation is too low. Corporate lawyers are locked into a habit of arguing whatever advantage they can, and probably only determined corporate leadership can set the industry back on a sane track....As I write about the new technology, I do wonder whether it will be a technical dream or a legal nightmare.[7]

This is why there is an elephant in the living room. Although patents were designed to provide profits that would in turn foster new research and development, they actually slow the progress of an industry when the ideas being patented are too small or obvious. Even the medical community is complaining about broad gene patents that are stifling research. Every industry must consider the ideal balance between sharing knowledge in order to build something far larger in the long run, and holding on to a very small piece of something that would make everyone have to go around it unless they paid the toll. As long as extreme forms of territoriality persist, the sharing of discoveries so necessary for rapid progress will be strangled.

Fortunately, the market is mightier than the law. When we discuss the open source movement a little later on, or distributed computing, or convergence and mergers, in every arena, it is not simply one case that is being tested, but a worldview that is being challenged. It doesn't matter who appears to *win* the endless series of court cases that are about to emerge in every digital domain from graphics to video to games to software. The issue of ownership will continue to be tested over and over again in new and intriguing variations. It is at the heart of what will eventually throw our once stable business models to the wind. It will change the very DNA of commerce.

MARKET VOLATILITY AND THE FORCES OF CHAOS

Think about this: *In 1991 the Internet was a business-free zone.* You signed an agreement *not* to conduct business on-line in order to gain access. This bias toward communication continues to be the foundation of all that we see.

These social dynamics continue to define the space. Yahoo!, one of the most heavily trafficked portals, says that its fastest area of growth is conversation.

Whenever consumers and suppliers come together in new ways, the boundaries between who controls what get fuzzy. This has been referred to as market volatility, but volatility is possible only when past assumptions about ownership are no longer well defined. Volatility can *only* occur when past forms of control have been deconstructed.

The following trends are contributing to this never-before-seen level of volatility. As you consider these impacts, you will see that they are not just new directions. They are paradigm shifts, forcing us to reorganize our familiar attitudes toward control and dominance.

- Information technology now makes it economically feasible to produce and distribute very small volumes of a product or service. With lower barriers to entry, more players can enter the game. They have little corporate history to defend, so they care less about preserving the current standards. ***Thus, once well-defended markets are vulnerable to outsiders and subject to all the ways these trespassers will go about breaking the rules.***

- Radical hackers and insurgents are the new research and development arm of every industry. These outsiders forge new directions, work out the bugs and invent the markets. The big guys either play catch-up or buy their way into innovation. In fact, the big guys eat start-ups for breakfast to fuel their insatiable need for new ideas. Many find it cheaper to buy the innovation they desire. ***In every industry, the edges are now driving the center.***

- The well-known joke is "on-line no one knows you're a dog." It is not so much that those with limited resources can approximate the look of larger, more established businesses, it is that *contexts can't be owned*. You can patent a formula, but you can't hold on to a context. Anyone can copy what you've done. So e-commerce businesses regularly cannibalize and steal from each other, creating a far more aggressive and destabilized landscape. The more a *product* rests on information, the more ownership can flow through your fingers. ***It is almost impossible to keep up with the torrid pace at which others can reinvent your business.***

- Palm broke into the handheld computer market like a hurricane, quickly dominating. Then several lead designers broke away to develop Handspring, which showed signs of being the next hot must-have toy. Next-generation companies splinter off at a staggering rate. Digital pioneers have little patience to wait for corporate permission to proceed. They also know that ideas have far shorter life spans, so rapid response is vital. Often when individuals have really, really good ideas, they will move on to form their own ventures rather than contribute their breakthroughs to the companies that employ them. *Businesses once counted on the intellectual capital of their key employees to make plans and build their futures. Now, that commodity is far more fleeting and no longer an asset that can be counted on.*

- The early buzz for the low-budget independent film *The Blair Witch Project* was created almost entirely on-line. One continuous thread led from the gossip about a recently discovered documentary made by some lost kids to the beginning of the film. The jerky camera motion kept the rumor going that this was a homemade movie. It drew the viewers into the plot long before they ever saw the film. The line between fact and fiction was deliberately blurred. It was far more than a clever on-line campaign; it was a new dimension of storytelling. With new avenues for marketing narratives, it is far easier for anyone to access guerilla marketing. *Entrepreneurs now view the entire digital landscape as their stage, traveling across mediums to get the word out in ways that continually defy normal channels and traditional gatekeepers.*

- Integration is yet another dynamic that will bend our notions of creative territories. Your refrigerator will soon be able to tell your grocer to add milk to your order and send that information on to the farmer so he can modulate production. When your family needs milk, the farmer will know. For an event like this to occur, dozens of companies must cooperate and share information. The boundaries between the software company, appliance manufacturer, grocer and farmer will be blurred as they plan and develop future directions together. With convergent products and collaborative services such as these, no one is the sole owner of the end result. *We will no longer have distinct products and services; instead we will have consumer events that tie vast networks of providers into a single system and force them to share once closely guarded knowledge.*

- Once stock trades became inexpensive and easy and in-depth information became readily accessible, day trading was born. Thousands of small trades made on very small shifts in price began to create their own *weather* that had nothing to do with real conditions. The capacity to trade built its own feedback loops independent of real-life events. Many discovered they could make as much or more by trading on pulses of information and the flow that followed than by following real-life valuations. *There will be a whole new breed of entrepreneurs and business endeavors that are designed to capitalize on very small windows of opportunity. They get in and out fast, leaving slower-moving entities to deal in their wake. Often they will reap rewards from the pockets of more committed enterprises.*

- Further, the digital world will always race ahead of the law, our favorite form of control when all else fails. There are sites that freely expose the weak links in corporate information networks. If these same individuals were offering known criminals the keys to a corporate headquarters, they would be considered accomplices in whatever crime was committed. These sites are the digital equivalent of breaking and entering, yet they are perfectly legal. The law has not arrived in this part of town yet. For the immediate future, the digital landscape will remain a relatively lawless land, which means no one is really in control. *And if ultimately no one can ever own the wind, there may never be truly enforceable claims to this land.*

- The World Wide Web was conceived as a forum for universal access, so researchers could freely share with each other. It is a principle that the players will fight hard to defend. It is a driving passion similar to that of the founding fathers who wrote the American Constitution and envisioned a land of the people, by the people and for the people. Many who are shaping the blood and guts of this new economic beast are not just doing business; they sincerely believe they are building a new world. This spirit shapes the attitudes of many residents of this world and should not be dismissed lightly. *This intangible, egalitarian ideology will always permeate the digital landscape. Key players in this world believe information wants to be free—freely exchanged, freely shared, freely available. We have seen it happen many times before; passionate visions are often the prelude to a new reality.*

If you peek beneath the surface of each of the points we just made, you will discover that they each force you to think in new ways about creative territories. The boundaries between companies, industries, consumers, suppliers and even between product categories become increasingly fuzzy. Ideas travel to seek out their best homes and little can be done to stop them. New dimensions of products and services arise with greater frequency, forcing everyone to let go of what they know in order to keep up. The future is no longer tied to predictable events and channels that the major players can control and dominate.

But ultimately, it is not all these remarkable trends—the fluidity of intellectual property, level playing fields, slippery contexts, fractured markets, fleeting intellectual capital, dissolution of gatekeepers, convergence of industries, hit-and-run players, lawlessness or free-spiritedness—that will define this landscape. *The foundation of this emerging terrain will be formed by the new kinds of power that are now in the hands of many.*

Leading business theorist Peter Drucker says that the most far-reaching impact of the information wave is e-commerce.[8] A software program that allows an architect to do in a few hours what once took weeks is not really anything new. This kind of change is actually more reminiscent of the industrial revolution, where the means of production were continually streamlined.

The real impact of e-commerce is a power shift, where the individuals who shape knowledge can also rewrite the rules. Andy Grove, Chairman and former CEO of Intel, has been known to say quite dramatically, "E-commerce is taking us into the valley of death." Despite the dot-com collapse, the pecking order is more easily challenged. But more important, those who shape the knowledge hold the most power.

Capital is still the dominant way businesses hold on to people—throwing money at them, tying them to stock options. *Golden collars* is the term for programming whizzes that make far more money than their bosses ever will. Drucker believes that financial incentives are only a short-term solution. In short order, knowledge workers will no longer be satisfied with financial reward; they will want to run the show. ***It is a revolution in every sense of the word; we just haven't noticed it because it is not being fought on the streets.***

A Parallel World

American Airlines slowly built its dominance over the course of decades. It has hundreds of planes, a well-respected name, and key routes all over the world. It also developed Sabre, a computerized reservation system.

As the travel industry came on-line, American Airlines aggressively worked Sabre into many on-line formats. The value of Sabre unfolded almost overnight. With almost no hard assets and in a few short years, Sabre became *greater* in value than American Airlines.

This kind of startling growth has caused bricks-and-mortar businesses to evaluate whether or not they can offer viable on-line versions of what they do. But often they find that the knowledge gained in their traditional businesses must be translated to a world that speaks a very different language. Some will form a company within the company and others will hire out—realizing that what you know in one world doesn't necessarily translate to the other. But, let's compare American Airlines' world to the world where Sabre lives:

American Airlines	Sabre
Prices rise by limiting volume	Value rises by increasing volume
Hard assets dominate	Intellectual property is highly vulnerable
Very high barriers to entry	More level playing field; competition from outsiders
Fixed rules of operation	Slippery contexts easily copied; constantly changing
New directions require large investment	Small, customized, low investment ideas can be profitable
Major players create the rules	Edges drive the market; the center plays catch-up
Highly skilled staff tend to stay put	Employees easily break away to start competing ventures
Predictable ways of getting word out	Innovative and varied vehicles for visibility
Product is clear and stable	Product evolves, converging with new areas of market
Growth is assured through domination	Growth is assured through alliance and networks
Well protected and monitored by the law	Law has not yet arrived in many parts of their town
Rules of exchange are well defined	Revolutionary spirit pervades every effort
Changes in the market happen slowly	Hit-and-run players can wreak havoc on established markets
Knowledge is closely guarded	Knowledge must be shared to facilitate service and growth
Hierarchies are necessary and useful	Empowered individuals must be encouraged to bend the rules

Once a business or industry acquires this virtual mirror of what it does, it is initiated into a new world. When intangible assets become as significant as hard assets, a company naturally becomes more fluid. The more chips embedded in your product, the more you must consider the rules from the column on the right. When a business spins off an information product, it turns once rigid management structures into moving rivers of change. Ordinary planning often goes out the window.

It is a parallel world that sometimes echoes real-life transactions and sometimes defies them. Although organizations face having to learn a new language, the people working in this transitional environment face the same set of cognitive and emotional challenges. The people working in the world of American Airlines may be bold, clever and imaginative leaders, but the challenges they face are most often observable, tangible and rest on familiar problems for which they have been trained. For them, ordinary senses are enough. Incremental problem solving is sufficient.

The people who work in the world where Sabre lives are faced with mostly invisible factors that they must learn to sense. They have to be loose and unencumbered. They can't hold on to what they know, because it will hinder their ability to perceive what lies ahead. Growth will always hinge on forging entirely new arenas of partnership and embedding your company's products and services within the context of what other companies offer. These are the kinds of shifts in consciousness that will move us past litigation and control into mind-sets that will allow us to follow the wind. These are the kinds of personal strategies that will open everyone's eyes to new kinds of values.

If you look at the Napster phenomenon through the eyes of those who live in the American Airlines world, then of course Napster-type events seem destructive and should definitely be stopped. Napster-like sites are a clear violation of intellectual property, and without these rights the system of exchange we now have would collapse.

However, if you look through the eyes of those who live in Sabre's world, suddenly Napster's actions make a lot more sense. Flexible, adaptable, and yes, more affordable data no longer seems like such an awful predicament, but merely the next stage of unraveling how information will travel through society.

I must admit, a large part of my brain still lives in the American Airlines world. And I would certainly hate to see my intellectual property become completely irrelevant. But in my heart of hearts, I do believe that intellectual property as we now know it will become far more transparent. Books will no longer be static events. They will arise in conjunction with idea communities that shape the direction of how new ideas are offered. The day will come when all forms of authorship will live in a world with far fewer fences. I also know deep in my gut that the more I surrender my personal biases in this area, ultimately, the more creative I will become.

The Net economy has allowed for *dynamic pricing*, where the price of a good changes moment by moment depending on supply, demand, amount of goods purchased, frequency of purchase and whatever other factors the business chooses to place in the equation. ***We will probably move toward a system of dynamic copyright, a system of reward that fluctuates based on what is being brought to the table at any given moment.***

Fuzzy ownership is just one piece of this puzzle. By the close of this book you will see how it connects with a much larger conceptual metamorphosis that is well under way. The on-line world is not just an informational highway with commerce following along its paths. What may prove to be most significant in the years to come is the potential for this landscape to evolve in a way that fractures the economic and business models that have ruled for so long. Thousands of directions will emerge that the power brokers will no longer be able to control. The edges will become increasingly inventive and drive the center toward ever more radical transformation.

And the *only* reason we are not seeing more dismantling of the traditional models of exchange is because we are only a decade or so into this process and still living deep in the shadows of the industrial world. The further we travel on this digital path, the more these shadows from the past will fade. More rapidly than anyone expects, we will be moving into a world of strange new creatures and never-before-seen events.

1.1 PLAYING THE DIDGERIDOO

An aboriginal nomad traveling through the Australian desert carries little on his back. Yet when he arrives at the next water hole, he finds his favorite musical instrument, the didgeridoo, hanging from a thin reed, dangling in the water, safely protected from the dry climate.

He plays to his heart's content and then moves on, leaving it for the next person. This beautiful reed instrument with the low haunting sound belongs to no one, yet encompasses the spirit of everyone who passes by. The context for participation is the art form as much as the music itself.

Many of you know the following story, but it is such a powerful force in our current landscape, it deserves retelling. In 1991, a Finnish computer student named Linus Torvalds decided a far superior computer operating system could be built. Frustrated with cumbersome systems that the advanced user had little freedom to modify, Torvalds wanted a more elegant system. He circulated his initial ideas to a network of hacker friends all over the world. Eager to jump on a challenge, and perhaps fueled by a bit of Gates-bashing energy, they poured in contributions.

A key feature of this product is that it is free. No one can compete by offering a cheaper product. Anyone can modify the system according to his or her own needs without paying a licensing fee—this concept is called *open source*. It is free not because of some radical ideology, but because of how the product evolved. If anyone had tried to own it anywhere along the way, the high level of participation would have broken down. Torvalds has publicly said that, contrary to the media hype, he was not driven by wanting to compete with Microsoft. His purpose in developing this system was so everyone could have *"maximum fun!"*

Now, that's a novel motive. The Linux operating system has quickly garnered an extraordinary piece of the pie, with megaliths such as Dell and Compaq equipping their computers with it and dozens of new Linux-

compatible applications showing up every day. It is one of the faster grow-
ing operating systems for wireless devices and the AOL Time Warner and
Sony consortium is using it for their new set-top TV box. IBM is using a
Linux-based operating system as the platform for its middleware.

When a company like IBM joins the open-source movement, it is a
powerful endorsement of the operating system. IBM has also hitched its
star to the research capacity of social community. It is connected to a
body of knowledge that will always be shared. A profit-making company
is now in partnership with a self-organizing, freewheeling artistic community. In fact, IBM is freely contributing to this renegade group by lending the technical support of two hundred workers from its research facility in Oregon.

Even without IBM's support, this international network of hackers
continues to upgrade its creation and develops free software on an ongoing
basis. The Linux world gets bigger with every passing year because it is so
very easy for new players to jump on board. Few want to miss out on
Torvalds's generous invitation for everyone to have maximum fun.

The Linux community is one of the larger providers of operating
systems and relevant software, yet it is not a business in the formal sense.
There are no salaries or stock options. It is a learning community
composed of high-level hackers creating ideas together. It is not a business
and yet it has developed a fiercely competitive product. Much like the
didgeridoo in the water hole, the operating system is a record of all who
pass through, yet the property of no one.

It is important to note that open source has been around since the
beginning of computing and is key to that free-spiritedness we discussed
earlier. In fact, the Web itself was built on a series of open-source platforms and nonproprietary contributions. Apache, another open-source
system, has been around a long time and is the leading software for Web-
based portals. Linux is also based on a preexisting operating system called
UNIX. And many of the key players, including Torvalds, have gone on to
lead profit-making businesses based on supporting the Linux product.

What *is* striking about Linux is its rapid commercial success at a point in time when proprietary systems appeared to have the market locked up.

In part, this incredible marketing clout was possible because the designers themselves were the early adopters of the system. The original designers were often employed as decision makers about product choices for high-tech companies; thus it was rapidly introduced into the larger industry. *The customers were also the creators of the product, collapsing the normal cause-and-effect relationship between product and sale. Creation and adoption were a single event.*

At first the real meaning of this event may slip past you. You might file it as another one of the crazy new developments on-line that is not immediately relevant to your world. But forget that it is a software and look at the facts. The Linux collaborators successfully challenged the dominant supplier in their field. They continue to develop and upgrade their goods with no investment behind them, and are expanding rapidly with no business plan, no one leading the charge and no one who will ever own the product! If this were happening in your business, you would be very worried.

The key to understanding the open-source movement is not so much that it is free, but that it is profoundly social. And because it is based on open dialogue, it is lightning fast. In the early days of the Web, a related platform called Gopher was getting a lot of attention and acceptance. One day the University of Minnesota realized that it had some proprietary claim to this software and announced that it reserved the right to act on this claim at a future date. Gopher was dropped like a hot potato. No one would touch the software if down the line they might have to tangle with lawyers about its use.

The real impact of open source is that a wide variety of people can contribute in a way that is just not possible with proprietary models. Thus when open source becomes the vehicle of choice for a vast number of profit-making companies, they will be hitched to a body of knowledge that can often move faster, and definitely more freely than systems that are controlled by a single provider. In an idea community, discoveries serving a small market are relevant. Thus diversity blooms, a creative middle class flourishes and the surrounding companies further adapt.

The open-source movement is a large and rapidly growing community driven by highly committed and resourceful members. They are the kind of artists who may no longer be content to be hired hands, no matter how well they are paid. As Drucker suggested, they will want to run the show. A book called *Rebel Code* suggests that the Linux movement is not just a threat to Microsoft, but could also challenge the foundations of the entire software industry.[9]

It is a creative model that has implications for almost any industry. It is an absolutely defining moment in digital history; the knowledge designers rewrote the rules of a very major game. The creative model is brilliant. If translated to other fields of endeavor, it could be the genesis of a very new economic landscape.

In 1966, a comparable event occurred in an entirely different field. Dee Hock was hired by Bank of America to *fix* its credit-card operations, which at that time were hemorrhaging losses. For years, Hock had been harboring secret dreams about organizations that truly empowered people. In response to Bank of America's offer, he helped design an organizational model *that had never existed before.* It was a nonstock-for-profit business entity that he called Visa. Today Visa is a 1.25-trillion-dollar enterprise with 750 million customers and twenty-two thousand representative banks. Similar to the Linux community, it is owned by no one, yet responsible to all its members. It is driven by fierce competition and persistent cooperation. In fact, Hock coined a term for the model he forged: *the chaordic organization,* a blend between chaos and order.

Hock offers the model of a chaordic organization as a vision for how businesses of the future will need to think. Like dynamic pricing, our prediction regarding dynamic copyright fits perfectly with the image of a chaordic organization that balances order and flexibility.[10]

In much smaller ways, we are seeing similar collaborative trends such as books written through on-line exchanges and in turn marketed and sold through the very same networks that created them. Farmclub, now joined with Get Music, launches new musical groups, not through promotion but through its listeners, who have sole responsibility for ferreting out the new stars.

And it's not just media artists who are pushing the envelope. After three years of recession due to low prices for cranberries, Ocean Spray had to generously show the growers who had contracted to sell to them how to boost profits and grow more cheaply through more effective knowledge management. Ocean Spray could no longer remain separate from its suppliers if it was to survive as a viable company.

Like Visa, Ace Hardware has functioned for years as a centralized buying and branding unit owned by, and responsible to, its local members. Similarly, when the expansion of CVS pharmacies threatened to almost completely obliterate the corner drugstore, Bergen Brunswig Corporation, a distributor of health and beauty aids, orchestrated a purchasing system that allowed small players the same advantages as chains: aggregated purchasing power, sophisticated software and integrated logistics. Like Ocean Spray, by helping those around it, Bergen Brunswig Corporation furthered its own position and is the country's number two distributor.

Collective models are gaining ground all over the world, from the garment industry in Denmark to the Mondragon Cooperative Corporation in Spain to the CAMA furniture makers in Italy. Each functions as a shared, self-managing vehicle to further the interests of its individual members.[11] Similarly, Worklaw Network links twenty-four small law firms together as a way of approaching the clout and presence of the big national firms. This type of collective is one of the fast-growing business forms in the legal community. This new kind of connectivity means that small players can more easily aggregate their power. Thus creative alliances are no longer just the domain of the mighty.

Economist Jeremy Rifkin offers a perspective on why these models are picking up steam, again tying the artistic transformation to the commercial one.

> Hypertext undermines one of the central features of print consciousness—the idea of an author who owns his or her own ideas and words. Because the medium is based on inclusivity and connectivity rather than exclusivity and autonomy, there are often no clear boundaries separating one's contributions from another's . . . . When material of all kinds becomes part of an open-ended process, involving multiple parties distributed over time and space rather than a finished product resulting from a single person's creative effort, exclusive ownership sometimes becomes difficult to assign.[12]

This hyperlinked capacity is allowing businesses to share in product development and forge links for everything from cobranding to interactive supply chains. Lockheed Martin allows its clients to look in on the design process and offer suggestions. Large industrial shippers allow customers to track the progress of their shipments and make changes in the route if they want. Cisco drives product development based on the questions, complaints and requests of customers. As the digital landscape unfolds, the creation, marketing, supply and sale of a product will become irrevocably intertwined. The players who focus on these different sides of the equation will see their organizational roles become far more blended. Shared information will weave them together. More and more industries will discover that rigid interpretations of ownership are an obstacle to connecting with a greater web of economic forces and creative possibilities.

1 • 2 THE INEVITABILITY OF GENEROSITY

The Maori, the indigenous people of New Zealand, did not own land. They did not even understand the concept. But they did have a very gen-

erous tradition of giving. When you met a stranger it was expected that you would offer him a gift. But what this really meant is, use it for a while and when you are finished give it back.

So when Captain Cook landed in New Zealand, they welcomed him. In the spirit of generosity, they asked if he would like a particular piece of land. Thrilled with such a gift, he accepted the land, which is now the city of Auckland!

Roughly 350 years later, a beautiful promontory with views of the downtown, which, of course, had become very prime and expensive real estate, was returned to the Maori people. They won the case based on the thesis that they were merely generous and did not have a word for the concept of ownership.

Information-based businesses are continually faced with the dilemma of seeing their ideas appropriated by others and deciding whether their energy is best spent defending their copyrights or focusing on the next new thing. Ideas now have such a short life span that many companies often let go, because the next generation product will make what they are currently doing obsolete anyway.

In fact, a common practice of up-and-coming information-based businesses is to give away product for free in order to build a client base. Giving stuff away is even an acceptable competitive strategy. Microsoft gave away their Internet Explorer browser to compete with Netscape. Although Microsoft was accused of violating anti-trust laws because of this strategy, it will continue to be a critical feature of this domain, because it is so easy to disguise as enhancing the features of your product or service. Without facing a legal challenge, Oracle gave away a comparable customer-management software that Seibel Systems was charging for. It not only attacked Seibel's core product, but it also got people in Oracle's doors to buy more advanced software to piggyback on the entry-level platform. One company that we know of is on the ultrathin edge of the next horizon and is *purposely* allowing another company to infringe on its copyright merely to establish some visibility for what it does. Up there where the air is very thin, this cutting-edge company feels that having at least one other company offering a similar product might actually help establish a market.

Faced with the need for an on-line presence, Zagat Restaurant Guide courageously posted all its information on-line for free. Soon after offering all its material without charge, sales of its printed guides grew 70 percent. Like many smaller, specialized software companies, Homestead built traffic by offering free Web-building software and charging only for the professional version. MIT announced a Web-based curriculum of over two thousand courses, with lecture notes and assignments carried online. Amazingly, it plans to release all this material for free so anyone in the world can view it. It must be assuming that by increasing its visibility, MIT will become even more central to the future of higher education.

This is the Grateful Dead Theory of Marketing, now also used by such popular musical groups as Phish. For years the Grateful Dead encouraged bootleg recordings of their concerts and even cordoned off an area near the front of the stage for *tapeheads* so that their recordings would be of higher quality than what you could get from the seats. The band facilitated the sale of bootleg recordings at concerts, eventually adding on-line referral once that technology became possible. And, curiously, their records still sold. More significantly, for decades the Grateful Dead always made the top-ten list of the year's most financially successful tours, although they rarely had a hit song, received almost no radio airplay and were never in rotation on MTV/VH1.

Where else in the world would generosity bring such rich rewards? This kind of strategy makes absolutely no sense if you are talking about physical products. *How in the world would it benefit an appliance manufacturer to give away toaster ovens for free, thinking it will make its money on selling recipes and servicing the oven? How in the world could it ever link a free toaster oven to the purchase of a higher-priced product like an oven?* But this makes perfect sense in a world built on communication. **Physical prod-**

ucts can't blend into each other, but information is destined to merge and weave new patterns with neighboring products and services.

But now that chips are making even old-line physical products smart, everyone will soon be in the communications business. Suppose our hypothetical toaster oven now includes a link that allows it to connect with your cell phone and twenty minutes from home you can turn it on. If you are paying for that service, then suddenly it just might make sense to give you that toaster oven for free. Set your entire kitchen up with a service contract for relevant communication and perhaps all your appliances will be nearly free. Suddenly you are no longer being sold an appliance; rather, it is a communication device with all sorts of potential for extended service contracts. Suddenly generosity makes sense.

Kevin Kelly, editor at large of *Wired* magazine, says that the on-line world will always move in the direction of products becoming closer to being free. Further, it will always move in the direction of systems becoming more open, rather than closed.[13]

At first, AOL refused to allow nonsubscribers to instant message with its subscribers. Microsoft, a master of leveraging access to its own advantage, cried foul. Microsoft said it should be illegal to prohibit the exchange of another person's product. AOL can't refuse to allow people who speak another language, in this case MSN, to communicate with its people. AOL finally relented, but not because of Microsoft's legal pressure. The company understood that setting up barriers would ultimately be detrimental. If AOL's customers couldn't go anywhere, ultimately it would make AOL seem limited, and its customers would drift off toward more open pastures. In this new landscape, closed systems are never as viable as open systems.

So now AOL's instant messaging software can be downloaded free and is freely licensed to anyone who wants it. In the court hearing concerning the AOL/Time Warner merger, this exact issue came up as a cause for concern. Steve Case publicly said, *"Instant messaging is a feature; it is not a business."* In this new world, players can no longer survive by being gatekeepers. If they try, the flow of distribution will just go around them.

This suggests that the future role of entertainment companies can no longer be focused on dominating the airwaves, but instead should be focused on developing contexts and platforms that foster multiple streams of talent. Even in the face of continued mergers, the industry will become decentralized, and new economies of scale will allow much smaller exchanges to be financially viable. If these companies wish to survive, they will have to focus on adding value to the exchange between artist and public in a way that makes their place in the middle relevant again. They will have to transition from focusing on a few stars, to paying attention to the entire galaxy of players.

Subscription models, simplifying purchase and lowering the prices of what they do, are some of the directions that have already been triggered. They will have to allow the star system to collapse, where just a handful of artists dominate, so a creative middle class can be heard. Books, music, games, software, etc., will all lean toward becoming nearly free, and fees will be charged for features that add value to the initial document such as learning communities, windows into the creative process, added service, etc. This will all happen not because of Napster-like predators, but because of the natural flow of artistic communication.

Ultimately, free sites don't offer much service and don't have the bucks to make things user-friendly. A host of quite successful Linux-based companies now service this free software. They customize it, teach it, service it and charge for their work. This is definitely the wave of the future. More and more products will morph into service. Service will morph into communication. Contexts for social exchange will be the new source of income streams. Your core business will always lean toward becoming more free as you locate new domains of information that the customer may be willing to purchase.

CNET runs three different sites that allow you to download free software. The software designers have never even talked about taking CNET to court; in fact, they consider CNET an ally. Within five minutes of someone downloading a free piece of software, the designer is notified and he or she is able to immediately make money by offering the receiver of this free product the opportunity to pay for technical support. The reason the CNET model evolved so effortlessly is because it did not involve bringing an existing industry that defined itself in a particular way kicking and screaming into a new land. CNET was dealing with nomads, who expected to travel light. They had no corporate history blinding their sight.

Turbo Squid is an interesting business form, sort of a Napster run by the artists. It provides a platform for animators who have developed 3-D characters to offer them for use in other projects. Each artist sets his or her own price, ranging from free to thousands of dollars. The response by both artists and customers has been encouraging, and again, no one is going to court. The social equation rules.

> "In an open system we compete with our imagination,
> not with a lock and key... And a truly open system is in
> the public domain and thoroughly available as a foundation
> upon which everyone can build."
> NICHOLAS NEGROPONTE[14]

The decentralization of everything we know is not only continuous but also accelerating. Resistance is futile. We *will* have to learn a new language if we want to make this world our home. The ancient nomad didn't build fortresses against inclement weather; he moved when the wind changed. A nomadic mind-set is based on nonresistance and keen instinct. The only choice now is to quickly absorb new trends and make them your own.

Everything in the information economy will move toward becoming almost free and more open. Savvy travelers in this land must always be anticipating this eventuality and be heading in this general direction if they want to ride the flow.

1.3 THE URGE TO MERGE

It was almost impossible for an aborigine to go to war. An elaborate social system allocated responsibility for a particular area of land to the person who resided there most of the time and also to his neighbor. An interlocking mesh of social relationships meant that everyone was connected to someone else. Since your neighbor took care of you, you could not go to war with them.

Joel Stoner was a well-respected music engineer. As his recording projects became more complex, he found it harder and harder to keep track of information. Not finding anything adequate for his needs, he wrote his own software called Studio Suite and founded Altermedia to distribute his information-management tool.

Early on, he went to one of the larger distributors of media software. It was beginning to form an on-line distribution system and community for its software users. Joel's software was a natural next direction. The distributor was also a partner in a business-to-business (B2B) operation for studios to collaborate on-line, bid projects, find specialized musicians, etc. So Joel followed the trail to the next player in the chain. Rather than building his own empire, Joel was seeking partners in a vision. He knew that his dream was not isolated from a larger wave sweeping the industry. He did not try to hold on to his idea; rather, he deliberately and actively tried to merge it. He *wanted* to be absorbed into a larger vision.

This is not an unusual development; businesses develop strategic partnerships all the time. Andersen's global research initiative into the alliance phenomenon found that:

- Alliances account for 6 to 15 percent of a typical company's market value.
- Alliances are expected to rise to 16 to 25 percent within five years.
- A striking 22 percent of all companies expect alliances to account for 40 percent of their value within five years.

■ Eighty-two percent of executives cite alliances as the prime vehicle for future growth.

They quote General Electric's Jack Welch on this trend. "If you think you can go it alone in today's global economy, you are highly mistaken."[15]

Multiply the scene with Joel by many, many thousands, extend it all over the world, blend it across industries and you have some idea of the kinds of conversations that are happening in every business arena conceivable. The latest buzz being whispered in some circles is that the next wave of innovation will be forged by large companies partnering with very, very small businesses, even solo entrepreneurs, as a way of participating in the more nimble and customized capabilities that individuals have. Sony, Bertelsmann, Viacom and almost every media group has an in-house venture capitalist whose sole purpose is to sniff out these lone programmers to see if anything is brewing on the edges that these megacompanies can catch early on. They never want to be in the position of being napsterized again.

What was unusual about Joel's discussions was that these distinct companies held such inclusive attitudes toward each other. Their conversations were closer to those of scientists sharing data about a discovery than potential rivals jockeying for position. I can't imagine two fashion designers seeing each other's collections and saying, *"Wow, it seems we are using a lot of the same colors and materials this year. Why don't we put out a shared collection this season? It seems silly to have separate shows since we are working on such similar designs."* It is just harder to share physical objects. Two people can't each put out half a dress. But the moment a chip is involved, merging is far more natural. Joel would have been thrilled to put out half an idea. All it takes is a shared vision, and a few programs later your actions are blended.

Although digital pioneers do guard their hot ideas, once they are in motion they tend to bump into each other far more easily and consider collaboration much more naturally than old-line businesses. In part, this is why the new economy has merged at a rate that dwarfs the marriage rate of industrial empires. And since the new economy has all but devoured the old economy, the urge to merge will soon be a key feature of everyone's plan for the future. Fluid territories have made it a very sticky world. Ideas get drawn to one another, through some strange new gravitational pull that makes it more fun and efficient to share a ride. *Most entrepreneurs are not tapping into existing markets that they are trying to dominate; rather, they are inventing and designing markets that never before existed.*

Carrier has teamed with Microsoft to make all its air-conditioning units Web ready. This partnership allows the two companies to address what Evans and Wurster describe in *Blown to Bits* as the *richness versus reach* problem that every business faces.[16] Every company must balance its desire for reaching a wider market and thus becoming a force to be reckoned with, with its need to provide more depth or richness to the exchange and thus getting more from every client. Alliances afford a rapid solution to this issue. In this case, both Carrier and Microsoft get more reach and become more central to those who want to join their network. They each get more richness and service to provide to their customers. Both are blessed by the forces of synergy.

It takes more than just a logistical maneuver to place a chip in an appliance. It requires a creative interface between two companies; organizational borders must be a bit more permeable. This forces companies to not only share what they know, but to develop strategies in tandem and partner with customers in a very new way. For reasons such as these, Andersen Consulting's global survey of alliances also found that nearly half of these alliances fail or wind down. It is a process filled with many of the same risks as any marriage.

In a complete turnaround of everything we have learned, value is now created through access rather than scarcity. In the world of physical goods, the less something is available, the higher the price. If gold were found in everyone's backyard, then it wouldn't be worth much. However, in the on-line world, the more people use something, the more valuable it is.

So in a strange bit of superfluid logic, even if Microsoft did lose 40 percent of its Windows revenue through pirating, it still gained value from it. More people with Microsoft software, means that more people will continue to purchase it, merely to stay compatible with the status quo. This is why the boundaries defending products and proprietary knowledge have often purposely become somewhat permeable.

This is also why hitching a ride is one of the fastest paths to critical mass. Despite popular opinion, you don't need to be the first out the door with a product in order to win. You don't even have to be the best. Whoever reaches critical mass first is the one who wins. Critical mass means that a great enough proportion of the market uses your product, which makes others come on board just to be compatible with what everyone else is doing. Success is contagious.

One of the critical stumbling blocks to the open-source movement is that the varied players developing diverse innovations don't always make sure that these applications are able to easily talk to each other. Without this common language, no matter how good the product, its success is doomed. One of the critical features of living in a world of blended ownership is that it requires heightened collaboration.

Palm is hot on this trail. It has been very aggressive in pursuing a role in corporate solutions. For example, a salesperson can check a product code right from the floor using his or her palmtop and see if the item is in stock or perhaps at another store. Companies that have used this system, such as Famous Footwear, see mistakes drop and service rise proportionately. The Navy has used Palm to track the performance of pilots. Palm has also entered into an agreement with Zagat so that when you point at a restaurant, the menu and reviews can appear on your screen. Palm also recently licensed its operating system to Visor. Visor has come up with forty different applications like cameras, music players, global positioning systems, etc., which can be attached to the Palm device. It is alliances such as these that are allowing Palm to pull ahead in the wireless wars. You can also envision a time when Palm's licensing agreements become so numerous and lucrative that the Palm device tends toward free merely as a way of further expanding market share and getting more of those great service contracts.

Game companies will spend almost as much time on their networks of delivery as their products. When Alain Rossman founded WAP (Wireless Application Protocol), the language for connecting cell phones to the Internet, he spent the first couple of years getting firms like Microsoft to sign up. Then others rejiggered their software to meet his standards. Similarly, Quicken software became the program of choice for home accounting. Quicken was also aggressive about becoming the language for many financial platforms such as mortgage and insurance sites. And the more sites that use Quicken, the more it becomes an industry standard. Which leads Kevin Kelly to suggest yet another maxim of the digital space: The more you place yourself in the center of a network, the more powerful you are.[17]

This is also why we will no longer have discrete products and services; we will have consumer events that tie vast networks of providers into a unified delivery system. Already, cobranding is a well-developed and frequently used idea, where two companies such as American Express (Amex) and Hilton Hotels advertise and promote each other's products. Amex customers will want to stay at Hilton, and Hilton customers may want an Amex card. Cobranding will become an art form as more and more companies mine their overlaps and share their customers.

This is also why nimble careerists will find that interdisciplinary degrees and experience that bridges industries will make them hot commodities. Everyone will need good *translators,* people who can speak the language of two or more different fields.

For Palm to help a retailer with inventory management or the Navy with pilot performance, it had to get inside its neighbor's corporate skin to envision viable services. When it relates to a customer at this level, is Palm helping the Navy with its future, or is the Navy helping Palm to build its? Where does Palm end and the Navy begin? What happens to the employees in such a blended environment? Where do their loyalties begin and end?

The Japanese have always done business in the context of keiret-sus—networks of businesses that support each other and lend a hand in hard times. In practice, the Japanese system was beset with formalities and a history that often hindered goals as much as it supported them. In *The Shape of Things to Come,* Richard Oliver suggests that a new breed of nimble electronic keiretsu is emerging. For example, amazon.com, with its vast associate program, 3M's Technical Forum, which brings together its leading scientists and engineers, or Motorola's international network of scouts often function more like a learning community.[18]

An interesting battle is unfolding that will be decided purely on how developed our urge to merge really is. XML and HTML are languages that allows your home computer to talk to your telephone and your refrigerator and all those chips that are swarming through everything imaginable. Whatever becomes the standard for this language neatly places itself in the center of all the action. Of course, everyone wants to be the winner in this battle over protocols, but no one can agree. Meanwhile Microsoft is quietly setting its own standard. Like the much earlier Apple/DOS battle, Microsoft may dominate the Webbed world, not because it has a better product but because the motley crew of over five hundred players are still competing with each other. If these smaller players don't get the urge to merge very quickly, they will find themselves shut out of the game. Thus, skills for partnering, cobranding and sharing are now as critical as design, innovation and product development.

1.4 MINISTERS OF DECONSTRUCTION

Symbolic death-rebirth rituals are central to every shamanic tradition. Those who do not regularly shed their psychological skin in order to become new again become old before their time. Death-rebirth rituals allow you to reemerge in the present, free to perceive without the veil of personal history that may dull your perceptions and keep you from detecting the road ahead.

The CEO of a sixty-million-dollar software company had just seen a variation of his company's core product appropriated by a larger company and bundled within its entry-level offering. The CEO told us his company had six months' cash reserves to figure out a new identity. In this new freewheeling environment, it's an experience that more and more people have come to know. This is one of the more challenging emotional experiences for any business or individual; suddenly who you are is no longer relevant.

But this is also why wise businesses invade themselves. Wise businesses are not afraid to die. They seek ways to devour what they do before anyone else does. Consultant and best-selling author Tom Peters is a leading evangelist of this philosophy. He recommends that every company designate a *Minister of Deconstruction,* someone who gets paid to actively address paths for cannibalizing the existing business.[19] Obviously, creative deconstruction is not new; organizational theorists have been promoting this principle for decades. What is new is the heightened necessity to master this art, because of the speed of the market. What is also unprecedented is the ease and magnitude of deconstruction that is possible because so many business functions rest on bits of information and can bypass the more sluggish resistance of the human hand.

In January 1999, an idea was floated through the ranks of Cable and Wireless. Like many companies, it was searching for a way to add clicks to its bricks. In true Net time, by late August 2000, Bluefield was launched to develop the capacity for marketing and selling its products on-line. It was a company within a company, given its own identity and considerable latitude for making choices. More important, it was launched with the express purpose of devouring the way Cable and Wireless currently did business. A key player in this project told us, *"We are destroying from inside. Ultimately this will be the only way you find us."*

If the team at Bluefield wants something to happen and the existing bureaucracy resists, it has the authority to go outside to get what it needs. Bluefield doesn't have to fight the status quo. This is a key point for those considering this path. If in the end your internal start-up is bound by the edges of the existing system, you can never really escape the gravitational pull of business as usual. Bluefield is designing from the ground up, using the existing system when it is helpful and going outside when there is resistance.

Many businesses are consciously destroying themselves from within, but most often it is a particular product or service that gets deconstructed. In this case Bluefield will not only change how Cable and Wireless acquires and provides service, it will shift the entire identity of the company from that of a telephone company to that of an Internet company.

The larger company is documenting this creative process every step of the way. It transcribes meetings and notes critical transitions. It is developing an internal guidebook for creative deconstruction. Once this project succeeds, the company hopes to transport this model of change to its operations in Europe, Asia and the rest of the world.

Further, this deconstruction process is not a one-time shot, which once implemented will become the new status quo. Bluefield is viewed as a process. It is expected to continually cannibalize itself and reinvent its products and approaches on a regular basis. The key players who are building this new possibility have been told not to think about advancing up the ranks of the new organization. They are expected to go out and multiply, moving horizontally through the system as experts on corporate death-rebirth rituals. (The deconstruction process was so successful, that during the course of our discussions about this topic, Bluefield had already morphed into a more far-reaching vision called Sapphire.)

These attitudes are possible only because forward-thinking companies realize how fluid this world is. They understand that there is often not much security in having a *hot property*. A nomadic company needs *hot process*.

When Watts Wacker and Jim Taylor surveyed three hundred of the largest companies that had been in business for over one hundred years, they found that not one was still doing business in its original area.[20] Obviously, creative deconstruction has always been the way of long-term success; it's just that now we do it a lot more often and lot faster.

Let me offer an example of creative deconstruction that perhaps did not go far enough. Newspapers derive 30 to 50 percent of their incomes from classified ads. With the advent of the on-line world, hundreds of offerings infringed on this space. Sites like Monster.com began to build a presence for job offerings. Others absorbed automobile ads and added value by facilitating a customer's search for the exact vehicle from a much wider inventory. Even personal ads found new venues for display.

The newspapers were not completely asleep through these developments.[21] In an extraordinary and unprecedented act of cooperation, five key papers collaborated to build a national classified service and database. This move definitely helped stave off some of the income drain. But in my perception, the newspapers did not go far enough.

For the most part, they still run their papers like papers and their on-line classifieds like ads. The newspapers were looking for a solution to their income problem; they did not consider a total redefinition of their identity. With their incredible journalistic resources, they might have built a powerful information platform. One could click from an article about new research on learning, to more in-depth reporting on the local school, to ads for learning software or ordering books on the topic. They could have been building cognitive maps linking news with ideas and commercial exchanges in a seamless web. The newspapers would not have had to compromise truth in reporting. In fact, these types of links might have allowed them to separate the conflicts of interest that already exist and allow these influences to be more clearly established. Further, a local paper is a powerful mirror of the local community, and it is in a perfect position to build a virtual city. For efforts like these to have taken place, the newspapers would have had to redefine themselves at a much deeper level.

The CEO of a popular e-commerce site irreverently stated the company's business strategy: *"First we make the rules. And then we break them!"*

This is the language of the future. Whenever you sense a boundary, relentlessly pursue its breakdown. There is often a pot of gold on the other side of the wall you have just deconstructed.

1.5 WHEN ASSETS ARE LIABILITIES

Irene Jacobs and Neil Samuels could be considered poster kids for our digital aboriginal mind-set. They were up-and-coming fashion designers when they stumbled upon a process they called *cooked images*.

They didn't use the *phrase* digital aboriginal; they did it. They took sacred images from various cultures and cooked them by digitally altering and modernizing the look and providing a means of transfer to very high-end T-shirts. They might take a Tibetan Tanka painting and merge it with modern patterns to fit just right on the fabric.

In a world dominated by slick images, they believed ancient forms would carry extraordinary visual impact. They felt this *digital aboriginal* look would stand out in today's visual environment. And they were right. Their T-shirt line became the darling of rock stars and actors, and they became the hottest kids on the block, for a while.

Within months, dozens of firms had co-opted their look and lowered the prices. Irene and Neil had been in the fashion industry for years. They knew how predatory it was. They had experienced the appropriation of many of their past designs by more powerful companies. In the past, they would have spent huge amounts of energy defending their territory by romancing wholesalers. Although they did do some defensive maneuvers, they also redefined their company.

They were able to do this because for the first time their product was not just clothes; it was a way of putting information together. They had the freedom to explore new options because they were not tied to any factories or workforces. They rapidly adapted their technique to all forms of merchandising, successfully selling their look to companies like Disney and Sony.

Even as these endeavors progress, they are thinking further ahead and adapting their graphic process to animation and film. They are still producing clothes and using their lead to stay a step or two ahead of the pack and keep a lock on the higher-end market, but they no longer define themselves as just fashion designers. They are image makers, free to apply their craft to any industry. *As a result they can go anywhere with what they know.*

Nike is the most often used example of a company that has stayed focused on its intellectual capital and kept things like factories, trucks and stores of inventory off its books. Nike merely puts its brand name on goods produced by others. It manages the brand and little else. It's not only a cool way to stay focused, but it becomes imperative in a world where methods of production get outdated as fast as they are set up. Those who get stuck with long-term obligations are not as free to move. Assuming they have the intellectual capital and the emotional will to stay responsive, outsourced companies will always be freer to move.

Irene and Neil were free to explore their potential as image makers because they had fewer fixed obligations to factories and staff. In yet another *Alice in Wonderland* turn of events in the new economy, *fixed assets can actually be a liability.*

As quickly as companies join neighboring ventures, they are just as quick to outsource tasks that are not directly related to what they want to do. Old-line companies used to do everything in-house. Sometimes their workers were so involved in maintenance that creativity had to be outsourced. Now, all manner of housekeeping functions are outsourced from billing to printing to human-resource tasks. Companies want to stay lean so that their core people can remain focused on the true intent of the business.

Further, when something like billing is a housekeeping function, the people who do this work are not central to their company's purpose. They don't feel important and are far less likely to naturally innovate. Since the company doesn't value their services as a source of income, it tends not to really look at that department as a source of innovation. Yet when a company only handles billing for other businesses, it is highly motivated to innovate. That *is* its business. The company cares about it. Billing is important again; it is an art form and a science. The people who work in this billing company are no longer housekeepers, they are pros. They are experts in their field, so they naturally act smarter.

Outsourcing is the modern equivalent of the ancient clan. Clans were family groups responsible for a particular piece of knowledge, such as boating and navigation or basket weaving or healing arts. Each clan was dedicated to perfecting its area of knowledge. The clan could channel its natural inclination to make a better, more beautiful canoe or more elegant basket, because all its focus was on this expression. We are returning to this ancient form of specialization, where each group stays focused on its creative purpose. ***Outsourcing not only allows for nimbleness, it is great for creativity, both for the business who takes on the task and the one that lets it go.***

A key path to productivity in the new economy is to have everything *just on time.* Everything from capital to inventory to workers are streamlined so they arrive only at the moment they are needed. Anything that arrives too early or hangs around too long is a drag on profit. The only way to achieve this ultimate just-on-timeness is to streamline everything so that there is a minimum viable commitment to any particular direction. Just-on-timeness is a state of dynamic equilibrium that allows maximum freedom of choice. Commitments to preexisting systems are the very conditions that cause a company to resist change and defend its territories.[22]

1.6 THE NOMADIC ECONOMY

"A fine wind is blowing the new direction of time."
D.H. LAWRENCE

As long as products are shrink-wrapped, ownership as we now know it can reign. The more content is available digitally, the more vulnerable it is. The more the Internet grows as the medium of dissemination, the more the power of traditional gatekeepers is diminished. Volatility explodes when almost anyone can copy your form and new ideas are relatively easy to implement. Creative boundaries become very fuzzy when distinctly different companies must share ideas in order to generate a future together. And ownership becomes far more fluid when neighboring entities want to participate in the profit of an idea. Then you discover that what you are selling just barely exists and you should probably divest yourself of any physical obligations as fast as you possibly can.

It is no accident that the digital economy is playing with our ability to hold on to physical objects, and in doing so is providing a path for our journey back to this more nomadic mind-set. The dwellers within this world must value change more than stability, adaptability more than control, freedom more than clarity, fuzzy unpredictability more than fixed solutions, collaborative products rather than fixed authorship and designing new markets together with others rather than competing for a share of the old market.

We are witnessing the *de-evolution of control*. A nomadic economy requires that we:

- Release our strict notions of authorship and explore cocreative forms of distribution and dynamic forms of copyright and compensation.
- Plan for generosity, since systems will lean toward becoming more free and open and dialogues will be the new products.
- Learn to merge as a path for leveraging impact and hitting critical mass, focusing on getting involved with as many consumer events as are relevant.
- Continually deconstruct and redefine our core businesses, before anyone else does.
- Outsource as much as possible to stay nimble and focused on what lies ahead.

These are not unrelated factors. They contribute to a larger commercial environment of convergent products, codependent services and blended futures.

The new economy is not unlike those lava lamps from the sixties. The heat from the lamp causes the colored wax to merge and then separate, taking on new and unexpected shapes effortlessly and in ways that are quite amusing to watch. The cyberpunk mentality that gave rise to free software and edgy new values at the fringe is now standard fare, penetrating deep into the heart of suburbia and businesses alike.

The more we have to live with shared visions, the less rigid we can be about what is yours and mine. In fact, holding on to stuff slows you down. It dulls your perceptions because you are no longer free to see options that challenge what you currently do. Attachment to your personal or corporate history drives you to dominate your surroundings and preserve your place, rather than to hear what's coming. The metaphor that no one can own the wind reveals the essence of the nomadic spirit. Nomads are not oriented to acquisition, they only seek the next horizon. They have little need to hoard since they survive on what lies ahead. It's not that ownership or intellectual property will cease to exist, but our expectations about this concept will be continually redefined situation by situation. What we thought we owned today may be nearly free tomorrow, forcing us to continually ride the next creative edge.

In time we will come to understand the digital world in much the same way that indigenous people related to Dreamtime—as a realm of pure, unadulterated, infinite rivers of possibility. As we enter more fully into this landscape, we will discover its infinite capacity for ever-increasing complexity and adaptability to any creative direction we might wish to pursue.

The thesis that no one will ever own the wind is not a new rule; rather, it is an artistic palette. There are no fixed solutions to this proposition, it is merely an image designed to spark your imagination. We will soon come to understand the notion of authorship or ownership as a

field of influence that may look a particular way this month and be redefined next month. The fences we build around our ideas will no longer
define what we have. Instead, ownership will rest in the essence of what
we are able to take with us to the next stage of our nomadic travels.

New paradigms for understanding ownership will act like a pebble
dropped in a lake. Ripples will affect every dimension of the innovation
process. The reverberations of more dynamic intellectual property, com-
mingled corporate boundaries, products that morph into pure service
and collaborations that weave together vast consumer events will continue to send out profound organizational shock waves. The players who
are willing to treat property as a dynamic social equation rather than a
fixed line in the sand will be the visionaries who chart this new social
course.

If understood wisely, ownership is like the wind. It is the force that
pushes you along. It is an energy you can ride. But try to put it in a bottle, and its power is quickly lost.

In the eighties Australian aboriginal art was all the rage. A savvy dealer in Sydney signed one of the best artists. Every few months she would make the arduous journey to the outback to pick up the artist's completed canvases to bring back to the gallery.

When she arrived, invariably one of the canvases would have food stains from a time the artist's family used it as a picnic table. Another would have tire tracks from the time the artist's son rode his bike over it. She would plead with this artist to keep his canvases pristine and not use them as props in his daily life. Once again, the aboriginal artist would respectfully appear to agree.

The moment she disappeared from view, the artist would shake his head. Why didn't it add value to have his lines of paint infused with marks from everyday life? He could never understand why city folks had such a need to separate art from everyday experience.

When art is merged with everyday experience the quality of the piece must actually be more profound. It can no longer rest on the strength of the frame and the starkness of the white wall to provide the necessary contrast that will show it off. It must fully stand on its own merits.

THE RETURN
OF THE
STORYTELLERS

The ancient Greek site of Delphi was famous for its oracles. Their powers were so revered that before any battle or major decision, leaders would make the long pilgrimage to this breathtaking mountain site to gain some prophetic insight. However, if you visit Delphi, north of Athens, you will discover that the temple to the prophets is at a lower elevation than the theater. The prime real estate is devoted to the theater.

Epidaurus was another equally distinguished ancient site located in the Peloponnese, where Hippocrates wrote his famous medical oath. Wounded and ailing individuals would walk through pits of poisonous snakes in an effort to make it victoriously to the other side, and thus be healed. But once again Epidaurus's famed theater has the most stellar view, towering above the area devoted to healing.

If power is location, then clearly the dramatic event was the center of the Greek world. The theater was where new ideas were forged and social dilemmas enacted in the hopes of catharsis and resolution. As in almost every ancient culture, life was examined on the stage.

> "The birth of a child, education, hunting, marriage, war, the administration of justice, religious ceremonies and funeral rites—every important event in life is made by primitive man ... the occasion for a purely theatrical spectacle."
>
> RUSSIAN PLAYWRIGHT NICOLAS EVREINOFF[1]

In the days before advertising, way back before even the written word, people established their presence in ways that did not involve persuasion. Storytellers were the power brokers. They wove tales that would carry their tribes forward. Traveling minstrels were eagerly welcomed and fed by the local villagers since they were the voices of tomorrow.

Well, the storytellers are back! Where ideas and intellectual capital drove the information economy, pure, unadulterated imagination will drive the next phase of the commercial evolution.

This chapter begins by challenging traditional advertising and marketing beliefs, but as the pages unfold, you will discover a far deeper message. You will discover why myths, stories and modern-day rituals will again come to the fore as the substance from which culture is built and commerce is shaped. When the lived experience returns as the centerpiece of our culture, commerce will have to realign around this new axis.

THE DAY THE ADS STOPPED WORKING

Marketing as we have known it is history. Fewer people are listening, and those under twenty-five are already out the door. Hipper ads won't be enough to get them back.

The proliferation of easy publication means that everyone is vying for our attention. At the same time we have less patience for looking at anything. The average person will wait 13.2 seconds for a page to load and 51 seconds looking at that page. So, if your story doesn't come down quick and have a message that is immediately accessible, you don't exist!

As if these armies of professional attention-grabbers were not enough, average people have opened their own digital destinations. Friends beckon to other friends to check them out and tune in to their on-line chronicles. It is so easy to forward jokes, surveys, petitions and tidbits that even casual acquaintances shower you with constant mementos of their presence. Everyone wants a piece of your attention. *As a result, the impact of traditional advertising is collapsing in the wake of our rampant information smog and the ensuing time sickness that leaves us with never enough time to do what we want to do.*

It is not so much our privacy, but our attention that has become a closely guarded asset:

1. The typical business manager reads one million words a week.
2. Sixty percent of our time in the office is now spent processing documents.
3. The average person experiences more than three thousand advertising messages per day.
4. During the eighties, third-class mail grew thirteen times faster than the population.
5. By 1990, there were over thirty thousand telemarketing companies employing a mind-blowing eighteen million people.[2]

In case you are still not yet impressed: We also have 260,000 billboards, 11,520 newspapers, 11,536 periodicals, 27,000 video outlets, plus dish on demand and 100 million computers. Forty thousand new book titles are published in the U.S. every year; three hundred thousand worldwide. Sixty billion pieces of junk mail will enter our mailboxes every year. Forty-one million photographs were taken every day in the U.S. before digital cameras came into widespread use.[3] The number of images in circulation now is incalculable. Telephone lines now carry more bits of information than actual talk between people, and the wireless devices now exceed the ones that need a line.

At this pace little gets absorbed. Research has shown that the *more* you are surrounded by input, the *less* you retain. Information gets blurred. You can't remember where you heard what. Decision making is slowed because there are so many opinions to integrate. Even important inputs blend together in an ever-present undifferentiated background noise that no longer receives your full attention.

Millions of Americans have been clinically diagnosed with Attention Deficit Disorder (ADD), which causes restlessness, short attention span and the inability to focus on a task. "With so many of these [distracted] people running around," writes Evan Schwartz in *Wired* magazine, "we could be fast becoming the first society with attention deficit disorder." He nominates ADD as "the official brain syndrome of the information age." [4]

David Shenk compiled an excellent survey of this problem in his book *Data Smog.* He cites Stanley Milgram's landmark study of information overload and six adaptive responses that arise from it:

1. We allocate less time to each input.
2. We disregard low-priority inputs.
3. Boundaries are redrawn in social exchanges so that the burden is shifted to the other party in the exchange [i.e., you have to prove yourself; the listener doesn't help you out].
4. We block off reception of messages through unlisted phone numbers, unfriendly expressions, etc.
5. We use filtering devices to diminish the intensity of input. [This includes the auditory insulation provided by Walkmans, MP3 players and constant cell phone use.]
6. Specialized institutions are created to absorb inputs that would otherwise swamp the individual. [5]

And I'll add a few more ways that we have of coping with this deluge of data:
7. Information of all types becomes blurred, indistinct and quickly

fades from memory. A curious result is that despite mountains of data, decisions become more immediate and less informed.

8. Interrupted by beepers and cell phones even in the presence of friends or in the midst of important work, we become accustomed to having our attention constantly fractured. It is acceptable to never be all there, no matter what we are doing.

9. *Wombing in,* a self-imposed isolation and avoidance of input has also become socially acceptable. People can proudly announce without shame, "Oh, I never read the newspaper."

In addition, many find it difficult to slow down from the fast-paced imagery of TV and music, to the slower pace of prose. A favorite phrase among teens is the term *too much information,* liberally used when someone gives a lot of details. E-mail etiquette says keep it short and sweet. Not only is 13.2 seconds the maximum time we will wait to download a Web page, it's the *official conversational attention span* we will allot to almost anything.

More troubling is that approximately 20 percent of the U.S. population is considered partially or functionally illiterate. Compare that to an illiteracy rate of 4.3 percent in 1930, just after the huge waves of non-English speaking immigrants arrived here, and this number is more staggering.[6] Even among the literate, there has been steady decline. The average newspaper is now written on a sixth-grade level. Sadly, even the *New York Times* downgraded its vocabulary in order to stay *competitive.* In the last fifty years, the average vocabulary of a six- to fourteen-year-old in the U.S. has shrunk from twenty-five thousand words to just under ten thousand.[7] *A key impact of our modern media diet may very well be the gradual deconstruction of the written word as the centerpiece of mass communication.*

If you are an advertiser or merely someone who wants people to know what your business offers, these adaptations are cause for worry. These symptoms are showing up for you, all the people you work with and all the people you are trying to reach. You can no longer hope to connect by merely having another clever piece of input.

Response rates for mail promotions have just hit an all-time low. In dozens of states you can remove your name from phone dialing registries, making it illegal for anyone to call your home or business and solicit sales. About one-third of the public has left network TV for other venues, usually those that are commercial free. Sixty percent report that even when the TV is on they don't pay attention as much as they used to and mostly use it for background noise. The Yankelovich Report on Generational Marketing states the dilemma quite clearly: *"Browsing will begin to characterize the way all age groups relate to all media. Yet our marketing strategies are still based on them watching and reading."* [8]

Once the remote control came on the scene, we became a nation of data dodgers, with highly specialized skills for ignoring vast stretches of the information terrain. We can walk down the street and never notice the change of a billboard right above our office. We have an incredible talent for thinking about something else the moment a radio ad comes on and tuning back in when the music returns. ***The remote control no longer rests in our hand. It has become part of our brain, allowing us to screen out uninvited information with incredible accuracy and effectiveness.***

Perhaps the only audience left who still listens and more important the only people who still believe what they hear are young kids. So it's no surprise that 20 percent of all ads are targeted at them. Research shows that kids influence 20 percent of all purchases in their home, so they are powerful folks. Advertisers also know that kids under seven have a hard time distinguishing between fantasy and reality, so when an ad says a sugar cereal will make you stronger, kids think it really will. And parents are well aware of this susceptibility; just witness the in-store tantrum of a child who has been denied a purchase. Of course activist parents are horrified by the influence of advertisers. For years they've lobbied congress for action, to little avail. But now TiVo will do what the government never will. This is a key piece of TiVo's marketing hook—*it allows mothers and fathers to easily assume a new parental role, that of media editor.*

This takes the remote control mentality a few steps farther. A series of programs can be personalized for each member in your family, allowing everyone to have their own *customized channel*, designed from an almost endless series of offerings. The early data suggests that 88 percent of all commercials go unwatched in a TiVo household. The moment TiVo-type products become widespread, the price of TV ads is bound to drop precipitously. And that moment is fast approaching. Forrester Research projects that by 2004, fifty million homes will have such devices on their sets. So the trend is clear. You no longer have to avoid, edit and screen unsolicited intrusions; you can design a world where they don't exist.

By 2004, most cars will have satellite radio capacity as a standard feature. Lead companies like Sirius and XM Satellite Radio have already partnered with the big automakers. When asked if radio really needs fixing, their response is simple and to the point: Fifteen minutes out of every hour of traditional broadcasting consists of commercials. These companies will offer one hundred channels, mostly commercial free. And once Web radio is established, the home listener will be able to personalize this medium just as effectively. With services like PointCast you can select your news, so classifieds are no longer the price you pay to stay informed.

Agents can be programmed to search out on-line information according to your specifications so you don't have to encounter a single ad. Software programs like WebWasher allow you to avoid spam, filter out banners and delete unsolicited content. A similar filtering program called AdSubtract expects to be on five to ten million PCs by 2002 and will be preinstalled by three of the ten best-selling PC manufacturers. Go-Video's VCR advances right past the commercials.

The media industry is proud to announce that it can offer *anything, anywhere, anytime*. But as Nicholas Negroponte points out, the average consumer is far more interested in *"nothing, never, nowhere,* unless it is timely, important, amusing, relevant or capable of reaching my imagination."[9] **In every media domain, the public is about to officially graduate from an editing mentality to a world of complete unadulterated choice.**

Marketing guru Regis McKenna has gone so far as to declare the *end of brands.* Brands don't matter; distribution does.[10] The most famous example of brand management is Coke, said to be the most recognized brand name in the world. But McKenna says Coke's clout rests far more on its distribution channels than its name. People buy Coke mostly because it is so relentlessly accessible. McKenna offers ample evidence that just because your brand name is profoundly familiar, it still does not mean the customer will actually choose your product over another. *To consumers dulled and jaded by constant input, proximity and access is what creates behavior, far more than name recognition.*

In fact, brand loyalty has decreased 20 percent in the last eight years. Price tied with brand is the number one reason customers make a particular product choice, and there's little doubt it will soon pull ahead. In other words, a company that focuses primarily on brand management is still living in the fifties.

The Yankelovich Report on Generational Marketing examines attitudes of three distinct target markets:

- the Matures, born before 1945
- the Boomers, born before 1964
- the Xers, born after 1965

It offers extensive polling data showing that the influence of brands will diminish in impact as each successively younger generation comes on board and reaches the peak of their purchasing power.[11] Thus with every passing year, the public will become ever more immune to the advertising agenda.

Don Tapscott goes a bit further and attributes the biggest part of this change to an even younger target group: the growing impact of the Net generation, born after 1980. In his book *Growing Up Digital* he says:

There is considerable evidence that the combination of the new generation with the new media may spell trouble for the brand, at least as we have known it. It can be argued that in an interactive world with N-gen customers, the brand will be harder to establish and may evaporate.[12]

Eighteen-year-old Andy Puteschegl sums up the on-line mentality of his generation in a few easy sentences:

I love being able to skip all the fancy advertising if I'm in a hurry. I don't wait for something to load. I just click onto another page. I don't even pay attention to the ads on search engines because I am there for another purpose—to look information up.[13]

The remote-control mentality, which took us through the last decade, will be dwarfed by the TiVo-ization of every media stream. *Despite the hype, the digital world is* not *a new channel for advertising opportunities; it is a medium for personal choice and ultimately a vehicle for the avoidance of any unsolicited intrusion. It will eventually render traditional advertising obsolete.*

More Is Less

Believers point to the fact that telemarketing brings in nine billion dollars a year and that an effective ad campaign can still increase product sales. This is only because we are still dwelling between two worlds, partly swayed by persuasion and partly well on the road to building an ad-free media diet. Based on the trends, the world of persuasion is bound to bring diminishing returns.

Nevertheless, most still carry on, completely ignoring the looming shadow of ever more effective editing devices. One dollar out of every six in expenses is spent on marketing, using mostly traditional advertising channels. Completely denying the fact that they are dealing with media grazers, the advertisers are still investing heavily in five-course, formal, sit-down, media dinners. Amazingly they still assume everyone is sitting back enjoying the jingles, absorbing the message.

Thus most are still trying to get noticed, fighting ever harder for an ever less meaningful piece of the attention pie. Calvin Klein used provocatively posed, half-naked preadolescent models in underwear ads. Now everyone does it, and the very same look that caused many to attack Calvin Klein for skirting the boundary of what could be called child pornography is background noise. Benetton had the same experience. Photos of death-row criminals adorned its yuppie catalog. People talked about it. People complained about it. Then ten companies ripped off the look and the shock value was instantly absorbed and rendered ordinary.

To a public that has seen it all, it is harder and harder to find an edge that is truly new. This leads market profilers to say that the new generation would rather you get to the point and give them the facts straight up. Tuning in to this sentiment, one Nike ad says: *"We don't sell dreams. We sell shoes."* Keeping on message, another says: *"Don't insult our intelligence. Tell us what it is and what it does and don't play the national anthem when you do it."* In the lower right-hand corner the ad reads, *"I am not a target market. I am an athlete."* [14]

If you see one of these give-it-to-me-straight-type ads you can assume it is targeted at Generation X and younger. But in this media dense environment this direction will soon be most effective for every target group.

In part, this is because even memorable ads are making less and less connection. Maybe you remember my personal favorite, where a group of weather-worn cowboy types sat around a campfire and told stories at the end of a long day on horseback. They told of the trials, tribulations and rewards of *herding cats*. The tag line was so memorable that the phrase *herding cats* made it into the popular vernacular. It's an advertiser's dream to have his or her tag line infiltrate daily talk. But can anyone remember the name of the company that claimed to be so good at herding cats? I can't and I loved it. A memorable ad means nothing if the viewer doesn't link it to you. With the increased information-blurring caused by data smog, the inability to connect messages with the speaker will happen even more. Fewer people are listening, and when they do, they can't seem to get the message straight anyway. *What's an advertiser to do?*

Early research also suggests that the responsiveness of the on-line viewer may be far lower than that of the TV viewer. As a result, any dot-com company whose main income stream was based on advertising found itself in very treacherous waters. Peter Martin, Founder and CEO of ExpandMail, agrees that using traditional advertising to get people to come to a Web site has not worked. He's hawking the capacity for e-mailed video brochures with no browser download required.

Of course, all the hip ad agencies tout their ability to conquer the illusive domain of on-line media. Mostly they play around with more invasive formats in order to break through the numbness barrier. They use side pieces to catch your peripheral vision, pop-ups in the middle of the page and full-page displays that emerge every time you go to a new page. But these new visual assaults are still bound to have limited effect. We are rapidly moving away from interruptive advertising to messages that interact seamlessly with the events on the screen.

This is why the original *Blair Witch* on-line campaign *did* work. In hushed tones one person told another about a group of kids lost in the woods who left behind a documentary, the only record of their amazing adventure. Long before the movie opened in the theaters a huge electronic buzz had already been created. Similarly, Farmclub has launched several hit musical groups by allowing its listeners to be the judge and jury. A particular sound is not pushed down your throat; the listeners decide the future of the musicians they hear. Farmclub has no money in promotion, so it has no investment in your choice; it wins no matter what.

Viral marketing was born the very same day we switched on the big beautiful Web. Yahoo! membership exploded overnight. Napster broke all records by getting millions of hits in a few months. Even more rapidly fifty million users left and found new destinations when Napster was reorganized.

An animation site offers a daily image of a guy on a toilet. It received an astounding thirty-five million hits a month, rivaling the largest entertainment sites. The developer was offered a contract by Sony, not so much because of his animation skills, but for his knack at creating buzz. Friends telling other friends about a product is how things get heard. In fact, this new generation has been called the *Chit Ch@t Generation* since they have an incredible talent for talking themselves through a purchase. We all delete our spam without even looking, but when a friend forwards something, it is six times more likely to get a second glance. Much like being at a party, there is a very fine art to becoming the topic of conversation without turning people off by dominating the space and talking too much about yourself.

So an army of viral specialists arrived on the scene. At first, they seemed to apply the old persuasion paradigm to this new participatory one, by planting messages or *fake buzz* in various chat rooms. But that got old quick. M80 Interactive Marketing President Dave Neupert, one of these viral experts, says, *"The community can always smell a rat."*[15] So these specialists have now been relegated to lurking around conversational scenes and passing the word along to their clients so that they can adjust their actions based on the chat. At most, a particularly vocal customer, either positive or negative, may be contacted, either to encourage or assuage them. In this new world, you can't power your way into people's hearts and minds. They have to want you there.

Scarce attention may actually save us from being buried in drivel. When attention becomes a valued commodity, everyone will demand improved mythmaking. ***Crowded markets require more compelling tales. Weary listeners demand more authentic conversation. Experienced viewers who tend to buy more, also tend to seek out the most intelligent dialogues.***

Push to Pull

Google claims to be the only search engine that offers listings based on *merit only* and not because the listing site paid to be placed near the top of the search. Google makes its money on pop-up ads coordinated with the nature of the inquiry. It also boasts a click-through rate *three times higher* than other search engines, merely because its ads are so carefully crafted to be relevant to the search.

Amazon.com has also forged a partnership with Yahoo!, so that when you conduct a search for a particular topic, you can click to receive a listing of books related to that topic. The *New York Times Book Review* finally offered a link to Barnes & Noble. The *Times* was hesitant to link its reviews to commercial gain, which probably resulted in many heated meetings. But the truth is, if it hadn't done this, the prestige of its list might have fallen from public view. The link only improved the *Times*'s standing. *Atlantic Monthly* and others have done the same.

Here's where the real promise lies: ***The on-line world offers an extraordinary ability to connect the moment of hearing about something with the immediate possibility for receiving it.*** Business consultant and writer Rob Reid calls this the *impulse economy*. The key problem with traditional advertising is "there is no direct link between the demand created in the traditional off-line media and the fulfillment of that demand. This structural disconnect has huge ramifications."[16]

It opens the doors to all the problems we cited earlier that are linked with information smog and data drift, where you can't remember where you heard what. All advertising is a plea to buy, but its effectiveness is muted when you need to shift contexts *before* acting on the desire to buy. In that gap, your impetus diminishes, you forget what it was you wanted to get or some other direction distracts you. Or as Reid says, there is *leaking demand*. An opportunity to find out more about a product, properly placed within the context of everyday on-line behavior, allows you to bridge this gap. Impulse and fulfillment become best buddies, living just a click away from each other.

Already British Sky Broadcasting allows viewers to shop with its remote. Domino's Pizza claims that 2 percent of its sales come through this channel. Imagine what this capability could offer a QVC or Home Shopping Network. The line between the PC and the TV, and between e-commerce and broadcasting, is poised to evaporate. Convergence, or the blending together of different media modalities, has been called the trend of the next decade. It is not just channels of delivery that will blend, but the underlying purpose of news, entertainment, and marketing will begin to merge.

This shift in perspective, from pushing data to pulling in the viewer, will also reframe our entire understanding of how to position a product or business. The new marketing approach will rest on defining layers upon layers of information relevant to a product or service and finding ways to connect this information to the everyday on-line activities of the public. In his book *The Digital Estate,* Chuck Martin calls this marketing from the inside out versus outside in. With smart agents and targeting programs, marketers are approaching the ultimate marketing goal: to reach every unique customer at exactly the right moment.[17]

This has resulted in a new wave of marketing services—programs that allow you to track precise information about each and every customer. You can discover that they like jazz music, baseball and gourmet foods. When they visit a sports site to check out the latest score, a personalized pop-up ad can appear offering a coupon for gourmet cooking sauces and an announcement for a jazz club in their hometown.

This level of targeting is quite extraordinary, and it is not even the best part of the story. The best of these services allow customers to choose how much they let you know about their personal preferences. They decide whether to reveal or not. Already many sites allow you as a customer to refine your tastes in music or books ever more precisely. The better the information you offer, the better the recommendations become. This means that potential customers view the recommendations that pop up as a service, as choices they have made and, *voilà*, you have the ultimate advertising goal—*they have invited you in.*

Thus, marketing becomes more about understanding the cognitive spaces that surround a product. Once the behavioral terrain is mapped, then real, authentic, meaningful and entertaining information must be developed in a way that is useful. Maybe you only want your jazz club announcement to pop up on Thursdays, just before the weekend. Or maybe you want your ads for jewelry to pop up only in the weeks just prior to the customer's wedding anniversary and his wife's birthday.

NBCI.com took this immediacy to a whole other dimension. Its ads boast: Click on *any word, anytime, anywhere* and you have immediately conducted a search based on that word. If a friend sends you an e-mail and mentions a trip he or she took, all you have to do is click on the name of the city, even though your friend had no intention of referring you, and immediately you have relevant information. If an on-line magazine mentions a product, again you can click and shoot. Of course, the price you pay for this service is that every click is recorded, analyzed and fed to companies who would like to know more about you. Since you are clicking on words from your daily conversations, they get a remarkable read on your everyday environment. But that's another story, covered in the next chapter.

Assuming privacy concerns continue to fade into the background as we believe they will, it is imperative that a connected company establish a great information environment to surround its product or service. It is not marketing in the traditional sense of defining target groups; instead you are immersing yourself in existing markets so that your presence merges seamlessly with ordinary activities.

HOT TO COLD

Marshall McLuhan called TV a hot medium. The hotter and more captivating the better. Special effects, big, bold, beautiful graphics and recognizable celebrities all work well in the hot, steamy world of broadcasting.

Print is cool. The viewer plays a bigger role—scanning, jumping around to different sections, viewing in whatever order he or she likes. In a cool terrain, customized information works far better. Thousand of *zines* focused on ever narrower topics and personalized content are ideally suited to this medium. Print doesn't tend to launch stars. If it did, you'd know the names of the top-five columnists for the *New York Times,* the *Wall Street Journal* or *Fast Company.* Even famous authors pass through the airport unnoticed and without disguise. Flash, celebrity, special effects are all less relevant in a cool medium.

Well, if print is cool, then the on-line world is downright freezing. Flashy graphics, 3-D viewing tools and bells and whistles actually make the user experience more difficult. eCompany now publicly confessed its own on-line mistakes and detailed the kind of disasters created by overly fancy strategies.[18] Creative Good, a strategy consulting firm, found that 43 percent of buying attempts failed, up from 39 percent in the previous year. As sites get more complicated, customers are giving up more often.

The Boston Consulting Group (BCG) found that 20 percent of all customers give up before a page finishes loading.[19] If you add that to the 43 percent who are lost after the page loads, it means that two-thirds of all potential buyers are disappearing primarily because of impatience. When Creative Good did some consulting work for Gateway and helped it improve the customer experience, conversion rates went up 40 percent.

Further, people don't seem to visit because they remember who you are. They visit because you just happen to be in the way of their on-line path. Regis McKenna's advice is even more relevant to the on-line world: Distribution, or in this case access, is vital. Ads are less important than proximity and links. The more on-line roads lead to Rome, the more Rome will get visited.

This is what built Amazon.com. Its banners are almost always just a click away. Amazon.com built much of its permeating presence through associate-type programs where the referring party receives a percentage of the sale. Associate programs run the gamut from single individuals who have developed a small community of interest around a niche topic, all the way up to the largest portals and mightiest search engines. It is also a model that helps with that stickiness problem—getting people to stay around long enough to buy. With an associate program, sticky customers are thrust straight into purchasing mode.

Beginning in 2002, Jupiter Media Metrix projects that 24 percent of on-line purchases will be driven by affiliate sales.[20] Widely used by the big retailers, associate programs have also been critical to legions of small businesses that can't afford advertising and have niche products, like live lobsters or dating services, that make them prime targets for referrals. But even the affiliate approach has evolved over the last few years:

- Amazon.com introduced this strategy by offering a commission on books you recommended on your site. By 1999 it had over one hundred thousand affiliates boasting the Amazon banner. Its name was everywhere, mostly through unpaid spots on other people's sites reaching precise and active niche communities.

- Naturally, Barnes & Noble had to get in the game. It one-upped Amazon.com and expanded its offer to include all the books that were purchased by the individual you referred, not just the ones you recommended. Barnes & Noble went on to sign up some really high profile partners like the *New York Times Book Review.*

- Then Amazon.com forged a link with Yahoo!, so that an on-line search triggered an Amazon banner for books or products on that particular topic. Amazon.com also partnered with such popular niche sites as Intuit's Quicken.com to become its exclusive bookseller.

- eToys, although now defunct, discovered that when it raised its commission rate from 12 percent to 25 percent, it actually did better by attracting more serious affiliates.

- Building on this line of thought, Procter & Gamble (P&G) and Yahoo! launched an Internet promotion that tied payment to results. P&G paid only for people who actually clicked through to its products. The ads themselves acted like associates.

- Since every on-line business builds a community, why not share your entire neighborhood? *Virtual City,* a New York City magazine backed by *Newsweek,* agreed to carry a dozen pages of Web site reviews from Excite in exchange for banners on Excite's homepage.

- Some have discovered that real-life associates can add even more value. Bolt, a teen Web site, has an army of fifteen- to twenty-year-old reps who tell their friends to check out the site. These reps show up at schools, skateboard parks and malls and act as culture scouts so that Bolt can stay on top of what's really cool. With four million users and growing by five thousand a day, Bolt has built yet another variation on the associate model.

- Commissions are great, but if a viewer leaves through a link, you've lost a customer. Because of this, some companies were resistant to this model even if it was useful. New associate programs allow the viewer to purchase from a neighbor, without ever leaving his or her living room. Problem solved.

- Sites like Greatergood.com and 4Charity.com are linked to dozens of brand-name retailers. They return their associate fee, allowing 2 to 20 percent of your purchase price to be donated to a nonprofit cause. It is an associate model that is growing rapidly in popularity and allows consumers to tie purchasing to what they care about.

- Other popular software allows links and sidebars to appear, at the customer's discretion, as they go about their normal activities of surfing the net. Many feel this model may replace the traditional pop-ups, with advertisers paying only when a click-through occurs.

The next chapter will take this model even further. We will suggest that roaming consumer gangs may run more and more of the consumer world and associate arrangements will be just one aspect of their growing power.

In *Digital Darwinism,* Evan Schwartz provides a compelling economic argument for moving in the direction of associate-type models.[20] If a typical banner ad costs thirty dollars per thousand and has a 1 percent click-through rate with 10 percent buying, it takes one thousand customers for one sale. Your cost per sale is thirty dollars. If you pay an associate two dollars a pop or even ten dollars, your cost per sale is still dramatically cheaper.[21] "Ads become more like salespeople working purely on commission, rather than something you pay for ahead of time regardless of the impact it produces."[22]

Another striking development of the digital landscape is how easily people are willing to put their private lives on the line. If you think celebrity pales in print, it is almost useless in the on-line world. People want to display themselves, more than look at anyone else. The early statistics bear this out. Sanford Bernstein polled D-generation kids and found a 27 percent drop in whether they considered athletes role models compared to a decade ago. More important, when they were asked if athletes were cool, there was a 50 percent drop. Sanford Bernstein links this shift to the new kinds of individualistic sports that are now popular with kids, like skateboarding and gravity games, but a critical factor has also got to be that everyone wants to be star, and now they can.

Jaron Lanier, a musician and originator of the term *virtual reality,* is working on a program that allows an on-screen avatar to reflect your movements. A camera allows the screen character to smile or scratch its head just because you do. The upshot is that not too far down the line you will be able to insert your own face for an actor playing a part, in effect playing the lead in any movie you choose. Once this capacity is in place then celebrity will fade even farther into the background.

For these very same reasons, letting the viewers take your ad material and make it their own is exactly what works in this domain. They want to insert their biography into your material. As you learned in the previous chapter, it's hard to own the wind. Therefore *stealing* is rampant. Thousands of fan clubs *stole* the cute little fat characters from Comedy Central's show, *South Park.* Their images freely roamed the web. Some shows, like *Star Trek,* have sued when people took their precious licensed characters for personal use. But this natural on-line buzz was critical to *South Park's* early success. It's a shame to put a lid on such natural enthusiasm.

If that stealing can help you get your message out, then instead of theft you have *viral marketing. South Park* was able to welcome this attention because it had contracted with a company called ThingWorld. ThingWorld's technology allowed *South Park* to place copyright information and hyperlinks into these images and characters. When the cute faces were ripped off, the characters pointed the *thieves* back to the legitimate site, where they could then purchase all the legally licensed products. The fan clubs were thrilled that their activities could flow unimpeded *and* it helped make the show.[23] Ads of the future may be raw collage material for interested fans to make their own.

One more point about the benefits of this transition from push to pull, or hot- to cold-type marketing strategy. One of the more depressing stories I read in all my research for this book was offered by Tom Petzinger in his excellent book *The New Pioneers*.[24] He describes a telemarketing firm in Virginia that is hired to make all those annoying solicitation calls you get every evening. The work in this place is so repulsive and the morale is so low that supervisors have to continually walk the floors just to keep people's spirits up. They serve popcorn in the afternoon to give people a tiny bit of cheer, so they can make it through the dreary day. If you hate *receiving* the calls, it is even worse to be on the other side! The company's success rate is about one sale per 170 calls. Two sales in a shift is considered a very good day. In fact, this work is so depressing that it is sometimes farmed out to low- and medium-security prison inmates who have little choice about their line of work.

Petzinger contrasts this low morale with the high spirit at a Staples phone facility. Workers in the Staples phone room take the initiative. They display excitement. They continually go the extra mile and enjoy what they do. The only difference between the two facilities is that *the calls are coming the other way.* Customers call Staples, Staples doesn't call them, and that makes all the difference in the world. Can you imagine the day when everyone stops selling? What a relief for everyone involved. ***The motto of the new millennium customer will definitely be: Don't call us, we'll call you!***

IF THE ADS STOP WORKING, WILL A LOT OF PEOPLE BE OUT OF WORK?

If you make your living in a field related to advertising you have got to be a bit worried by now. If all this energy is being taken out of traditional advertising, what will these people do? In part, advertising will be reparadigmed. Old attitudes will be reworked. Personally, I believe advertising will have a long and prosperous future; it will just look very, very different. It will be far closer to the role of the ancient minstrel who was welcomed at each of his stops along the way. Here's a quick overview of the changes about to transpire.

Marketing in a Broadcast World	Marketing in a Connected World
Push info at customer	Allow information to be pulled from the context of other activities
Interrupt the viewer as much as possible	Integrate with the viewer's activities so you disappear
Make data hot and more captivating	Make data cool, simple and useful
Profile target market to homogenize message	Keep file on each individual so message is personalized
Blanket media with high volume/low response	Focus on low volume/ high response strategies
Repeat message constantly to drive it home	Change message constantly so viewer will want to stay
Develop catchy hooks	Don't be so clever—be relevant, imbed message in real issues
Make them come to you	Get invited in
Make them remember you	Become so accessible, they never have to remember you
Focus on building sales staff	Provide avenues for everyone to sell your product or service, focus on associates
The sale is the end of the line	Sale is the beginning, an entry point for continued service
Differeniate your product, make it stand out	Affiliate your product, make it central to what everyone else does
Talk about yourself constantly	Provide substance and interest, so others talk about you constantly
Build your uniqueness	Build your ubiquity, be immersed everywhere
Wow the viewers with your cleverness	Support the viewer with material for his or her own creative endeavors

Doc Searles, one of the authors of *The Cluetrain Manifesto,* was hired to create public relations for a French computer firm. This firm was hush-hush about its new product, not wanting anyone to get ahead of its game. When it was time to launch, the firm contacted Searles to spread the word. He informed the company it was too late.[25] Publicity, marketing and sales must begin at the moment of product conception. Announce your birth, if you want people to care about your development. The approaches in the right-hand column of the table are all oriented to keeping people connected all through the marketing process.

An interesting footnote to the TiVo phenomenon is a provocative comment offered by Marc Andreeson, one of the founders of Netscape. *"(TiVo) is the Trojan horse for the computer industry to take over the entertainment industry."*

Consider the possibility of a movie review linked to the ability to screen that film. When the final scene is over, you have the option to visit the fan club, order the soundtrack, examine available fashions or perhaps view some interviews with the director and actors. A school could transition to the study guide. Someone in the industry could receive material on how the special effects were created or how the titles were designed. You could also view a particular scene in slow motion, perhaps linking to some additional material relevant to that image, such as where a spectacular beach scene was shot. Or if you were viewing a film like *Saving Private Ryan,* you might want to tap into some relevant World War II information and perhaps see a few related documentaries. Yes, the information industry would have a big role in all this, potentially taking over what the networks now do. At the very least, the lines between entertainment, information, product development, education and customer service would get a lot more fuzzy. Yet another reason for getting an interdisciplinary degree.

Here's a story that should give even more hope for those in traditional advertising and marketing fields. A very unusual design firm called Imaginary Forces has built a lot of its award-winning reputation developing titles for movies like *Seven* and visual images for ad campaigns. IBM approached this company to define the voice and image of its new Centers for IBM e-business Innovation. One of the founding partners, Peter Frankfurt, explained, "They wanted us to do the media. They wanted us to be the AV Guys. And we said we don't really want to do that, but let us show you what we think this could be." Thus, these players jumped outside the box right from the start.

Imaginary Forces proceeded to completely redefine the Center—from furniture to floors to typeface. The entire space became a performance piece. Walls reconfigure to create new and changing images. The conference table has interactive projections at each seat. Another founding partner, Mikon van Gastel, explained, "The model of just one person behind a lectern and everyone following him is not real anymore because media are now interplaying and even architecture is thinking about motion and transformable surfaces. So [organizations] need to borrow from companies like us to think about how sound, images and projections can influence and shape architecture." This firm redefined their traditional creative role to fit the direction it wanted to offer.[26] This is the kind of shift traditional advertising and marketing people will learn to make. They will discover the creative elements that can be tapped in services that are not their traditional domain.

All these factors we have just discussed are still only part of the reason that traditional advertising paradigms will collapse. ***The biggest reason traditional advertising will continue to lose relevance is that selling will eventually become completely embedded in ordinary life.***

RL (REAL-LIFE) RETAILING

How many times have you heard a great song on the radio, missed the name of the group that performed it and then forgot about it altogether? Well, no more. A company called I-Tag allows you to point and click at the radio; when you arrive home, all the songs you clicked appear on your home computer. You can listen to them again, get background information on the artists, hear their other songs, get a concert schedule and, of course, immediately order the song.

Using the nomadic principles described in the previous chapter, I-Tag quickly merged its ideas with other companies. They quickly established themselves by selling their technology to thousands of radio stations and forging collaborative agreements with major players such as CDNow and Amazon.com. Using nomadic logic, the I-tag people are not thinking in terms of fixed territories; they are going everywhere. They have already talked to wine producers and restaurants to offer the same capacity to them.

If you like the wine you just ordered, run your I-Tag over the bar code and all the relevant information will await you at home to peruse at your leisure. This same technology could soon allow you to target any item for future purchase. Perhaps you like the jacket a friend is wearing—run your I-Tag on the bar code in the collar and information awaits on your computer with fabric and color options. Does your child like a friend's toy? Point and click.

Comcast Cellular is exploring the same concept. If you like a song on the radio and are a Comcast customer you can dial them up. They know what station you are tuned to and will provide song details, and you can order the CD straight from the same call. Many are betting the cell phone will be the central vehicle for this consumer interface. In Europe, you can already point your cell phone at a Coke machine; the soda pops out and the charge appears on your phone bill. Of course, the handheld devices are hot on the same trail. BeamCast allows Palm users to collect data on products just by pointing an infrared beam. The central vehicle that will organize this kind of purchase is still in flux, but the direction is clear. If you like that wine on the table or that song on the radio, the information and capacity to order will be immediate.

Forecasters also estimate that virtually enhanced goggles priced low enough for the average consumer are just three to five years away. With these goggles you could look at a product and instantly access reviews, best prices and support material. You could walk down the street and switch on their enhancement functions as desired. Thus for the average shopper, the phrase *just looking* will take on new meaning.

How can traditional advertising ever keep up? How can a print ad of a dress ever compete with your spontaneous reaction to seeing that dress in real life? That's why stores put so many small items right near the register; they know that spontaneous purchases are how many things are bought. **Who needs ads when the real world becomes a huge, ever-changing showroom with real-life models? Daily life and all the things you admire could become the biggest mail-order catalog in the world.**

Let me give you a taste of where this could all go. For decades, people have paid premium prices to have designer logos imprinted on their wares—perhaps DKNY on their shirts or Louis Vuitton on their handbags. The public are primed to use their bodies as free advertising. Further, a majority of the public has either participated or bought products through some kind of multilevel marketing venture, where essentially friends sell to other friends. And most have encountered some form of associates program, such as the MCI friends and family program or E*TRADE's well-publicized referral system, where they get benefits for bringing in new customers.

Imagine this: With an I-Tag-type capability and a good associates program, anyone could be a walking catalog for a vast array of products. You could get a cut if your friend clicks and buys the Tommy Hilfiger jacket you are wearing or your hot new combat boots. Individuals could represent any product they wanted just by wearing and using the stuff. Already, famous artists and musicians receive free, unsolicited computer equipment, just so others will see them using it. Why not ordinary folks? A popular high school athlete could be a representative for Nike. A golfer who improves his game could offer his buddies an easy link to the new club he is using or the instructor he credits with improving his swing. Peer marketing—friends telling friends—would take on a whole new dimension if people could serve as walking catalogs and then get referral fees. My husband would be a prime candidate for this; when he likes something, he is obsessed with getting everyone else to use it. He insists that everyone buy the digital camera he uses, or the palmtop he prefers, easily citing reviews and specs. He hands out as many business cards for the people he recommends as he does for himself.

Michael Dertouzos at the MIT Lab for Computer Sciences and leading imaginaire in this field describes the day when chips will be integrated with the body. He describes the technological underpinnings for body nets and smart clothes that would allow the fantasy I have just described to easily take place. He also claims the technology for all of this is only about seven to eight years away.[27] The new mu-chip will only hasten this scenario. Small enough to sew in a clothing label, the Gap and others are using these chips to track inventory and more important, follow customers. Factor in the new *outernet*, digital broadcasts placed at the gas pump or cash machine and Real-Life Retailing is good to go!

Marketing *will* become more and more embedded in real life; it is only a question of how fast. Promotion will no longer be something that invades our natural patterns of attention and recreation; it will be embedded in real-life events. The day is fast approaching when the billboards come down and the thirty-second ad goes the way of Betamax. Newspapers, magazines, TV networks, movie studios, record labels and publishing houses will all become personalized subscription services where you pay for the information you use and unsolicited intrusions never enter. The capacity for Real-Life Retailing will go hand in hand with this larger evolution of the commercial experience.

To someone born before 1970, Real-Life Retailing may seem even more repulsive than the relentless bombardment of unsolicited ads. But to the Net generation, it is a hop, skip and a jump from the sensory world in which they grew up. They naturally expect that their virtual worlds will become ever more real. More important, they expect that the real world will become ever more virtually enhanced. They will be far more natural about translating real-life recommendations into virtual selection. But soon, when a friend says, "You have got to see this movie!" you will be able to order tickets on the spot. DRM software is being shaped to be viral friendly, offering you a percentage of any media product you e-mail to a friend, that they decide to keep.

THE UNUSUAL PSYCHOLOGY OF THE FUTURE CONSUMER

With our cell phones on steroids, and wearing our new smart clothes enhanced with chips, going from off-line to on-line, outernet to internet and back again, will become immediate, effortless and yes, natural. The veil separating the two will become ever more transparent.

The group who is about to come on board is called the Echo-Boom generation. Their numbers are vast, thus their impact will have teeth. In the U.S. they are seventy-seven million at last count, almost 25 percent of the population. And almost all of them will be wired, about 90 percent, according to current projections. They have a new kind of literacy, that is far more visual than verbal. As with every generation that has come before, they will make their mark on the culture and persuade all of us to become a little bit like them. Whatever one generation is capable of, everyone soon absorbs. A key reason entertainment will ascend in importance is because this new generation has grown up playing with multimedia toys. They expect everything to be merged with entertainment, and soon we will all share this bias.

MIT professor Sherry Turkle is one of the leading pioneers studying how computers act on us and change how we in turn see ourselves. In her groundbreaking book, *Life on the Screen,* she describes the sensory world of this next generation as a shift from calculation to simulation. The on-line generation no longer looks for things that can be measured, counted, held and acquired. They look for windows that can be opened and experiences that can be entered.

One of her teenage interviewees says he thinks of his personality as a series of windows. *"RL is just another window . . . It's just not my best window."* [28] If you experience your own personality as a window, then you will also come to expect that everything you encounter will offer this same fluctuating potential.

Robert Logan, a professor of communications and physics at Toronto University, an avid student of Marshall McLuhan, echoes this thought. He suggests that we are re-creating the fundamental dynamics of an oral tradition:

> In tribal society, the users of information are also its creators. In the tribal council, every voice is heard and every pair of ears is part of the system. Even when the storyteller told his or her tale, it would change depending upon the mood and reception of the audience. Internet participants can shape the story by indicating their mood, they can change it by adding their comments. The story being told over time becomes their story, a never ending story. [29]

This is a critical expectation the Net generation will bring to the commercial exchange; they will expect products and services to become *their* products and services. They will expect to make them their own, not just through customizing the details; that's old news. They will want to make the commercial experience their own by participating in the creative process.

Tim Berners-Lee, an architect of this world, saw the future early on. He says that interactivity is not about sitting in front of a screen that has interactive features. Real interactivity is based on the ability to cocreate an event. The on-line experience is returning us to the participatory style that once characterized all ancient oral cultures. Stories are not initiated by a single author; they are told and retold and developed through community participation. Thus the dramatic event, the theatrical experience, *the telling of the story,* becomes central to everyday life, far more than all the products that were the ground of the industrial era.

Sociologist Robert Lifton, another early voice in the exploration of on-line psychology, [30] suggests the emergence of a new kind of self-concept, the *Protean Self,* capable of using multiple personas. He suggests that it is an evolutionary response. It is a more mature way of coping with competing demands, ambiguities and the new complexities of modern life. The self becomes capable of morphing into unlimited shapes in order to connect with the *window* that is before it, virtual or real. Attention is redirected toward developing the ability to mutate and reform one's identity in the moment. Pleasure and self-esteem are derived from fluidity, far more than acquisition.

Mark Pesce, cocreator of VRML (Virtual Reality Modeling Language), the language that delivers 3-D images over the Web, goes even farther out on a limb, suggesting that this morphing sensory reality will extend into the real world. In about fifteen years we will be able to shape everyday objects according to our needs. It is a world where the idea of fixed objects will be almost nonexistent.[31] This is not the empty rant of a digital futurist. Industrial designers already translate their on-line designs into physical prototypes. Think of it as a printer that spits out objects. Mark Pesce is suggesting that as soon as the price of this *printer* comes down, everyone will have an object-replicating capacity in their own home, downloading products as needed, according to their personal specifications and in response to their creative input.

This kind of imagery goes quite a bit farther than the editing mentality or even the *TiVo-ization* of every media stream. It suggests that commerce will become a totally collaborative experience, where the lives of the storyteller and the listener become hopelessly intertwined. The public will use the raw materials and windows provided to design never-before-experienced consumer events. They will not only participate in information, they will interact with their products through creative input.

The reason this psychological imagery is important is because a direct result of living on-line is that you project these metaphors onto everything. The cocreative, dynamic theatrical experience becomes more than just an on-line event; it colors all your commercial expectations.

Economist Jeremy Rifkin says:

The new postmodern man or woman is constantly casting about for new lived experiences, just as their bourgeois parents and grandparents were continually in search of making new acquisitions. The new cultural industries, in turn, are creating an almost infinite number of scripts for acting out one's life experiences, just as the manufacturing industries provided a vast number of consumer products to buy.[32]

In simpler words, a D-generation kid says the same thing:

If your product is so great and offers all this great capability, why are you trying to sell it to me? There must be something wrong with it, if you are trying to get me to own it, i.e., get stuck with it.

If a company is really interesting, it will never want to saddle you with owning something that is bound to become obsolete or that takes you out of the buying loop. It will want you to subscribe to its never ending stream of *Really Cool Stuff*. Many software companies have already discovered this subscription strategy as a key to a more stable income stream. Obsolescence is bound to become obsolete. Or as Tom Sachs, an artist at the Mary Boone Gallery says, *"In the future, art will look like an incredibly complex, high tech, handmade, clumsy, expensive, broken, dripping service contract."* [33]

At just about the same time the ads stopped working, we also started buying fewer material goods. We kept on buying, but it was mostly invisible, intangible, weightless goods and services. We subscribed, leased, and partnered. We began to want adventure more than acquisition. We wanted amusing simulations, rather than objects that just collect dust. *We began looking for things to do, rather than things to have. When you begin marketing experiences, then you are entering a whole different ball game.*

THE EXPERIENCE ECONOMY

Several researchers figured out how to render thousands of different odors into digital code. Their company, Digiscents, offers a desktop device with a core group of scents. The unique digital rendering of the scent in question is downloaded through your personal computer and wafts out through this device. The smell of hot pizza could emanate at lunch time, just as an ad for local pizza delivery floats across your screen. (Remember, we will have a keen ability to target the individual customer.) Naturally, smelling pizza when you are hungry will accelerate your purchase of pizza. It's marketing nirvana.

The Digiscents folks assumed advertisers would be the core market for their product and they pitched it heavily to this group. To their dismay, hardly any ad people showed up at their initial presentation.

But the gaming industry knocked down their doors. In the first six months, two thousand designers of video games signed up for the Digiscents product.

Why? Because the gaming industry is on the forefront of designing new experiences, far more so than the ad industry. The gamers are on the leading edge of designing sensory impressions to create ever more seductive worlds. They get it. Anything that enhances an experience is gold. Already a successful game designer, Kenji Eno, has turned his energy to reconfiguring databases and portals to make them more fun. He claims to be bored with games, and sees this direction as a new artistic challenge. *These digital artists will probably be critical to the next layer of the new, new economy.*

1. *Entertainment represents an ever larger percentage of the total economy.* More than 10 percent of all non-medical consumer spending goes toward entertainment. It is growing faster than almost any other sector of the economy and provides 12 percent of the new job growth. It is also the largest U.S. export. Sixty percent of all TV seen internationally is produced in the U.S. and 90 percent of the revenue from the worldwide film audiences goes to American filmmakers. English is now spoken by 20 percent of the world, another clear tes-

timony to the power of this industry. Many believe it was CNN, rock music and American movies that brought down the Berlin Wall far more than economics, diplomacy or politics. For decades we have been exporting American culture—obliterating local cultures and annihilating ancient traditions in a single generation. No war or enemy occupation could have ever achieved the incredible domination attained by the dancing electrons on a blank receptive screen. As the digital divide between the industrial and poor nations continues to fall, the last dam holding back the flood of entertainment from having worldwide impact will crumble.

2. *Even as traditional entertainment soars, the underlying foundation of this industry is changing dramatically.* Video games are a seven-billion-dollar industry. They are *bigger* than Hollywood. Sony, one of the largest media empires and suppliers of entertainment hardware, receives *one third* of its income from its video game division. Sega spent seventy million dollars to develop one game, about the budget for a major Hollywood blockbuster. Devices for screening these games, like Sony PlayStation 2, have been referred to as *stealth PCs* due to their sophistication. The new games have traveled far beyond the fast trigger-pulling of early *twitch games* to complex, multidimensional story lines with collaborative capabilities and moves that require complex strategies. A generation that grows up on these highly sophisticated, interactive simulations is different than a generation that grows up watching TV. Gaming lets you interact with the story. The outcome is not fixed; you help author what happens. A lot of people are still betting on interactive TV as the future of programming but even if this is the case, the influence of the game mentality will be critical to how this plays out. This participatory expectation will further color our commercial expectations.

3. *As a result, the line between fantasy and reality has become so blurred that our expectations of real-life events are often unrealistic. When real life seems less sensational, screen life continues to gain in importance.* Eight out of the ten best-grossing movies of all

time were action blockbusters with major special effects. The public loves this stuff. The screen has offered so many windows to the future that the general public thinks that doing the same thing in real life should be no big deal. *Star Trek* had replicators and holograms a decade ago. Surely they should be commonplace by now. *What is taking those slowpoke scientists so long?* Some believe that Reagan was able to push through the initial Star Wars proposal, despite strong congressional opposition, because the major TV networks began airing animated scenarios of how the missile defense system would work. The animations made it seem pretty easy and straightforward. The public couldn't understand why congress was still complaining that it wouldn't work. For the commercial world, this means that imaginary events become more interesting than their slower-moving physical counterparts. Who wants a plastic action figure when the one on the screen can do so much more?

4. *As a result of this new generation and the media excitement we have all come to expect, every industry will have to consider the entertainment value of how they interface with their customers. To some degree, every business will become show business.* Every industry will have to consider whether it connects with its customers, clients and employees in a way that creates meaning, excitement and interest. Boeing lets its clients watch the progress of the new jetliner being built. This allows them to customize the product—but don't kid yourself, the entertainment aspect is also part of the value. A small business that sells houseboats saw its sales boom when it offered 3-D on-line visits to these homes on water. A furniture company we work with had to develop 3-D imaging of their proposals in order to keep their customers engaged and wowed by their products. You can't just sell the stuff, you have to surround it with an environment. The experience is as important as the product. *Those who offer the best experiences will always win.*

5. *In this new, new economy we will pay for access, although increas-*

*ingly we will **never really** have **anything**.* Economist Jeremy Rifkin's provocative treatise on this transition, *The Age of Access,* asks the question, "Why are we spending more and owning less?" He describes an amazing array of temporary economic structures that allow you to gain access to something but never really own it. Physical products may be on their way to becoming the dinosaurs of the entertainment age. Gateway computer with its effortless trade-up policy is well on its way to becoming the Gateway subscription service, providing an ongoing stream of upgrades and services for a never ending monthly fee. Parents no longer buy their children handmade toys that they will in turn hand down to their children. They buy representations drawn from the latest hot movie. And when the next hot movie comes along, the old toys get discarded in favor of the next fantasy moments. We lease, we subscribe, we pay for use, but soon we will never get stuck with the goods.

6. *Thus, the next dimension of technological evolution will be targeted to serve the insatiable imagination of the ever more powerful entertainment economy. In a self-reinforcing spiral as entertainment becomes more effective, it will become ever more important in every domain of commercial exchange. As it becomes ever more important, it will in turn be able to demand ever more effective technology.* For decades, the defense industry drove new technology. Everyone designed for it, because that's where the money was. Michael Wahrman, who runs digital production and special effects for Viacom says: "Pretty much everything you're seeing in video games, computer animation, and networks is financed by the military. Everyone you know in the media industry was funded by the Department of Defense."[34] But lately there has been a curious turnabout. For a decade, Silicon Graphics Inc. (SGI) developed advanced software for scientists and engineers. Now its main client is the entertainment industry. Lockheed Martin, one of the major defense contractors, cites *entertainment applications* as the area of its most intense-

ly concentrated growth. Interestingly, Lockheed Martin headquarters are located in Orlando, literally in the looming shadow of Disney World! Much of the bandwidth race has the entertainment industry in its sights. The latest crop of digital designers will definitely be looking for ideas to please the storytellers. And in an amazing turnaround, the military is actually turning to the game industry to develop training simulations because it now has more advanced applications! Soon *everyone* will want to hire the entertainment folks to redesign advertising, retailing, product development strategies, human resource functions, training and education. In other words, if you can make it in Hollywood, you can make it anywhere.

In the next new economy, products will become ever less important. Service will count a lot, but experience will drive the show. Imaginative windows will be the hot properties of the future. Products and services will become mere props for entering the larger theatrical flow of the market. The digital artists will soon be coming to a boardroom near you to show you how to transform what you offer into a tale that can really involve your buyers.

How might this all look in real life? I will now describe a series of paths for meeting and greeting the opportunities of an experience economy. The key to accessing the larger electronic culture will be entertainment, entertainment, entertainment. And the key to accessing entertainment will be imagination, imagination, imagination.

2.1 CLICKS, BRICKS, SLICKS AND FLICKS

The ancient storyteller plied his wares in the marketplace. That's where the people were. And the merchants encouraged him to stand very close, so the gathering crowd would be near their stores.

An e-commerce site combined with real stores, combined with *slicks,* or a mail order catalog is the triumvirate of market power. Even with premium prices, The Sharper Image continues to thrive on its excellent capacity to drive all three elements. If you have clicks, bricks and slicks, the impact is synergistic. But few have really mined the depth of synergy that could exist between these paths.

Jeff Bezos of Amazon.com fame has said that Barnes & Noble is crazy not to use its real-life stores as showrooms for its on-line capacity. With the exception of its e-book offerings, Barnes & Noble almost treats its physical and on-line stores as competitors. He has wondered why Barnes & Noble doesn't sprinkle terminals throughout the store, allowing staff to facilitate their customers' on-line journeys. *Why give them the opportunity to go home and perhaps order with someone else?*

For that matter, walk into Wal-Mart, Gap or most large retailers and you might never know the inroads they have made with their on-line presence. The floor staff of all these companies could easily support the customers' on-line adventures, acting as *retail librarians* who show you just how much is possible.

Clicks, bricks and slicks definitely give you a mightier marketing sword. But to reach the new consumers who choose their media diets, who were weaned on simulations and who have an insatiable appetite for new experiences, you will also have to have flicks, or a tie-in to an entertainment strategy. **Stores need to become part showroom/part theme park. Consumers will expect virtually enhanced real-life realities.**

Trend watcher Faith Popcorn says that stores of the future will be fantasy wonderlands.[35] She cites examples such as Bass Pro in Springfield, Missouri, where customers are taught to tie flies and can practice fishing at an indoor trout pond. There are pistol and crossbow ranges on-site and a resident taxidermist. Virgin Entertainment Group opened the largest music and entertainment store in Times Square complete with live performances, a four-screen theater and a restaurant. The Smithsonian National Museum of Natural History is using immersion cinema, which allows viewers to direct their exploration of a particular topic through touchpads. Such developments raise the bar for what the public will expect to see. The days of the normal retail store that merely displays its wares are numbered.

REI, the mega-supplier of camping and adventure gear, has turned its Seattle store into a one-hundred-thousand-square-foot simulation of an outdoor experience. When you purchase climbing shoes, you can practice on an indoor climbing structure. You can test harsh-weather gear in the rain forest room. You can get a visceral sense of your next adventure. You purchase camping gear within the context of the best virtual reality program currently available: *real life.*

Of course, REI knows that right now every store can't be as large and fantastic. At its smaller stores, computer terminals offer full access to the entire REI inventory, even when that particular store can't stock the full array. If you offer on-line access straight from the floor, suddenly even your small stores can approximate the clout of huge retailers. *No one is limited by current inventory anymore.* One day soon, you might enter your favorite neighborhood retailer and sit on a comfy chair while your favorite retail librarian takes you on a personalized journey to select what you want. Of course, they will expect you to leave the store empty-handed, since all your selections will be delivered.

Far away from the retail experience, Coldwell Banker Real Estate Office in ritzy Woodside, California, has opened a high-end restaurant next to its office. And plans are in place to open boutique hotels at other California locations. Coldwell Banker has caught the drift. Clearly, high-end real estate must be linked with a much larger gestalt of a life lived away from the everyday hustle and bustle. Fine dining and stylish comfort put you in the mood for a home that is equally stellar.

Paul Allen poured megabucks into his urban theme park in Seattle, which is based on Jimi Hendrix's legendary album that provocatively asks, *Are You Experienced?* There is so much entertainment value there, that the park can charge $19.95 for admission and the opportunity to shop. A summer event called Europe Expo 2000 had everything from sandy beaches to dirt-bike paths to restaurants and dance floors, all enclosed under one gigantic roof. Again, you paid to enter the space, which was part community center, part rave, part sports park and part pick-up scene, with the opportunity to purchase items distributed throughout the event.

Very wisely, Hallmark has redesigned its entire business structure. It no longer focuses on target populations; it focuses on target events such as high school graduations, births or weddings. This shift has allowed Hallmark to forge tie-ins to vendors who cater to these kinds of affairs; it has opened the doors wide to new kinds of creative collaborations.

The Metroplex in San Francisco is a full-spectrum entertainment extravaganza with movies and *game bars,* where you can order up the latest computer game. Commercial realtors are already hip to this trend. The new anchors for large shopping malls are not the big department stores; they are the big movie/entertainment complexes.

Michael Baynard of the Urban Land Institute, a nonprofit research group in Washington, D.C., says that every civic project these days has an artistic component: *"It's a long-term trend towards the introduction of entertainment into every land use development project. Everyone is demanding entertainment."*[36] If the government gets it, then you know this trend must be really well entrenched.

Once retailers invest in this new paradigm, stores will become imaginary playgrounds. The plot of a movie that is being screened at the theater may trail onto the floor as related images play out in the window displays and flow out onto the streets of the city. A sci-fi thriller might lead to futuristic fashions, electronic music, next-wave gadgets, science projects from the local school, a literary contest for sci-fi stories and town meetings about the future. A historical drama might set a very different mood. The existing malls will have theatrical directors to orchestrate these performance pieces. Similar to visiting Disneyland, the day may fast approach when you enter a mall with either a single ticket, multievent or all-day pass to whichever theatrical events, i.e., retailers, interest you.

The next few sections focus on the retail experience; after all, consumer spending is two-thirds of the GDP, but the very same principles apply to all commercial exchange. *Contrary to popular belief, physical stores and real-life representatives will take on even more relevance in the on-line world; they will just function differently. In fact an on-line vendor that does not have a tie-in to a physical one will be at a disadvantage. The next wave of marriages are bound to be on-line communities and retailers looking for physical representation.*

2·2 EVERYONE WILL PRACTICE STREET THEATER

Ancient clans formed according to marriage and bloodlines. But another feature of this bond was the right to tell a story. Every clan had its own tales that no one else was allowed to tell. Each new generation embellished the core stories of the generation before, thereby growing the wisdom and value of the clan.

Let me take you back in time to two people who had a very early understanding of this strategy. Mel and Patricia Zeigler were masterful practitioners of street theater. Their first business venture began with a small shop in downtown Mill Valley called *Banana Republic*. They had been traveling all over the world and had slowly assembled a line of clothing that was ideal for adventure travel. The original store was a total hit and their stores soon spread all over the country. Frequenters of the stores were able to follow the couple's continuing saga of safaris and escapades to exotic lands.

Temperatures from foreign cities were posted daily on the walls behind the register. Expensive floor space was devoted to a rich selection of rarely purchased travel books. Snapshots of the couple's adventures adorned the fitting rooms. *Of course inquiring minds wanted to know what to wear on such adventures!* By buying those safari pants people were getting a piece of the adventure. I can remember specifically walking into their stores just to see if they had gone anywhere new, and often walking out with a shopping a bag on my arm.

Based on the Zeiglers' extraordinary success, Banana Republic was bought by Gap. The retail professionals viewed their store merely as a recognized brand. The trappings of the store were quickly dismissed. The travel books were the first to go. Foreign temperatures and photos of safaris were taken off the walls. The stories that surrounded the clothes were deemed irrelevant; the name was all that mattered. Financial repercussions persisted for a while. Although Banana Republic recovered much of its earlier profitability, its current stores are a pale, pale reflection of the original magic. Urban safari is a lifestyle image no longer tied to real-life escapades. I used to walk in because I wanted to hear the story, now I walk in only if I want a shirt. And I walk in a lot less.

This was all done in an era when the brand was considered everything. Maybe if this buyout had occurred today, and the new owners had understood that we were well on our way to becoming an entertainment economy, the original story might have been kept more intact. It would have been natural to book exotic travel adventures right from the floor of the store. The stores could have offered crafts from these exotic locales or fabulous photographic prints of far-off lands. Why not house a Banana Republic Café inside the store with drinks like Chai, Yerbe Matte and assorted specialties from foreign lands?

Maintaining the story would have insulated the new owners from competition. A look can be copied, a marketing strategy can be approximated, but if anyone had copied the store's curious, unusual story they would have looked foolish. The Gap executives just did not understand the power of what they had, mostly because they did not think in these terms. They completely missed the opportunity for spinning even bigger tales. (A hot trend in New York City is for furniture stores to carry clothes, and vise versa. Why not have your clothing style match your home? And Roots, Canada's version of Banana Republic, has in fact opened resorts. So my idea of blending these genres is not that far-out.)

Interestingly, several years later, the Zeiglers used their same story-telling brilliance and street theater style to launch a tea company, The Republic of Tea. In fact, the company began as a book describing the creative process of the founders, told through a series of fanciful written exchanges that revealed the inner workings of their imaginative process. The business appeared *after* the book had already been published.

The company's mail-order catalog was a manifesto for a slower life. High-quality tea and traditional Asian brewing pots were merely the props for this journey. Fans relished the Zen-like advice about seizing the present moment. New advice appeared in each edition of the mail-order catalog so that customers could continue to advance their knowledge on this topic. There was a quirkiness and spontaneity to these early catalogs.

Once again, the Zeiglers and partners had a major hit on their hands. Once again they were bought out and the storytelling aspect was thinned so that the professionals could market a brand. Once again I can envision ways the story could have been expanded to include Zen retreats and relaxation products. The Republic of Tea was perfectly positioned to become the Sharper Image of simplicity, well ahead of a trend that now boasts countless Web sites, several magazines, numerous catalogs and pushed Oxygen Media to launch a site on this topic with fourteen marketing partners.

Marketers will eventually realize that a good, imaginative story is far more valuable than a recognizable name. A good story has untold dimensions and never ending spin-offs. You can build on a story, whereas a name is static.

Land Rover is well on its way to turning its dealerships into fantasy wonderlands. It offers its own clothing line. TV sets screen dramatic footage of off-roading events. Once you purchase a vehicle, you get a formal invitation to take off-roading trips guided by its staff. Land Rover's biannual catalog reads less like product promotion and more like an international adventure magazine. The company was even a founding member of an environmental group devoted to healthy land use. You haven't just bought a car, you've joined a club. It's called *lifestyle marketing*—where you weave a spell so that the buyer walks through an imaginary doorway into a new way of life.

But Land Rover could go even farther in spinning its tale. Most people who buy SUVs never take them off-road, but if they did, they would see yet another reason to take the step toward this kind of purchase. Why not develop a travel division that markets off-road adventures directly? Most national car rental companies rent four-wheel drives, but according to your rental contract, you can't take them off-road. Why doesn't Land Rover supply the vehicles and allow this possibility—factoring dings and rapid tire use into the equation? Land Rover should be the king of off-roading experiences! It could be publishing books on the topic, developing guidebooks, facilitating discussion groups and helping adventurers in local areas meet one another. It could become *the resource* for everything you might want to know about this kind of outdoor adventure in every part of the country. It could also become a more visible advocate for open space policies, which are large and growing political forces, especially in the West. All this would represent a next layer in the emergence of Land Rover's already budding story.

The technical marketing term for this direction is *brand extension*—meaning that you spin off another application from an existing brand. Condé Nast Travel Magazine spins off Condé Nast Fashion. Or Quicken becomes Quicken Consulting. In his excellent survey of the new economy in *The Digital Estate,* Chuck Martin recommends that you think like a spider. Take any product and spin out the potential ramifications.

Although brand extension is an accurate term, there is something to gain by using more imaginary terms like *street theater* and *spinning the myth.* Any product or service can be turned into theater. You just have to stop thinking *brand management* and begin thinking *story management.* It's a click-on, click-off culture. If you are not providing new drama, your customers will be left with no choice but to seek a new sensory fix.

2.3 BRANDTAINMENT

Today what matters is brandtainment; ever unfolding features to delight and amuse the audience.

It's no accident that when Sarah Jessica Parker, lead actress for *Sex and the City,* opens her laptop to write her newspaper column, she is perfectly placed so that when the camera sweeps in for a nice tight shot, the Apple computer logo is in clear view. It's no accident that when an actor drinks a can of soda, it is perfectly tilted so that the viewer can read the entire logo. Companies pay for these plugs.

Recently I saw a rerun of *Jurassic Park* on TV. Watching it for the second time and no longer surprised by the action, I decided it was the longest, most expensive consumer ad in history. Early on, the camera does a long slow pan over the T-shirts, lunch boxes and all the other Jurassic Park paraphernalia that will be sold when this imaginary park opens. Later you are offered a quick visual reminder of the theme park merchandise because the escaped raptor almost knocks over some of it. Then, lo and behold, the very same items that you saw on the screen are for sale in real life. *Jurassic Park* didn't just translate characters into merchandise; it offered a blatant ad for the merchandise it would sell.

Frankly, I am surprised that movie theaters haven't realized that they could offer these items next to the popcorn. Why break the spell by having to go out into the mall to find it? Walking out of the theater, still in the haze of the fantasy adventure you have just experienced, naturally you would want a memento of your *trip*. Theaters already know that they only break even on ticket prices—their profits are in the refreshments. Why not become an outlet for all the stuff people have just seen on the screen?

Hollywood and merchandising have been in bed with each other for a long time. Even in the fifties, Disney characters were already jumping off the screen onto every product imaginable. Merchandising can easily double the profits of a film, and the really powerful writers and directors can demand a cut of these proceeds as well. Hollywood insiders have revealed the ugly commercial truth—that studios will describe the kind of merchandise and the age group they want to target, and *then* get writers to write a film that will meet their merchandising goals.

Not to be left out, computer-game companies are also seeking product placements. A hot new game that allows you to play on-line pool sports a logo in the center of the table. Every time you place a shot, the Jack Daniel's insignia stares right back at you. With hundreds of thousands of hits a week, you can be sure this is just the beginning.

Most movie and rock stars get tons of free merchandise, from sunglasses to shoes to clothes. Do you think they really pay for all those couture clothes they wear? The moment a star is seen wearing a particular shirt, the next day that shirt sells out in stores across America. How can a thirty-second spot compete with a two-hour, forty-million-dollar budget for a blockbuster film and your favorite star endorsing the look? But while these strategies are still highly effective, they are old news.

But the media/marketing marriage doesn't really come alive until you can order straight off the screen. You will soon be able to watch TV or a film and point and click when you see something you like. If you like what one of your favorite actresses is wearing, point and click and the dress is on its way to your home. Of course, it is ordered in your correct size, charged to the right card and sent to the correct address because everything has been preprogrammed to your preferences. Once this technology is in place, ads will fade even farther into the background. All you need are agreements to place your products on the set of the story.

Unwittingly, J. Peterman was an early pioneer in this arena. This slightly offbeat clothing company began with one product, a long horseman's canvas duster coat and a great story about becoming a free spirit. It expanded its *clothing as fantasy* imagery into a large mail-order business. Then it did the product placement people one better. The owner became a character on the hit show *Seinfield* as Elaine's boss. J. Peterman was on every week, as Elaine agonized about the text for the catalog and had to deal with her boss's quirky demands. Similarly, AOL was given a starring role in Meg Ryan and Tom Hanks's hit film *You've Got Mail*. Matt Damon and Ben Affleck sold their reality show *Runner,* in part because of the ability to embed product placements within the action of the show. Although it was initally pulled, the show allowed advertisers to shape the content in ways that were unprecedented.

If thirty-second ads are on their way out anyway, advertisers will be even more compelled to look in this direction. They will have to sponsor shows and find ever more inventive ways to sneak their merchandise into the plot. If Gap sponsored the TV show *Friends,* it wouldn't need ads; it would merely outfit the show. Viewers would point, click and buy if something struck their fancy.

It is not hard to imagine movie scripts forging cobranding opportunities with a range of designers and product developers. A particular designer would be given the rights to develop outfits, place furniture or position products on the set. The designer would probably do it for free. In fact he or she might eventually pay for the privilege because the opportunity will be so lucrative. You can imagine kids watching a movie like *The Matrix* and being able to order the heroes' long leather coats on the spot. You wouldn't have to stage an expensive show in Paris or New York City to attract the attention of the public, the film would become your show. And with just-on-time, customized production, you'd never be stuck with inventory that didn't sell. In a post-Napster world of peer-to-peer distribution, studios might even be willing to offer their films for free, because of all the money they made from product placement and direct selling from the screen. Behind the scenes sponsors already wield this clout. Why not make it explicit?

The print media will evolve in similar ways. Suppose you are reading *National Geographic* on your e-book. If a particular adventure sounds interesting, you can point and click and all the necessary information, costs and booking possibilities will arrive on your desktop. Thus, traditional advertising will become ever more transparent and embedded in real life. *Everything you do in daily life can become a context for discovering what you might want.*

Once storytelling begins to rule, new business forms will also emerge. Once an entity like *National Geographic* can link you to a travel resource, then you have a critical cobranding opportunity. Suddenly every travel site, adventure outfitter, airline and hotel will want to be affiliated with *National Geographic*. Of course, *National Geographic* could also link you to conservation efforts in the area just described and sell photographic prints to help the cause. *National Geographic* would be in the position of power because it has the story. Product and service would flow from its tales of adventure. Naturally, the software provider and e-book developer would be in the copilot's seats as they advised future marketing directions that involved them.

The critical factor in this paradigm shift is that *an experience drives the purchase.* A great film and cool look will drive fashion. A bad story with no individuality will result in hardly a dress being ordered. A great description of a travel adventure will make customers flock to the destination and care about what happens there. Conversely, a poorly written story won't inspire anyone to go. Curiously, the more persuasion gets embedded in real life, the more good story-making matters. The more purchasing occurs within the context of stories, the more entertainment will define the commercial exchange.

Some of this may seem like a bit of a future trip, but remember: I-Tag is in place at thousands of radio stations, infrared palmtops and hopped-up cell phones are already in use and hundreds of distributors are hot on the trail. The technology for everything we have just talked about is waiting in the wings.

2.4 NEW SOCIAL SPACES / NEW FICTIVE FORMS

Ancient storytellers would often borrow characters from one another. So Hercules might come across Diana, Goddess of the Hunt, in one of his escapades and Diana's story might allude to Hercules. Once a story suc-

cessfully interfaces with another, it is no longer a simple tale; it graduates to the realm of legend and myth.

Lee Jeans launched a mysterious guerilla campaign based on three unusual characters who did not seem to be connected in any way to the brand. As the story unfolded, it became like an on-line scavenger hunt. It eventually required viewers to go to the store and get the serial number of a real pair of Lee jeans in order to keep playing the game. Lee's sites had a non-commercial feel. Despite some critique that there was not enough brand-building material, initial reports showed sales were up and on-line traffic included more store locator and product description activity.[37]

Now suppose these characters that Lee Jeans developed—*Curry* in his red leather pants, *Super Greg* a wannabe DJ and *Stranger* in a caveman garb—began to venture beyond the confines of the Lee campaign. Why can't Curry, Super Greg and Stranger wander onto some game show, appear at the MTV awards, guest star in a few music videos or appear in their own comic book? Who knows, Stranger might harbor a secret desire to be a rapper and Curry might want to have his own on-line game.

These are the predictions of Bruce Carter, creative director of Animal Logic, the special effects company behind *The Matrix:*

Things from the real world will be impossible to distinguish from the virtual one, and it will be fantastic, because we will have characters that appear on the cover of a magazine, that will appear in the gossip pages; they will be as real as the current ones are, but you will never see them in a restaurant, because they won't exist.

Ultimately the more these characters have a media life of their own, the more value it creates for Lee. Every time you see Mickey Mouse, it is a covert ad for Disney, because the character has such international recognition. This is what could happen for Lee. In fact, if the characters get really popular they could even produce a new revenue stream for Lee as animation celebrities deserving of their own shows and games.

The Net is mostly a playground of new social spaces, from the more ordinary extensions such as chat rooms, instant messaging, sampling, teleconferencing and hypertext, to the more exotic offerings such as MUDs (Multi-Users Domains or Dungeons), MOOS (Multiple Object Oriented Spaces) and MUSH (Pure Imaginary Spaces). Sheldon Renan produces videos, conferences and events for Fortune 100 companies that capitalize on these new social possibilities. He offers a view that is indicative of a whole new breed of digital philosophers and artists who are exploring the potential of this creative playground:

> Physically these places and spaces [like those listed above] exist in silicon-based servers, enabled by algorithmic synapses. But in the evolving human matrix, they are the locus of a new social reality.
>
> These new spaces literally create new ways of being. The universes the Network makes possible are also incubators of new fictive forms that, over time, will challenge past forms of Telling of the Story... Normal dramatic structure will, like Einsteinian relativity, become deeply compromised, radicalized and certainly complex. The new forms will be stretchy and throb between the tribal and anarchic.[38]

It's probably been a while since you last discussed the relationship of Einstein's theories to your current marketing campaign. But perhaps you should. If you accept that marketing, retailing and even product development will become more married to the imaginary space, then new fictives will be a place to look for opportunities. That's where Lee turned when it wanted to create a strategy that would get heard. Lee knew it had to fully utilize the dramatic capabilities now available to the cyberartist.

Interestingly, the guys that cooked this up, Linus Karlsson and Paul Malmstrom from the Fallon agency, had used a similar strategy for Miller

Lite a few years earlier and fell flat on their faces. Could it be that new fictional forms were irrelevant in a broadcast era, and yet are brilliant in a viral, communication-based medium? Maybe we have only just entered a sensory environment where these new fictional forms can come alive.

According to communications and physics professor Robert Logan, the on-line universe is oral and tactile, rather than visual and literate; right hemisphere rather than left hemisphere; synthetic rather than analytic; nonlinear rather than linear; simultaneous or synchronous rather than sequential and analogical rather than deductive. As a result of our encounters with the digital domain, our senses are finally stretched-out enough to fully embrace the intricacies of mythmaking.

Back in the seventies, two mystery writers, Richard Stark and Joe Graves, conspired to have two characters meet in each other's books at the same point in fictional time. The same scene appeared for a moment in each of their books and then each character went on to a very different future.[39] In a similar play of interlocking realities, Polaroid partnered with Fox to create a steamy on-line soap opera called *Polaroid Place*. Fox wrote the narrative and hosted the site. Polaroid provided the characters—by clicking on them you were magically transported to a Polaroid site with additional games and things to do. It was an extension of a forty-million dollar marketing campaign. Was it Fox promoting its characters or Polaroid showcasing its? Majestic, a hot new game developed by Electronic Arts, involves players through the use of e-mails, faxes, voice mail and a Web site. Clues are given that allow participants to solve an intricate mystery about a government conspiracy. This is yet another dimension of storytelling where the plot invades the daily life of players. (You can imagine the advertising implications, not to mention that Electronic Arts gets to assemble an amazing database of contacts.)

The HBO show *The Sopranos* is another one that is pushing the edge of parallel storytelling. On its Web site, the college-age daughter, Meadow, had to tape video confessions for a class at Columbia. The tapes are then leaked to a real-life site run by a mob aficionado. This, of course, causes all sorts of drama. Now you have the on-line destination creating its own dramatic spin-offs and interfacing with real-life events, which may perhaps at some point weave back into the TV show. A new Web audience that enjoys an enhanced story line and has additional information beyond that of the mere TV viewer is created.

Might we see story lines weaving in and out of multiple sites, through neighboring companies, and in and out of real life? Steven Spielberg's movie *Artificial Intelligence* (AI) carries a credit for Jeanine Salla, sentient machine therapist. On-line this same psychologist is involved in a web of mystery set in the year 2142. It is difficult to tell which story led to which. *If you thought it was easy to merge information products, good story streams are positively destined to flow onto each other's shores.*

The freedom, versatility and play that people have come to expect on-line will be translated into real-life experience and then enhanced. Lands' End already offers light imaging at its stores so customers can have virtual representations of their physical forms reproduced on-line. This then allows them to try clothes on virtually. The Lands' End Web site also offers instant messaging capabilities when you shop. Two teenage girls can shop on-line together, gossiping and talking about each piece of clothing, trying them on their virtual models, which approximate their height and size. A customer representative can even get in on the conversation if you need some additional help.

Now all retailers need to do is more fully integrate the link between on- and-off line. Every store should offer Web cams so your friends at home can watch you shop and offer comments. Or perhaps you see something your friend might like—you should be able to e-mail a 3-D image to his or her personal on-line model straight from the floor of the store. I guarantee, a savvy retailer who pushes the boundaries between on-line and off-line realities and creates new fictional forms will become *the place* to go. In fact, Lands' End was facing huge losses because of slow-moving inventory in its stores, but was saved by the success and inventiveness of its on-line space.

The retail world will become more committed to making its virtual rep-

resentations more real and its real world windows more virtually enhanced. The edge between on- and off-line reality will continue to dissolve as stories come right off the screen into the physical world and back again.

2.5 SMALL IS BEAUTIFUL AND THE EMERGENCE OF PERSONAL BRANDS

The real measure of an indigenous story's success was whether or not others began to repeat the tale and thus catapult it into the public domain. In fact, really, really good tales would inspire others to become storytellers themselves.

Some skateboard companies will periodically put out new lines of boards under new logos and pretend that they are new companies. The skateboarding subculture thinks a hot new upstart has come on the scene and the early adopters flock to be the first ones at the edge of a new hot product. ***This is the exact opposite of brand management! This is brand blasphemy!***

In this case, a successful company *denies* being the manufacturer of a successful brand. It disguises itself as an edgy upstart in order to appeal to the savvy practitioner of gravity games.

Farmclub, the site I mentioned earlier that allows viewers to guide the fate of unknown bands, is actually run by the cochairman of Interscope Geffen and A&M Records and is seeded with money from Seagram. Farmclub doesn't promote this fact too heavily, because in the music industry it is more valuable to be seen as a radical outsider rewriting the rules of the game. ***This new marketing environment is bound to launch a new breed of stealth companies—megaconglomerates who disguise themselves as new kids on the block.***

Many are still hanging on to the importance of branding, but in this era of increased customization and choice, people will want their own personal brands. It's great to have Levi Strauss cut a pair of jeans for your exact measurements, but while they are at it, why can't you have a personal label attached to the back pocket? And why not a choice of fabrics?

Just-on-time production allows your exact selection to be beamed to the sewing room floor and made on the spot. So why can't you completely personalize the entire look? Everyone has their favorite outfit that they would love to have in different fabrics. Everyone has tried on items they loved and thought, *if only the collar were different.* And if the style is classic, wouldn't it be great to be able to repurchase the item a few years later, when it has finally worn out—or to replace it with the current hot colors or perhaps a slightly larger size if necessary? The fashion industry is ripe for the emergence of personal brands.

Nike now lets you add your own personal tag line to the swoosh; it arrives stitched into your shoes. Many furniture sites allow you to play around with different fabrics and trims. Even cereal companies are experimenting with allowing customers to order their own personal mix. If the means of production are cheap enough to be used for a cereal, more intriguing variations are bound to be on their way.

- Virgin Megastore has installed kiosks designed by Digital on Demand that allow you to create personalized CDs. Why can't a popular club DJ contract with a record label so you can take home the mix you hear that night at the club and order right from the floor? DJs are often local celebrity figures and would certainly push their own personal labels.
- Why doesn't every gym have video-on-demand so that every personal trainer can print a video on the spot with customized routines for each client?
- Why couldn't magazines like *Metropolitan Home* or *Architectural Digest* launch a platform for their readers to customize their furniture designs and link to suppliers that want to bid on their business?
- Why can't chiropractors develop their own brands of vitamins and herbs tailored to their own recommendations with a label printed with their name?

- With advances in genome research, soon even drugs will be tailored to your unique personal physiology. Your unique genetic material will guide the formulation of the specific drug you take.

The more the public become coparticipants in designing commercial events, the more they will want brands that reflect their own personal styles. More than niche marketing, we will have niche brands tailored to niche communities. I know it's hard to believe in this era defined by about three media conglomerates, five large fast-food franchises, a couple mega-chain bookstores and a handful of nationally syndicated coffee shops, that people will ever want anything but the sterility and predictability that these megacorporations offer. But the moment a few companies offer the possibility of niche brands, they will spread like wildfire. In the increasingly local world of the global marketplace, people will no longer want large, generic, megabrands anymore; it will be considered *so nineties.*

Why have a DKNY label when I can have my own? Why be limited to the standard line of furniture offered by some company, when I can assemble a design of my own from a mix of available options? I'd much rather be able to tell people that the couches in my living room are my own creation rather than by some designer I've never met.

This kind of capability plays into the new consumer profile of those who expect to have input and impact on everything they touch. It plays to the new consumer profile of individuals who expect to author their own experiences and have a role in every game. It plays to new status trends, which purport that the highest-quality things are one of a kind. It plays to the well-known truth that the more customers are involved with you, the more likely they will be to use what you offer.

In line with this trend, the local experience is becoming more vital. Neighborhood and community events have risen 10 percent every year for the last five years. Marketing experts now point large corporations in this direction, suggesting they will get more bang for their bucks by sponsoring a bunch of local events rather than a single high-profile event like the Indy 500. A more politicized, creative, active public is getting more involved in creating these events and in supporting them. Once again the new generation may lead the way on this. Twenty-eight percent of European teens say they would rather buy local products. And in tight subcultures like the gay and lesbian community, eighty-seven percent say they are more likely to purchase a product that is targeted to them. Thinking globally is definitely driving people to act a lot more locally.

We may need to consider niche generations. Marketers conveniently lump generations into twenty-year blocks, assuming that a group that crosses decades will have similar attitudes and values. Some sociologists say a new generation now arises every four to five years. Any teacher will tell you that a twelve-year-old is a world apart from a fifteen-year-old. They are not the same generation. Because of the new connectivity, they can bond so tightly that they form subgroups within subgroups. A fifteen-year-old kid who calls him or herself a Goth is not of the same generation as a fifteen-year-old who calls him or herself a Jock. We will soon have niche generations and the smartest folks will know exactly how to tailor their products to ever more refined consumer profiles.

Throughout corporate America, regionalism is definitely in. Marketing consultant Yankelovich called this trend *glocal,* where global enterprises learn to become locally responsive. Watts Wacker and Jim Taylor have introduced nine paradoxes of the new economy.[40] One paradox is that the smaller you are the bigger you must look, and the bigger you are the smaller you must get. In fact, franchises of the future may no longer offer such fixed, homogenized experiences. Franchising is a model that flowered in the era of mass marketing; it too will transform, due to some of the same reasons traditional advertising will collapse. It is just not suited to the personalized, imaginative, responsive, local spaces that an entertainment culture will demand.

In this era of demassification, personalization and choice, a new breed of stealth companies will purposely disassociate themselves from their own successes in order to build ever more edgy products. More and more companies will commit brand blasphemy and let their own customers become the creatives.

2.6 CAUSE MARKETING IS EXPERIENCE MARKETING

If you want to connect with a customer's passions and interests, what better way than by becoming responsive to what he or she cares about? Environomics International surveyed individuals in twenty-three countries about how they perceived corporations. Corporate responsibility was at the top of the list. Twenty percent of all consumers internationally, and 40 percent of North Americans said they avoid products they consider irresponsible.

Paul Newman began a small company to produce his recipe for pasta sauce. Newman's Own is now a major provider of a vast array of food products. It has carved a niche in one of the most competitive fields with almost no advertising or traditional promotion. Much of its rapid success has hinged on one factor, *tremendous, tremendous word of mouth.* This word of mouth is so incredible in large part because the company gives all its after-tax profits to charity, one hundred million to date. The company has also become a leading spokesperson for stopping the use of genetically altered products by refusing to use them in their products and by lobbying congress. It gets real press for its exemplary actions, not faux-press about new products.

In the interest of full disclosure, I must tell you that I work for Newman's Own. Whenever I see a friend open a can of pasta sauce, salad dressing, pretzels or packaged cookies, I suggest that he or she purchase Newman's products and tell them why. I successfully lobbied our local grocer to carry these products. A few weeks later, I was happy to see that he had the pretzels, salad dressing, chocolate and pasta sauce. However, the cookies were not on the shelf. I pointed this out and encouraged him to carry the rest of the product line. About a year later, I noticed some of the line had been dropped, so I gave the store owner a pep talk so that he would continue his commitment to shelf space. (Even this well-designed plug is bound to convert a few of you.) I am an unpaid, highly successful sales-person for Paul Newman's products because I like the story behind them. Any company would be thrilled to have a few hundred customers like me.

Viral marketing can also work against you. Nike estimated that 38 percent of its drop in sales in 1997 was due to bad press about the poor con-ditions in its overseas factories. This could never have happened five years ago; people just weren't connected enough. When Kathie Lee Gifford was publicly accused of similar conditions in her clothing factories, she was on camera the very next day pledging to make changes. She even became a spokesperson for this issue and appeared before congress. With the cur-rent pace of chit ch@t, no company can afford to ignore word of mouth.

Everyone wants a viral idea—a concept that gets told over and over, passed from person to person, with no expense to the seller. Catchy fic-tives are important, personalized brands will help, but in this era of loud, crowded markets, only stories that a customer really cares about will get told over and over. Products that have good stories will naturally tran-scend the confines of the bottle in which they are stored.

One of the fastest ways to create buzz is to become involved in some-thing that people believe in. The consumer of the future is more active. Sixty percent of the public say they have either complained or praised a company by phone or letter. For these reasons, more and more companies are turning toward cause-related marketing. It will be a critical strategy for connecting with the wired, politicized, retribalized consumer of the coming decade.

Cause marketing is yet one more reflection of the tendency to tie marketing to customers' real-life concerns and passions. However, since the public has such immediate and accurate access to real information, this involvement has to be more than just a superficial. Like clothing designer Eileen Fisher, who gets real press for its progressive stand, you've got to *really* care.

With declining revenue, most newspapers are operating with minimal staff. They rely heavily on *news* fed to them by corporations. Corporations even refer to these press releases as *free advertising*. But is it really news that Windows XP is about to be released? Is it really news that a new line of gadgets is about to appear? Some estimate that over half of what we read is pseudonews fed by self-interested parties to news organizations. Further, with the ever-heightening demand for content to fill the 24/7 news day, pseudonews is bound to become the mainstay for many sources.

At first this seems like just another contribution to the decline of truth in our culture. But, ever the optimist, I believe the media consumer will become skilled at detecting this bias. Further, in this era of endless press releases, companies will have to have something of real value if they want to rise from the glut of pseudonews. Newman's Own or Eileen Fisher get press mostly because their actions are genuinely interesting.

2.7 Web Sites from Birth and Liminal Culture

Our friends announced the birth of their son with a Web site. They invited all of us from distant lands to watch their son grow up on-line. Regular postings chronicled his development. They didn't name their son Truman after Jim Carrey's film character, but the effect was eerily similar. I wondered:

- One day, when he is old enough, will he take over the site and continue the tale?
- Will people with the coolest on-line stories be the most popular kids?
- Like a director setting up a scene, will he begin to choose life events because they work well on the screen?
- Will he avoid other choices because they don't have visual appeal?
- Like an actor who remains in character, will he confuse his on-line story with his off-line persona?

- Will his virtual identity have power over his real-life self-concept?
- Will we all begin to focus on how to capture what we do as entertainment?
- Instead of ordinary relationships, will people share story lines, weaving ideas from one site to the next?
- And if this boy's personal story can attract the attention of public venues, where does he end and MTV, CNN or some interactive TV show begin?

Americans are primed for self-exposure. According to a Time/CNN poll, 31 percent claim they would allow a reality show to televise them in their pajamas and 8 percent are willing to be naked.[41] More than thirty-six million Web cams will be in circulation by 2004, enabling an entire nation to *go public*. DotComGuy received one million mentions in print and became one of *People* magazine's top twenty-five most interesting people by spending one year of his life shut in his house, surviving on-line and allowing twenty cameras to follow his journey. He even came out of his ordeal with a wife. He met her on-line and quietly proposed in front of a small, intimate, nationally televised family gathering. And in a quaint throwback to tradition, their bridal registry was posted on Amazon.com. Reality-based shows that create instant celebrities further the mind-set that visibility in and of itself creates value. Once anyone can get on screen, our current notions of celebrity will probably begin to crumble. We may become more interested in seeing ourselves and our friends up in lights, rather than whatever face the industry is pushing. *Who needs a celebrity? Why not insert our own biographies into this continuous flow of instant culture.*

CU-SeeMe-type technologies allow people to create visual connections in real time. Companies make their meetings available. Consultants simulcast their speeches. Physicians can examine and treat rural patients from their city offices or even guide operations on-line. You can make video calls to friends and easily insert streaming media into your daily e-mail. Lawyers, real estate agents and almost anyone will allow prospective clients to meet them on-line, so they can get a feel for what it would be like to work with them. *Once we have Web sites from birth, will we all begin to see ourselves differently?*

In this new communication environment, we will no longer be allotted our fifteen minutes of fame. Fame will be a negotiated event. It will exist for anyone, anywhere, anytime whenever someone is willing to give away fifteen minutes.

When I heard the early, early buzz on *The Blair Witch Project,* several media-savvy friends suggested with full belief that these kids *really* were lost in the woods and this documentary *really* was found. Everyone explained the film's explosive success by talking about media convergence and peer marketing. But the main reason the story got told and retold was because it walked that thin line—it was fantasy masquerading as reality. This blurring was critical to the early buzz. If the early messengers had thought they were spreading the word about just another movie, I guarantee the word of mouth would not have been so vigorous.

Ever ahead of his time, Marshall McLuhan warned of the discarnate effect, where the body becomes divorced from the mind and travels without regard to physical constraints. This is precisely what happens in the on-line experience of MUDs and MOOS. Although these are still relatively fringe experiences, one must remember that the future always lives at the edge. Emerging trends always live on this fragile perimeter so they can explore with few formal constraints. But, once the details are worked out, with the help of early adopters and culture scouts, these fringe experiences have a tendency to wend their way to the center of the stream.

Disney offered a movie version of the myth of Hercules. It was entertaining, but bore little resemblance to the original story. Culture has become divorced from the historical experience. We are fast becoming a liminal culture, where hard facts and soft fantasies are indistinguishable.

In a liminal culture, politics become entertainment and entertainment becomes political. Martin Sheen plays the president on *The West Wing* and has established clout with voters and campaigned with Gore.

I'm sure many confused his endorsement with the status of his screen character. The lawyers on *The Practice* regularly promote highly political issues, such as the importance of maintaining the constitutional rights of criminals in order to keep a society democratic. Forget *Survivor* and *Boot Camp;* these are the *reality shows* that matter! The real and unreal will bounce off one another, turning fiction into fact and real stories into public opinion. In every domain, storytellers ascend in importance.

2.8 PLANET ART

I know several successful musicians who can't read a line of music or play an instrument, yet they sample and compose away on their computer keyboards, spinning out a lot of musical hits you would recognize. A host of graphic artists are creating amazing digital renderings, yet know nothing about painting mediums or principles of composition. Armed with $2500 in video software, the average person can approach the special effects capabilities of the first *Star Wars* movie. CD burners, which allow the average person to distribute music mixes or short films to their friends, are one of the fastest-moving product areas. Sites like Blooger.com give you the tools to design the Web. Metafilter.com gives you the capabilities to create your own discussion groups. ***Thus, one of the extraordinary wonders of cyberspace is that it brings every form of artistic expression within striking distance of the average person.***

Both Swatch and Holiday Inn have asked the public to submit thirty-second ads for their company, offering to air the winners. This kind of offer is relevant only because large numbers of the general public are playing around with digital artistry. Which brings us to the interesting observation of fifteen-year-old Deanna Perry. "We have control over the computer. As a consumer it makes us more resistant. We may find a way to create the program or applications ourselves. Then we might not even need the products sold to us."[42] It sure smells like teen spirit!

A generation who has grown up on simulation is used to authoring their own creative products. They are Webmasters and digital artists from an early age. These are not resources they have to hire out. Many learning theorists say the ideal time to learn computer skills is around three to four years old—exactly the same time it is best to learn a new language. These educators say computing skills are not a new knowledge set like science or history; they are far closer to a new language.

Imagine this: Suppose you lived in a country of people who knew only English as a second language. They all arrived as adults from some other land and English was learned later in life. You would see frequent evidence of rather stilted, awkward language in formal written and oral presentations, due to the fact that English was not the mother tongue.

Then suppose the kids of these parents who spoke English as a second language grew up. Suddenly you would see an outpouring of extraordinarily well-written books, complex dialogue in films and public discourse that was far more interesting merely because this new population had grown up speaking the language from birth.

This is a perfect analogy for what we are about to witness. There is a lot of great on-line creativity, but it is still owned by people who, in the best-case scenarios, began speaking the on-line vernacular in their teens. Some are very good with languages, but computing is still a *second language*. The on-line world didn't gain speed until at least 1995, so most of the native on-line-speaking kids have barely hit elementary school. We cannot even imagine the economic and creative forms that will emerge from the first generation who speaks DFB, *Digital from Birth.*

"The fusion of art/music/fashion/film represents to me a strong futuristic vision. It's about the idea of a blank canvas. Many people have unsuccessfully tried in the past to predict the future in the image of science fiction. I believe the future lives in a vision of creativity that dares to open the eyes of the public. These artists, musicians and directors do this in a very real way. In the future, current laws and restrictions will no longer be valid. A new aesthetic will evolve, inspired by these visionary artists."

DONATELLA VERSACE[43]

The future always lives on the edge, where the radicals, revolutionaries and cognitive dissonants hang out. Jose Arguilles is definitely one of the future's more well-established residents. Arguilles is best known as the man who in the eighties popularized a global street theater event called Harmonic Convergence, based on his reading that the ancient Mayan calendar was about to end. His publications are often stream of consciousness rants. Several years ago a friend came back from one of his lectures and told me a provocative tale.

As I suggested at the beginning of this chapter, most early cultures were centered in the arts. For example, in the Balinese culture everyone was an artist. Everyone chose a form of creative expression that they then contributed to the larger society. They didn't even have a word for *artist*, since it was so integrated into daily life. As a result, the Balinese system of irrigation was so elegant that hardly a drop of water was wasted and labor was reduced to a minimum. Water effortlessly trickled down from one terraced field to another, guiding the mountain rain down what was in effect a man-made stream through everyone's personal gardens. It was beautiful, laborsaving and ecological in one fell swoop. Artistic cultures all over the world tend to be models of peace, prosperity, quality of life and sustainability.

Arguilles suggested that at some point in our early history we replaced the artistic event with the commercial event. Commerce replaced creativity. The marketplace replaced the artistic ritual as that which brought people together. That was when civilization started down the wrong track. Again, you only have to look at what has happened in Bali since tourism arrived to see how quality of life declines in a purely commercial society that no longer considers beauty its central value. Arguilles has suggested that the only way to correct our current economic, social and environmental imbalances is to restore the idea that we are meant to be an art planet.

I immediately latched on to this image as a way of explaining the hope I feel about the digital economy. The digital economy could restore the artistic experience as the central vehicle for building the larger culture. It is not that people won't make money, it is just that they will be making more of the money through intangibles and less through pure product. It is that imagination, meaning and creativity will define the road ahead far more than the relentless drive for market share without regard to impact. Beauty will begin to matter again, although it will probably be a more radical beauty.

Arguilles provides a powerful thesis. And Paul Schell, the mayor of Seattle, is acting on it. With his support, the city is undertaking one of the most amazing commitments to cultural expansion of any city in the country—with 1.2 billion dollars of arts-related projects begun or completed in the last ten years. To give you perspective, this is more than the entire budget of the National Endowment for the Arts during the same time period. Schell establishes the rationale:

> You have telecommunications, biotech, software, and the Web all coming together with great music, architecture and art. It's at the intersection of all these disciplines that sparks fly. That's where ideas come from. We are creating a place where the creative experience can flourish.[44]

Once people become more artistic as a result of every-day activities such as editing video to place in their e-mails or constructing their own personal Web sites, they naturally gain new values. The on-line world places the creative experience in the hands of every individual.

Codesigning experiences becomes even more interesting than consuming them. Producing, sharing and distributing creative events will be accessible to everyone. Content will be developed by everyone while commerce reshapes itself to support and further personal artistry. Cottage industries, personal brands, super-empowered associates who represent products they actually use in real life , activist consumers and a nation of digital artists will be the new loci of power. The depth and power of our organizational stories will matter like never before.

The Australian aborigines do not have possessive pronouns
for referring to relatives. They can't say, my husband, my wife,
my child, my parent.

Rather, they say, husband-me, wife-me, child-me, parent-me.

Their connections with others are so enmeshed that even identity
is a shared event. Who they are can be understood only
by who they touch.

3 TRIBALMIND

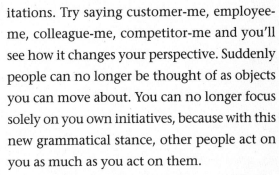

Language is a subtle bias. We are so immersed in it we rarely sense its limitations. Try saying customer-me, employee-me, colleague-me, competitor-me and you'll see how it changes your perspective. Suddenly people can no longer be thought of as objects you can move about. You can no longer focus solely on you own initiatives, because with this new grammatical stance, other people act on you as much as you act on them.

As a result of this natural interactivity, the aboriginal mind is deeply tribal. The most profound layers of wisdom can be touched only through relationship. Indigenous people believe they *borrow* their spirits from the tribe, and when they die their individual life forces again return to the whole. Thus, the *tribalmind* is an intelligence beyond the mind of any single member.

For this reason, the greatest punishment to which any indigenous culture can ever subject someone is banishment. But banishment for a tribal culture is not what you and I would think. You are allowed to safely sleep alongside the tribe. You partake of its food and your physical well-being is never in jeopardy. Rather, you are destined to wander among your friends and not be seen. No one makes eye contact and you are rendered invisible.

This is an acceptable, even welcomed feature of modern life—to be able to walk past others and not be noticed. It's hard to fully comprehend why this would be so incredibly punishing. Yet, it is pure agony for someone whose very being rests on the feeling that he or she belongs to a larger whole. Being rendered invisible is soul wrenching when even your brain waves move in tandem with those of your peers. Separation from this invisible web is equivalent to being deprived of air.

To have impact at this level, interdependence was invisibly coded in every act, infiltrating everything they did. Thus tribal members were telepathic, resonant and responsible for one another.

In fact, in most tribal cultures, crime is almost nonexistent. It is impossible to distance one's self from the group long enough to do anyone harm. The cohesion of the tribe allows individual problems to be absorbed and balanced out by the larger group. An African proverb that Hillary Clinton used and popularized says, "It takes a village to raise a child." This does not only imply the support of dozens of extra hands (although that is welcomed). The *village* refers to the resonant field of shared values that invisibly points every individual toward the tribe's greater good.

In a tribal world, individuals are enmeshed in a fabric that spreads far wider than what modern man has ever considered. *But as you will soon see, once again we are headed right back to where we began, and beyond.*

POWERSHIFT

Much of modern life rests on a separation not only from each other, but also from the sources of our survival. Few know which river brings water to their taps. Most can't identify the chain of hands that will bear food to their tables. Yet, we live under the incredible illusion that we are self-sufficient.

We have even come to believe it is a sign of weakness to need someone else in order to accomplish our goals. The greater our self-reliance, the freer we feel. Our role models are those who can do anything they want without challenge or permission. This, we are taught, is maximum power.

And it is upon these very values that most businesses are built. We assume we can survive without knowing our neighboring entrepreneurs. Departments are separate; there is little need to know what the other is doing. Dominance is rewarded. Secrets are expected. Individual accomplishment is all that counts. We may work with others along the way, but for the most part, relationships stay formal and fleeting. We spend more than a third of our lives at work, yet the years go by, side by side with our peers, and deep roots are rarely forged.

This illusion of separation permeates how information is exchanged, money is shared and the future is charted. A powerful business person annihilates the competition, dominates his peers and stands out as a commanding presence. Dozens of handy guides can help you become the Genghis Khan or General Patton of your very own business domain. Conquer and thrive. Wield your way to unlimited power. Claim what is rightfully yours. These maxims have worked for thousands of years and continue to bring ample rewards. It is hard to believe there could be any chink in such an invincible armor.

But warrior cultures always have their Achilles' heels. The city of Troy was impenetrable, the safest in all of ancient Greece. Its people rested easy knowing that no invader could ever make it past its mighty, towering walls.

Then, one morning, a large, beautiful painted horse appeared at Troy's gates. The people were suspicious at first; but a stranger led them to believe that by taking this horse inside their walls they would curry favor with the Goddess Athena.

Always eager to get on the good side of a powerful goddess, they wheeled this fine horse behind their walls. Everyone admired its beauty. It certainly added variety to their ordinary days. Filled with fun and bright chatter, the citizens of Troy went to sleep that night, satisfied and exhausted by their eventful experience.

When darkness fell, a trap door opened in the belly of the horse and a small band of soldiers climbed out. These intruders opened the gates from within and allowed their army to enter, quickly conquering the unsuspecting residents of Troy.

This is exactly the predicament many now face. We have innocently hooked our lives to the big, beautiful Web, hoping to curry favor with the Gods of Speed and Nimbleness. We offer our wandering teams the latest ways to stay in contact, and then discover they are using our airtime to vent their dissatisfactions. Graciously, we invited our customers in for some heartfelt dialogue and now they are giving each other information about competing products. We've kindly given suppliers keys to our inner workings and now we wonder if they will remain loyal. *Have our walls already been breached?*

Four journalists who have been observing the social shifts of the new economy wrote a rather irreverent and important book called *The Cluetrain Manifesto.*[1] Many companies still act as if they are at war, conquering the customer, targeting the opposition and bringing their employees into submission with the strategic plan. However, due to the incredible, informal and truthful exchange unleashed by the Webbed world, many realize the emperor has no clothes. The senior team will congratulate each other on how well a meeting went, while the rest of the players are already on-line telling the truth about how they really felt in the same meeting. And customers don't pull any punches either as they ruthlessly tell each other the score. Suddenly, truth-telling wreaks havoc with the best-laid plans.

In the blur of newfound economic speed, authors Stan Davis and Christopher Meyer echo a similar sentiment. They advise that customers have become partners in your business.[2] The more you treat them this way the more they will enrich what you do. And the people who work with you must also be entrusted to assume more vital decisions.

Bureaucratic forms of authority are giving way to adaptive structures, offering employees the freedom to explore directions you may not have considered.

If you distance yourself from the people who are involved in your business, you distance yourself from a knowledge that is now vital for survival. You distance yourself from a body of solutions you might never have considered. Businesses of the future will relentlessly break down these barriers to input. The most forward-thinking companies will steep in the forces of the market, allowing its chaotic twists and turns to be instantly felt, absorbed and incorporated into their next steps. Thus, those who have the best means to sense the pulse of the tribe will be at a considerable advantage.

Warrior attitudes are counterproductive in this new terrain. Nomads are deeply tribal people. You'd better be able to count on others when everything else in your world is completely transitory. When you travel to a new conceptual destination quite regularly, you need intimate and trustworthy partners.

Thus, business priorities have shifted to emphasize coordination more than production—alliances rather than self-determined initiatives. But no matter how hyperlinked and connected you are, intellectual capital can be stored only between the two ears of a living, breathing person. In fact, with the rise of intangible values and easily copied innovations, people may be the only way to hold on to what you have. *If you think the loss of fixed products and stable territories throws your current plans to the wind, wait till you see what happens when you have to start sharing your brain!*

WELCOME TO THE DIGITAL TRIBE

There is little privacy in a tribal world. You easily hear conversations through tents. If you fight with your partner, everyone is privy to the exchange. Private life is public domain. So it is curious that one of the first impacts of the digital culture is the loss of privacy. Thousands of little brothers now know everything we do. We each leave a digital trail, revealing what we look at, what we buy, how we buy and when. We may try to curb pieces of this capacity for continuous observation, but face it—our on-line wanderings are no longer private. And as we get used to it, we may even discover that having our on-line travels observed is actually quite useful. Others can come to know us and even watch over our interests.

In an inexplicable turnaround of public opinion, many don't seem to care about privacy anymore. The city of London has put video cameras on almost every corner. You can barely cross a street without a lens following you. You'd think its population would be rising up in revolt. Instead people say they feel safer under the eye of constant surveillance. And the cameras are not just trained on London streets; they are watching every square inch of the planet. Orbiting satellites beam back TV-grade images once available only to the military, images that can now be purchased by anyone for mere pennies per use. And business is booming! By 2004, thirty-six million people will have hooked up their Webcams, fueling an epidemic of people freely offering their private lives up for on-line view. This new generation wants their windows wide open. Talk about free love! *Welcome to the digital tribe.*

A nomadic tribe can pack up, shift camps and barely say a word. There is a telepathic resonance that allows every member to stay in constant contact. Once again, we seem to be craving this resonant state. The 24/7 day of cell phones, beepers, instant messaging, teleconferencing, intranets and virtual teams, puts us in constant touch with everyone connected to what we do. More than 80 percent of all businesspeople stay connected to the office even while on vacation. Happily, our day is no longer our own. It is shared with the stream of contact that flows from all the people vital to our lives. Immersed in continuous dialogue, we are rarely alone with our thoughts. With a phone to our ear we walk along, warmed by our blanket of continuous contact. *Welcome to the outstretched arms of the digital tribe.*

A high-tech world requires very high-touch skills for introducing new products to the average person. But even more important, a swiftly changing environment demands people you can lean on. Often, you don't have time to slowly develop structures and systems; you have to quickly marry or befriend the knowledge you need. It is no longer possible to know everything it takes to make things happen. The one brain we've all been given suddenly is not enough. Projects are rarely solo ventures shepherded by a single visionary; everything happens in tandem with someone else. The World Wide Web deepens the plot by offering the means for wandering electronic tribes to organize and communicate in bands of shared values. Nimble upstarts composed of packs of like-minded pioneers already use neotribalism to get the job done; now all of us must adapt to this edgy way of relating to others. *Yes, welcome to the woven wonders of the digital tribe.*

The global village is open for business! Anything happening anywhere happens everywhere. A huge *now* envelops the globe as we move to a universal drumbeat. But the more global we become, the more we seem to crave the local. The more networked we become, the more it is also a one-to-one future—demassified, individualized, coauthored and highly personalized. It's a cinch to act global; the real trick is to make us feel close and special again. *Once again, welcome to the digitally induced tribe.*

The everyday sights and sounds of the electronic universe are building the neural pathways of a collaborative brain. The voice of the self and the voice of the other are intermingling in new and provocative ways. It is no longer possible to keep the sound of the crowd separate from your own inner voice. Your brain waves are subtly intertwined with others in ways that prevent you from definitively claiming ideas as your own. In fact, you feel left out if your creative juices are not added to the bubbling group soup. Outside your conscious awareness, ancient wisdom is being provoked about what it is like to live in shared contexts. The unrelenting sensory cues of the electronic world are triggering a long latent tribal gene. *And once this ancient memory is fully triggered, we will all be magically infused with the natural wisdom of the digital tribe.*

THE COLLABORATIVE WEB

For his senior thesis in computer science, a student in England was exploring free speech on the Internet. He developed a piece of software that allowed users to share music, video, published material, software or anything rendered in a digital form with anyone they wanted. He launched Freenet, which goes a few steps beyond Napster-type sites, which have a central brain and therefore can be shut down.

With Freenet, the use of the software is untraceable. One-to-one exchanges can take place whenever and with whomever we want. At first, sites like this were cumbersome to use and therefore not very popular. But what is truly unnerving is that with platforms like this, there is no one to sue. It's just a piece of software dropped on the side of the road by a wandering nomadic hacker. As these sites become user-friendly and high-speed lines widespread, peer-to-peer computing will define both the commercial and artistic experience. ***One-to-one distribution is also one-to-one creativity.***

Like it or not, this *is* the underlying architecture of the World Wide Web. It is a network of one-to-one exchanges governed by the language (or software) you use to communicate. E-commerce merely sits on top of this vast network of personal conversations.

A hot new software called Groove lets small groups build their own virtual teams. Developed by the designer of Lotus Notes, it has become the darling of Free Agent Nation, allowing users to assemble teams that rival any in-house group. Interestingly, corporate teams are also using it, sometimes even inviting in people from the outside. Much like Freenet, it frees users from having to work through a central source. The exchange is nimble and self-organized. Software like this is helping to build a nation of players who love to share and know how to collaborate. It will also serve to further dismantle the formal organizational chart.

Tom Peters and his co-author of *In Search of Excellence,* Bob

Waterman, made separate lists of the main challenges they thought were facing today's businesses. Their separate lists bore no relationship to each other, with one, and only one, exception: *decentralization*.

> After fifty (combined) years of watching organizations thrive and shrivel, we held to one . . . and only one basic belief: To loosen the reins, to allow a thousand flowers to bloom and a hundred schools to contend, is the best way to sustain vigor in perilous, gyrating times.[3]

Decentralization is what happens when the randomness of the one-to-one relationship is allowed to thrive. Decentralization is what happens when conversations rise to the surface and begin to shape the critical dimensions of commerce. You are no longer just buying and selling; you are talking. This means that what happens right now between you and me *is* the substance of business. This is where policies are made, strategies are launched and innovations are born. This one central factor has driven every critical weaving of the Web. That is why the beating heart of commerce is now marching in time to a very different drummer.

In the early days of this revolution, the ARPANET (Advanced Research Projects Agency Network) was funded by the military to insure communication in times of war. The military purposely made it decentralized so that the central brain could never get knocked out. It was redundant and self-managing, so it could persist without any control from above. People like Vint Cerf introduced packet switching so each unit of information could follow its own path without needing a central guidance system. There is a wonderful irony to the military having played a key role in the breaking down of command and control models.[4]

In those early years, there were a few different Nets up and running, but one Net could not talk to another. If this situation had continued, we would not be talking about a new economy. One Net not talking to another is exactly what old-line business is about—I have my TV station, you have yours. I have my customers, you have yours. And the more I can prevent you from accessing or even knowing about someone else's stuff, the more powerful I am. But we *are* talking now, precisely because Tim Berners-Lee at CERN, Advanced Particle Physics Lab, Vint Cerf and many others introduced a series of protocols, a universal language that allowed one Net to speak to another Net. Thus began the breakdown of the separations between discrete players with differing agendas.

But this early system was still intended only for scientists and researchers. It was designed so everyone's doors would always be wide open. You could link your document to someone else's *without asking permission*. Since the original purpose was rapid exchange of knowledge, ease of sharing was wired throughout the early platforms. As a result of this early design peculiarity, putting in effective locks and keys has now become quite challenging. In fact, this underlying tendency toward accessibility has become one of the troubling features of this medium at least as far as commerce is concerned. But the deed is done. It is an irresistibly, irreversibly, undeniably collaborative domain. ***This irrefutable message of connectivity seeps out through every pore of the Web's vast, silvery electronic skin.***

These early visionaries dreamt of free-flowing information that would enhance creativity. Scientists would no longer have to wait for the slow pace of normal publishing; they could instantly keep up with one another. Idea creation would explode. Knowledge would grow in quantum leaps because everyone's brains would be hooked up together. And according to Tim Berners-Lee, gloriously, the World Wide Web would always remain "just a little bit broken," continually shaped by the unexpected, uncontrollable and unimaginable. It would always remain a turbulent, dynamic, pulsing force.

In those early days of the first digital dawn no one was dreaming of dot-com millions. The Web was expected to be a playground for researchers and geeks, of little interest to ordinary folks. The big money bet was placed on interactive TV. That's where the majority of us were expected to spend our time. Since the forces of commerce were preoccupied with building a bigger, better, buff TV, the geeks continued to play outside of their fields of influence. So Mosaic, the early language that enabled the first browser Netscape, was designed to support full-on, top-speed accessibility. Like the founding fathers before them, Mosaic designers Marc Andreeson and Eric Bina publicly said they were attempting to *democratize information.*

Once commerce enters the equation, then people begin to think about how can they build in proprietary features. They purposely design technical features so no one else can play. But these early pioneers didn't even know any venture capitalists. They were philosophers and dreamers, artists and innocents. They were painting new social realities. They built things as freely as possible so collaboration would thrive. No one even entertained the idea that profits would ever lurk in the strange synapses of this emerging beast.

Thus, these deeply collaborative principles were present throughout the early moments of conception. They are held in the digital DNA of every single on-line exchange. Like it or not, accessibility enters the code of each new generation of communication. ***This core image of free exchange was there at the big, digital bang that unleashed the amazing potential of this new medium, and its relentless presence cannot be avoided.***

On top of all this, a second equally big collaborative bang is just now being felt. The number of chips placed in computers has begun to level. It is now exceeded by the number of chips placed in the home, the office, appliances, cars, phones, etc. It is the intelligence that can now be embedded in every small item that is creating what Kevin Kelly calls *swarm intelligence.*[5] The tires of the farmer's tractor will be able to speak to the soil, and relay a chemical assessment of what is needed to the organic fertilizer company. The fertilizer company will in turn customize a personalized prescription for that farmer, mix and ship the prescribed product to where it will then be automatically loaded on the tractor for the next day's distribution on the field.

Another key digital visionary, Howard Rheingold, says that when these chips swarm through every possible activity, technology itself will begin to fade behind the cyber curtain.[6] The *conversation* described above will have a life of its own; the farmer, tractor driver and fertilizer company manager will never need to know what took place. The intelligence of the exchange will be embedded, rather than explicit. Decisions will become very specific and local, rather than generalized and global. Technology will become ever more transparent, taking over everyday decisions, and revealing new creative roles for the people who interact within these systems. The industrial era will die, not because we won't be manufacturing anymore, but because of the new roles that will be revealed in the factories. Product assembly lines and conceptual assembly lines will all be run by chips, allowing the rest of us to assume the role of the artist.

Because of this second big bang caused by chips scattering everywhere, all the socioeconomic forms that describe how we construct our businesses will not only become Web-like, they will echo the patterns of the swarm. We will learn to travel like a flock of birds—led, yet leaderless. Directed not so much by a goal on the horizon, but through constant and powerful communication between each member of the flock.

Now let's consider a third big bang, which was alluded to earlier: the explosion of bandwidth. Because of limited bandwidth, events like teleconferencing and streaming video still remain a bit flawed. Chat rooms, user groups, e-mail and all forms of on-line communication are heavily dependent on the verbal representation of knowledge. If you want dynamic exchange, you still have to go face-to-face. Once bandwidth can approximate the nuances and facility of face-to-face exchanges, the on-line world will truly become virtual. And as the Accenture ads say, "That's when it gets interesting." Real-life events will be able to travel anywhere, to anyone, at any time as effortlessly as going across the hall. This is what will unleash yet another dimension of intimacy.

The raging profits of the digital economy often blind us to the underlying conceptual architecture. No matter what ideas you drape upon a form, the underlying bones always show through. The power of the new economy lies not so much in the incredible new avenues for publication and distribution; the real magic rests on the unpredictable nature of layers upon layers of decentralized exchange. *As a result of the third big bang—cheap, accessible bandwidth—the next new thing will be revealed by the next dimension of intimacy we are able to forge with the people who are most involved in the thick of the most interesting dialogues.*

As a result of all this, the current economy is sitting on top of a fundamental architecture that was designed to promote sharing. It was purposely designed to break down walls, take away barriers and allow information to flow unimpeded. Thus, these warm, fuzzy qualities are insidiously infecting every facet of what was once a brave warrior economy.

The grandeur rests on the imagination of each individual player bumping up against the imagination of another and the forward thinking digital artists who have learned to ride this wave of social intelligence. Millions of random personal behaviors now have a way to interact at a global level. This creates extraordinary feedback loops, with untold numbers of conversations colliding with each other, provoking uncharted possibilities. Mining these new dimensions of social exchange becomes the substance of business.

The technical terms for this phenomenon are: *self-organization* or *the emergent qualities of a system*. They refer to the tendency of any social system to evolve new layers of complexity or, in other words, to get more interesting. One day people may be chatting, the next they are organizing a political protest and the next day they are lobbying congress. These terms refer to the loose-knit layering of ideas that triggers new possibilities without the direction of a leader. You cannot understand the future of commerce without understanding these concepts.

Complexity evolves because of the inherent intelligence that lies within any social group, which can be unlocked only through frequent, random and continuous exchange. No one needs to lead the charge. MIT director and author Peter Senge suggests that discovering how to surface and ride these forces of complexity is key to the learning organization. An organization that doesn't allow this natural chaos to surface, also never really learns. True learning organizations are destined to always feel just a little bit out of control.[7]

You'll also see the phrase *social life* used a lot. I borrowed it from John Seely Brown, former director of the wildly innovative Xerox PARC (Palo Alto Research Center) research facility. In his extraordinary book, *The Social Life of Information,* he shows over and over that when ideas are embedded in conversation, they progress faster, get more interesting and have more practical application. Ideas that are kept in isolation are rarely as useful.[8]

Bottom line: We have a communication medium being used for commerce, rather than a commercial medium such as print, radio or TV being used for communication. *And this makes all the difference in the world.*

Becoming a Tribal Company

The economy has become one big blur. No one has clear roles. Customers morph into partners and then set your strategy. Workers mutate into CEOs and take charge of critical decisions. Senior executives are no longer in charge, becoming servants of the decisions that now flow from everywhere. The processes defining the creation, production, distribution and sale of a product become inseparable. The new economy has decimated the role of middlemen, while ushering in new forms of intermediaries at the very same time. Customers are face-to-face with suppliers; suppliers are face-to-face with each other, and everyone is in cahoots with one another. All of them are involved in the inner workings of *your* business.

When MCI was first being built, it deliberately changed its organizational structure every six months so that its players wouldn't settle into comfortable positions. In lieu of job descriptions, W. L. Gore tells new people to look around and find something to do. The company trusts that these fresh eyes are sure to see something that the current residents have missed. A major computer company now gives people orange or blue badges depending on whether they are maintaining the existing businesses (blue badge), or deconstructing the existing businesses (orange badge). Some even choose half blue/half orange badges so they can divide their day between clear messages and crazy risks. It's an *Alice in Wonderland* world of dreamscapes and strange characters who have been freed to take on startling roles.

Even if your products are way ahead of the curve, you are probably still immersed in models driven by the imperative of individuality. We think we want team spirit, but don't really know how to get out of our own brains. We say we want to share, but will hold back our best ideas for that moment when we are assured to get maximum credit for originating the idea. We try to listen, but have little patience for the cognitive dissonance of conflicting information, so we freely discard any information that doesn't fit what we want to do. We are still using possessive pronouns—my customer, my supplier, my manager—thinking that we can really *have* another person. We don't really know what it means to say customer-me, employee-me, you-me.

I will now propose twelve core dynamics that will drive a tribal company. An old-line company, or as the Cluetrain gang calls it, Fort Business, rests on its plans and visions, persuading its people to join the campaign and win the market-share war. *A tribal company relies on its social life to define its future.*

These twelve core dynamics will fall under three main categories:

1. How businesses relate to customers
2. How businesses relate to workers
3. Their overall commitment to a quality of conversation

As you are about to see, a tribal company is not any one thing; rather, it is driven by a series of ever deepening dialogues.

3·1 THE END OF CUSTOMERS

Customers as we now know them will cease to exist. This is due to one very simple dynamic: *the symmetry of information.*

Simply put, the reason that car dealers always *won* when a customer bought a car is because they had more information about financing, used car prices and the real invoice price. The salespeople would juggle these factors so that they would always come out ahead. If the customers were determined to get a good price for their new cars, the salespeople took their profits from the trade-ins or the financing. The customers never had a clue about what happened except for those nagging feelings in the pit of their stomach as they left the showroom with their keys that somehow they had been had. But these kinds of exchanges no longer have to happen. With the advent of e-commerce, customers are armed with the very same level of information as the salespeople. Symmetry is restored. Customers are on equal footing with the sellers.

Once power advantages are removed from the equation, truth begins to prevail. You can no longer hide and manipulate information to maintain an advantage. Customers can easily access the information that will allow them to see through your smokescreen; therefore you just can't play that way anymore. As you will now see, marketing, sales, supply, delivery, compensation and even hiring are transformed into dialogues rather than powerplays.

Sue Brown had diabetes. During the course of her own journey to identify resources, she assembled an extraordinary body of information. At some point she wanted to share her knowledge with others, so she built a Web site. Information rapidly flowed in from others about resources they had found and the knowledge base became even more interesting and dynamic. She found herself the coordinator of a rapidly growing community with a very big social life.

Through her able editing, this body of knowledge became top of the line. She easily leveraged her site into a great book contract. She then proceeded to design a line of herbal products and vitamins based on her customers' expertise.

Like a good nomad, she didn't invest a penny. She contracted with an existing company to manufacture and deliver the product. She supplied the customers. Success of the products was immediate. The formulations were exactly what this community wanted, so for them, there was no better product anywhere else. Their continued input allowed her to update the product and keep it current with her customers' knowledge. Eventually she offered this community ways to invest in the company, so that the members could also own a piece of what they were buying and also developing, and therefore care about it even more.

If you listen to your tribe, they will always tell you where to go. Her community began talking about buying clubs for prescription drugs. So she helped them band together to negotiate better prices. This self-organizing gang didn't stop there. They lobbied for new research and more advantageous insurance regulations. For Sue, this site began as a labor of love; financial success just came along for the ride.

Although this is a composite tale and the details of the actual events have been somewhat fictionalized, we do know people who mirror each aspect of this story. And you can be sure there are thousands of Sue Browns building their labors of love in every field imaginable. There are bound to be people who are putting the whole sequence together. We just haven't met them yet.

Here are the core trends embedded in this story: ***Our first four dialogues focus on the relationship of any business to its customers and how this particular relationship may mutate and evolve.*** (A customer can be the public, another business or even a supplier. Ultimately a customer is anyone who buys something from you.)

A. To Brand or Bond?

Sue Brown never had a customer in the traditional sense. She practiced *permission marketing*—the ultimate dream of every business. Your customers give you permission to sell to them. They actually wanted to hear what she would offer next. The CEO of Rockport shoes said it dawned on him one day that his company's present system of marketing was equivalent to being at a party and telling stories only about yourself. The next day he introduced plans for Rockport to be able to hear the other side of the story. For example, a particular customer's frustration that a favorite model wasn't offered in tan leather.

Almost everyone knows that you must get involved with your customer base. Some experts in this domain even suggest that you lurk around preexisting communities and find ways to infiltrate a group that would want to know about what you offer. In Sue's case, the book publisher approached her through one of the many literary scouts that now prowl the Internet for interesting prospects. Similarly, a savvy vitamin manufacturer could have spotted what she was up to early on and been there before anyone else. Many companies pay big bucks to consultants who really just hang around chat rooms and forage for ideas.

The buyer and seller can now meet in a number of ways that were just not available before. Both can choose to participate in as many of these models as seem viable:

- Auction sites in the eBay model, also used for overstocks and the sale of floor models
- Reverse auctions like those in the Priceline.com model, where the buyer sets the upper limit
- Sites for soliciting multiple bids for service such as Lending Tree
- Buying clubs that negotiate wholesale prices for a group of buyers based on volume
- Sites for comparing prices and evaluating professional and customer product reviews

- Sites that offer product data within the context of information like WebMD
- Paths for bypassing traditional middlemen through usage of new intermediaries, like AutoNation and most travel sites
- Sites that match buyers and sellers and negotiate services—almost like a commercial dating service—often used in B2B sites
- Dynamic pricing capabilities that allow prices to fluctuate based on use, loyalty and bundling of combined offerings
- Associate sites that build interest and refer the sale for a commission
- Digital malls that offer an array of usually smaller vendors under a single roof so that they can benefit from consolidated advertising
- Filters and agents that select merchandise according to customers' criteria
- As well as models not mentioned and hybrids of the strategies listed above

The common theme is that the customer is asked to move from a passive role to an active one. Alvin Toffler calls them *prosumers*—customers who take charge of their purchasing power, use their knowledge and act on their desires for customization. Many patients now inform their doctors about the latest drugs. School-aged kids organized on-line and pressured several hamburger chains to stop using South American beef in their hamburgers. Customers with wide-ranging agendas have the means to take charge of their purchasing clout. They are the new marketers, telling companies what they want, when and how. Thus, the supply/demand curve is reversed; demand now drives supply.[9]

This new demand/supply curve means that every feature of a business is organized around one critical input: *the customer's choice*. The moment the customer chooses is the defining moment that sets everything in motion. To be guided by the customer's choice, every phase of production must be poised to occur just-on-time. This runs the gamut from operating a no-inventory business to having materials arrive at the exact moment you need them to just-on-time capital that arrives seconds before cash flow is needed.

By 2004, Ford will allow you to customize every detail of your car and will deliver it in four days. Of course, Dell was among the first to harness the power of this strategy by building each of its computers to customer specifications. Demassification turns normal retailing on its ear. Instead of homogenizing your product so it appeals to the widest possible audience, you build maximum responsiveness into the production line so that consumers can select exactly what they want.

Don Peppers and Martha Rogers have led the cry for a complete turnaround of much of what we hold dear about brand management.[10] In their classic book *One to One Future*, they talk about breaking the *market share* habit and beginning to focus on how to get a greater share from each and every customer you already have. They advise a core paradigm shift—moving from brand management to customer management. They then show how this transition, if made, affects every attitude in the organization.

PeopleSoft is a large California company developing software for the human resource needs of companies. Yet 40 percent of its employees are in customer service. It provides high-tech product, yet almost half PeopleSoft's employees are involved in real time contact. It's a company driven by technological innovation, yet much of its attention is devoted to the question of how to connect with others. This is one example of the kind of people-based priorities we will see arising in almost every business category. As product cycles become faster, customers return much more frequently. Because customers now visit more often, every business must become more and more service-based whether it likes it or not.

Pan Am was once a mighty airline with excellent real estate holdings accrued from years of profit. As the airline started to collapse, year by year it sold off real estate to keep its operations afloat—only to lose in the end. But if it had sold the deteriorating airline early on and kept the real estate, it possibly could have survived. It could have become the successful Pan Am Real Estate Holding Company. Bill Gates offers a similar suggestion for McDonald's.[11] In effect, he asks, Why not use the low-profit fast-food business as a loss leader and shift the company toward the higher-profit-per-unit business of toys and merchandising? McDonald's has proven success in this arena and its customers are already used to getting this kind of merchandising at its counters. It's a natural progression.

Ideas like these are clever, but few companies ever really embark on these radical redefinitions of their core businesses. To make such a transition they would have to redefine how they perceive the customer—that is a big step for any company that is still focused on pushing what it does at all costs. In this age of declining attention span, brands blend, names are forgotten and identity is more transient. Hot new entities bubble up overnight, while the brands of the century get toppled. With the whole world a click away, people wander more easily. ***Relationship is the only thing strong enough to resist the siren call of ten million other sites that are just a click away!***

Forget last year's advice that said branding was the path to fame and fortune, when even free agents were advised to brand themselves. It's a bonded, bonded world, and involvement counts as much or more than a cool personal signature. You may recall the twenty/eighty rule, also called Pareto's law, that states 20 percent of your clients create 80 percent of your income. In a bonded world, you may see this percentage stretch even further, to where 5 percent of your customers can create 90 percent of your business, if you just know how to grow with their needs.

Emerging tribalists will rigorously design ever-deeper connections with those they serve. If you have not redefined your image of your customer in the last year, you have probably lost some big opportunities. Forward-thinking companies will marry their personal futures with the futures of their customers, even though this means continual redefinition, far less control and the capacity to be changed by the ones you serve.

B. Dialogues Become Products

Tom Sawyer persuaded the other kids to pay *him* for the opportunity to whitewash the fence that he had already been paid to paint. The new economy is Tom Sawyer heaven; it's designed to allow your customers to do more of the work.

Sue Brown kept her community working—feeding information, researching ideas, offering one another support, scouting the next steps for what lay ahead. And they loved her even more because she allowed them to contribute. Similarly, when AOL first began, it spent a lot of money to develop content. One day it dawned on the company that its customers created their own content through chat rooms, instant messaging, etc. In fact, this self-created content was all customers really cared about anyway. Once AOL let its customers do the work, it began to make money. The rest is history.

The most fascinating feature of the new empowered customers is that they *like* helping you. On-line bookings let them act as their own reservation clerks. With their new e-tickets they can check themselves in and get their own boarding passes, saving the airlines yet another few moments of employee time. Whether it is checking out their own groceries at the market or taking care of the shipping information for their on-line orders, customers are thrilled to help you out. A standard practice for software companies is to release Beta versions of a new product, allowing the public to work out the bugs faster than any technical team ever could. Beta versions are usually free, but in a true Tom Sawyer move, Apple charged $49.95 for the privilege of helping it perfect its hot new operating system, OS X. And customers for this task abounded in Tom Sawyer heaven.

In *New Rules for the New Economy,* Kevin Kelly offers a fascinating image of the ultimate new economy business: *zero* employees—customers do *all* the work. Let's Go Travel Guides has almost reached Kelly's ultimate vision. It has only one full-time employee. Every summer it hires several hundred Harvard students to comb the next country where a guide is being developed for interesting tidbits.

Suppose it opened its research base to students from any school and paid only for entries that were used. It could open an on-line site to announce the next country to be researched and invite widespread dialogue. By expanding its *employee* base, it might also expand its customer base. Students at every school in the country would be even more likely to buy the guide that they and their friends had helped to write. To some degree, Lonely Planet and Zagat's already use this strategy.

The much-hyped and highly coveted concept of viral marketing—where friends tell other friends about you and you don't have to lift a finger—is a clear result of involving your customers. Far too much time is spent on trying to find a hot product when what you really need is a hot relationship. In my opinion, Napster missed the boat by not understanding that its main asset was a hot relationship. Contexts are easily copied. Every record company is fully capable of developing a similar capacity.

But if you ever watched teenagers cruising the Napster site, you've noticed their devotion is intense. Napster reverted to warrior tactics and tried to win in court. But in a nomadic economy it doesn't matter quite as much who thinks they own what. If Napster had thought tribally, it would have said to the record companies, *"No problem, we'll take your products off our site and only allow the exchange of music for musicians who want to play our game."* (Of course, this is eventually what the courts ordered.) But I am willing to bet, if Napster had done this well before the record companies had sought legal intervention, and if the decision was framed correctly and communicated as a revolutionary act, Napster's devoted, idealistic customer base would have gone along with it, at least for a while. In short order, the record companies would have sought out Napster's services on terms far more advantageous to them. Fifty million users downloading other companies' material and the big labels would have changed their attitudes so fast, you'd hear wind whistling past your screen.

Eventually dialogue becomes product. Anderson Windows noticed that high-end architects were ordering expensive custom windows made by local carpenters. Anderson then developed a program that allows these architects to create customized windows for their clients—calculating costs, easily changing the dimensions and ordering straight from their final design. The moment the architect's client makes his or her final choice, the architect presses SEND and production begins. No muss, no fuss. Clearly it is a great service that could make any architect choose

Anderson Windows simply out of convenience. But something deeper happens when dialogues subsume products.

Once an architect begins using your software, i.e., *your dialogue,* your product gets more sticky. It's easy to choose a different brand, but people have to be pulled kicking and screaming to learn a new piece of software. ***In other words, get your information in the door, and your product will be there to stay.***

Once they are using your software to buy windows, why not layer in other stuff? Anderson could partner with other companies to insert custom staircases or high-end plumbing fixtures. The dialogue Anderson has established with architects has the potential to be more significant to its future than its windows. Much like Mobil, which is going past the gas pump to push their customer technology, the Speedpass, or Coca-Cola, which is reaching past cans and bottles to market a customer-service system, Good Answer, an on-line mortgage site discovered that the software it developed for making applications was far more marketable. It dropped the mortgage side of its business, and now it sells software.

Based on dialogues being products, Jim Clark, founder of SGI, and then Netscape, launched a third bold enterprise called Healtheon. The book *The New, New Thing* chronicles this legend's eccentric, entrepreneurial travels.[12] The business model for his third entrepreneurial adventure was scribbled on a scrap of paper. It was a very simple diagram, promptly named *the golden diamond.* It described four communities in the healthcare industry who needed to talk to each other: patients, doctors, hospitals and insurance companies. *That was it!* That was the big master plan he took years to dream up. The business was based on a series of *conversations* that needed to happen. The product (the software) was the means to have that conversation. For many reasons too numerous to discuss here, Healtheon merged with WebMD, which was based on a very different business model. The original golden diamond was an elegant conversational model, and had the company stayed focused on this original path, even Jim Clark suggests that success may have been more swift.

On a much smaller scale, we know someone who was trying to find the schedule for his local movie theater on-line without success. Thus, he saw an opening for a service that did not exist. A few years later down the line, his new company helps establish neighborhoods in virtual time. His creative focus is to make the conversation so interesting and beyond what anyone else is offering that people will want to hang out on his street corners. *In the digital world, the one with the best conversation usually wins. And I assure you there are many dialogues out there still in search of a village square.*

Hewlett-Packard (HP) adopted the nonprofit agency Second Harvest, the largest distributor of free food to those in need. HP helped this organization implement an information system that made it effortless for supermarkets and restaurants to offer their leftover food. In fact, it became easier for businesses to ask Second Harvest to pick stuff up than to throw it in the garbage. Suddenly, Second Harvest was no longer a charity dependent on the goodwill of others, it was a legitimate service. By getting involved in the day-to-day dialogue of restaurants, groceries, shippers and wholesalers, Second Harvest had a window into their world and a path for getting in on decisions. Amex sponsored Summer Concerts in Blue using their new smart cards to let you buy a ticket. Entertainers such as Counting Crows, Sting, and Third Eye Blind were featured. You then used your card at the entrance booth as your ticket of entry—plus you got a free CD. In their relentless pursuit of new ways to utilize their smart credit cards, Amex has also offered a $50,000 prize to the Java programmer who develops the best new application.

An interesting question to ask yourself is: What kinds of conversations do your customers like to have and which of those conversations would be of interest to you? Almost any new idea can be reduced to who needs to talk to whom, and why. Once the dimensions of a new commercial dialogue are established, you have an elegant strategy for going forward. You have the critical social architecture that underlies any new product or service.

Tribal companies are not afraid to follow in Tom Sawyer's foot-steps. Customers are given clear tasks to perform. More and more products will read: some assembly required. *This is because an involved customer who is put to work tends to care more about what its vendors are doing. Tribal companies will continually mine the white space—the conversational gaps between products, people and services that no one has yet detected—and develop creative exchanges to capitalize on these gaps. Tribal organizations will get far more involved in the social settings that surround their products.*

C. The Invested Consumer

You've heard it a hundred times: Customers are partners in your business. But no one *really* means it.

Remember those million-dollar ads for the Superbowl, which most of the time didn't explain what the companies did? And even if one could figure it out, the average person watching the Superbowl is not in the market for switchers and fiber optics, which is what a lot of the ads were selling. And even if one was in the market for switchers or fiber optics, it is unlikely that a thirty-second ad would carry any influence.

The ads were often for investors. With 60 percent of the American public owning some stock, a new class of investor has been born—average people who can loan you money in the form of stock purchases. The public have become the new venture capitalists, buying and selling bright ideas with ever more critical discernment. Financial information companies boast that the average investor now has the tools of a professional trader at his or her fingertips. The public is on a steep learning curve, but rising fast. How a company appears to investors has become a highly sophisticated relationship. There are public relations companies who focus only on this aspect of a company's public image.

But most traders are not really invested in the sense of caring very much about the companies they buy. The average amazon.com stock is held for less than five days. Day trading, or at least short-term trading, is still alive and well. The public is gambling, but they are not invested. The next evolutionary step is to create a class of average investors who are involved in the future of the company's ideas, much like the large institutional investors who are around for the long haul and will even help out.

We are still in the very early stages of customers becoming partners in money making ventures. Associate programs and multilevel marketing have paved the way for even individual people to turn who they know into a marketable asset. One day soon companies may include a minuscule stock option with every purchase. Buy twenty Nike sneakers and you get one stock option—sort of a *frequent-flyer-type equity program*. You are more likely to tell your friends to support a company that you also own—however small that piece may be. Employee stock option plans are a growing and sophisticated industry. Customer stock option plans could become equally interesting. Delta Airlines proudly featured its employee/owners in its ads. One day soon we may see an equally proud commercial parading a group shot of customer/owners for all to see.

Someone we know is considering raising money for his company by approaching his substantial and devoted client base. The clients are already advocates of his product, so why not ask them to become stockholders in his company, bypassing traditional fund-raising methods entirely? Other ventures have made public offerings on-line, without the traditional financial institutions that take the lion's share of the profits in standard IPOs. A number of mutual funds now exist called *transparent funds*, where the customers contribute information and make collectively negotiated stock choices. These developments will further blur the boundaries between customers, employees, partners and the investors who allow the business to grow.

In a collaborative world, every relationship evolves and inevitably becomes more complex. When the larger public understand the power of being invested in the products they like, concepts like corporate responsibility, accountability and community involvement will all become far more significant. Already, environmental groups are using this strategy by buying one share of stock and then showing up at shareholder's meetings to express their views. If you really want to look ahead, expect that a real relationship with the investing public will become as sophisticated and demanding as any other relationship you have. A new, complex and rich relationship dynamic has already been born: B2I, business-to-investor.

A tribal company understands that it must chart its future in tandem with an invested public. It will seek out innovative paths to make the public not only involved, but also invested. It will strive to get the community of players who participate in its business to genuinely care about what it does.

D. Consumer Gangs

Here is where tribal forces may really come into play. Once we are full swing into the on-line world, we will get our groceries, clothes, toiletries, electronics and almost everything on-line. Then we will apply programs, called *know-bots,* to organize information around the parameters we choose. When we place our on-line orders, we will direct our know-bots to choose only green, socially conscious products or to select only the best-priced products or perhaps to choose items recommended by *Consumer Reports.* Or all of the above. Those who continue to rely on passive retailing will wake up one day and discover that the customer has passed them by. The bonded, involved, invested consumer is only the tip of the iceberg. These trends are early forerunners of what could evolve into full-blown, roaming consumer gangs.

It is very easy to form electronic tribes around shared interests. In fact, this is how much of the noncommerce side of the Web is organized. If you are interested in adoption or a particular illness or a political position, there are always numerous sites that collect useful information and gather people around who want to exchange ideas on these topics.

Many feel that the politics of the future will be driven by these communities of interest who are beginning to represent and lobby for shared concerns. Jesse Ventura says he would not have become governor of

Minnesota if it weren't for the Internet and the grassroots enthusiasm it fostered. When it looked like Nader might take liberal-leaning voters from Gore, a site sprang up that allowed voters in states where the electoral outcome was certain to trade their Gore votes for Nader votes in states that were still considered battlegrounds. It was not a useful system, since accountability could not be enforced, but it was a startling development. Once such events are perfected, you can see how consumers may begin to leverage their numbers to affect political platforms and influence critical decisions. Once we are able to vote on-line, any remaining barriers between commerce, entertainment and politics will fall.

Communities of interest are bound to become the drivers behind very new consumer forces. We may see these tribes evolve into buying clubs centered around different values or shared interests. Nonprofit groups, such as the Sierra Club and 4charity.com are moving in this direction, developing their own products and forging associates programs so their members can support the group in ways other than just donations. If you like what it represents, why not let Sierra Club become a buying club or super associate so it can reap profits from all your on-line purchases? Sites like these could license their name to products to ensure that more profits stay in house and get used for furthering the mission of the group. Nike focuses on building its name recognition, farming out its manufacturing to others. In the same way, well-focused consumer groups could license their name, supply the customers and profit from the products made just for them. *Mark my words; we will not only be selling a lot more wine without bottles, we will be selling a lot more homegrown wine.*

Electronic tribes are still a new and somewhat primitive social form. But because they were born in Net time, they will evolve faster than anyone can now predict. For example, a few bicyclists in Seattle wanted more riding paths. Within months they had organized tens of thousands around this issue and quickly had more bicycle paths. This group talked excitedly about how fast they had organized and how quickly they got results. They were also quite proud that no one had ever emerged as the leader. It was all self-organized. Now the question is: Will this highly influential group slowly disperse because its goal has been met, or will it think of something else to do together?

eBay aficionados freely refer to themselves as addicts; they crave the community they find there. Europe is predicting that in a few years 8 percent of all commerce will occur through buying clubs. New kinds of software allow communities to create Web circles, where hypertext links the content on one site to its neighbors. On-line visitors can easily move from site to site as they follow the course of their interests. As mentioned earlier, Yahoo! says that the fastest area of growth on its portal continues to be conversation.

People love the village square. They may also discover just how loud their voices can get. Once our tribal gene is fully unleashed, these communities of interest may become highly sophisticated in their ability to leverage their clout, politically and financially.

The noncommercial side of the Net is where you need to look if you want to have a really big, full-length panoramic view of the future. Self-organizing groups will forge templates for the commerce of the future. Once the Net generation really comes of age, they will begin to realize the true power of this medium and the original promise of its underlying architecture.

Take proactive customers and arm them with symmetry of information. Add in their growing interest to become invested in what you do and more evolved activism is the next natural step. Napster-like gangs will roam the landscape, defining how they want to purchase goods and who they will play with. They will effectively further blur the lines between money, responsibility, community and politics, *just because they can.*

Consumer tribes may eventually become the new point of entry for purchases. They will eventually turn commerce upside down and you will be bidding for their business. Truly tribal companies are already looking ahead to develop models for accessing and reaching emerging consumer clans.

3·2 WORKERS WITHOUT WALLS

Customers are not what they once were, but neither is the workforce. It's been called Free Agent Nation, the legion of self-employed or freelance workers who now work without fixed employment contracts. There are now twenty-five million such workers and growing. This way of working may soon dominate the labor force and represent a new avenue for relating to workers.

We have all heard many variations of what workers have asked for and received, from job sharing to day care to sabbaticals to flexible fringe benefits to flex time to bigger commissions. The workers are helping to build the current atmosphere of anything goes—name your price and feel free to change the system to fit what you need. As a result of their pioneering efforts, all workers have been far more emboldened to ask for what they want. In his book *Free Agent Nation*, David Pink calls this digital Marxism, when the proliferation of inexpensive computing, wireless handheld devices and ubiquitous low-cost connections to the Internet allow workers to own *the means of production.*

Everything we have said about customers can apply to workers. They are more involved, invested and empowered. They are leaving corporate America in droves, sometimes for the chance to play employment roulette and hit the big IPO. Sometimes downsizing is the cause of their departure, but once they make it outside the corporate walls, many never return. Sometimes they leave to gain a more intimate, creative work environment where their input has more visibility. About 15 percent, according to some estimates, are just seeking work conditions that will afford a better balance between their personal and work lives. The gist of this trend is that the employees of the future will be less inclined to define themselves by the job they do, and far more interested in charting a path that reflects their personal values and creative visions.

But this trend is so well established that a story about someone who made this kind of transition into working as a free agent would not be all that unusual. There are a thousand variations of those who have left the stable realm of salaried life to chart their next directions with fewer fixed obligations, and there are abundant resources on this topic.[13] It is far more interesting to look at someone who has never left the confines of the corporate space *and yet is a worker without walls in every sense of the phrase.*

While searching for an archetypal story of an individual who represents employment trends of the future, I came upon the following profile in *Fast Company* about the key players who contributed to the amazing turnaround of IBM.[14]

John Patrick had been a Senior Strategist for IBM since 1967, all through the days when IBM ruled. He also stayed when many said the days of Big Blue were over. Many were saying that IBM was a dinosaur that could never catch up with the nimble world of connectivity. In 1993 a new CEO, Louis Gerstner, was brought on board to address this very problem. Gerstner is credited with maintaining pressure from the top, but Patrick is credited for mobilizing the grassroots.

One day Patrick was playing around with a software program called Gopher. Gopher allowed you to literally go inside someone else's computer. In a flash of inspiration, Patrick realized that this capacity would change everything. He wrote a call to arms titled *Get Connected,* and the response from the ranks was intense.

Six months after this white paper, an informal and voluntary *get connected* team gathered together to build one of the most significant corporate Web sites of that time. This was IBM's starting point.

Soon after, Patrick attended the then embryonic Internet World conference in San Jose. Without asking permission from anyone, he signed up IBM to be a presenter for the following year. He asked the *get connected* team to design presentations for the next year's show and went from department to department looking for financial donations; five thousand dollars here, five thousand dollars there, until he had the money to go forward.

The following year, the night before the Internet World conference, Patrick still didn't know if anyone would really show. Fifty-four people from twelve different IBM units turned up. He has proudly said "We dominated the show...and the amazing thing was, you couldn't find us in any IBM budget." Less than two years from the day Patrick was playing around with Gopher, an internet division was formed at IBM with Patrick at its helm and six hundred people assigned to the mission. And now IBM is as big and blue as ever.

Naturally, it helped that John Patrick was a senior player with some big successes under his belt like the ThinkPad product. It's a lot easier for someone in that position to take chances, muster informal support and garner attention. But in hundreds of similar, although somewhat smaller stories of innovation that we have run across over the years, in every case the individual not only took the bull by the horns, but often used guerilla tactics to make things happen.

- Is John Patrick an employee of the future?
- Was he a free agent?
- Was he a servant of an idea community more than a corporate entity?
- Were his acts an aberration or were they behaviors that can be fostered?
- More important, how did he single-handedly change the future of a company without ever asking anyone to change?

The reason John Patrick was a worker without walls is because he was completely immersed in his own creative process and did not wait for approval from on high. The *big bad corporation,* as many have come to think of it, is largely a mirage. As companies fracture within their own boundaries, as more and more people work within the context of well-connected, self-determining, highly specialized teams, then who is really in charge? The more companies follow the decisions that are being made everywhere and in the moment, the more the patriarchal, all-knowing corporate entity that grants permission to go forward disappears. In the nimble, decentralized, fast-moving business of the future, the buck stops everywhere and nowhere.

The next four dialogues concern the business-to-employee relationship and how it may also mutate, evolve and gain a far more interesting social life.

A. The Transparent Company

John Case popularized the idea of open-book management and is a wise and respected advocate of the process.[15] If the edges are to be empowered, they also need to be informed. The people at the top make the big decisions, mostly because they are the only ones with the big picture. Case suggests that when everyone has the big picture, and they are trained in various principles of business, then suddenly an army of people will emerge who are capable of making very valuable decisions.

In the old days, information was power. The inner workings of a company were not disclosed in order to maintain an internal pecking order. The biggest resistance Case faces from companies considering this direction is that they are afraid the knowledge will be abused. Yet, in his case histories of hundreds of companies that have shifted to this open book model, the reverse is true. People become more caring, responsible and invested in their companies' future merely because they know what is happening. Information is no longer just power, *information is empowerment,* and access provokes people to act more intelligently.

Bill Gates calls it building the digital nervous system of a corporation.[16] He advocates not only the paperless office, but also paperless decision-making, where access to immediate and relevant information can power every choice. He puts the corporate nervous system smack dab in the center between customer relationships, strategic decisions and operations.

Perhaps unwittingly, this is how John Patrick began his creative journey into the future. He made his thoughts available for all to see. First through his initial white paper, and then through a groundbreaking Web site, he made the activities of IBM's insurgent group transparent, available and thus, accessible. He trusted that if he was thinking a certain way, there were bound to be others who did as well. *Every company has its grass roots, you just have to find them.*

The concept of a transparent company is straight out of the playbook of the tribal way. All tribes are redundant and holistic. Everyone knows the whole picture. People can easily stand in for each other. Leadership is decentralized. You don't wait for someone to tell you what to do; you know enough about the whole picture that you can look around and easily see what needs to be done.

If you want *radical* innovation, you will have to give voice to the *radicals*. Japanese information pioneer and digital artist Joichi Ito tells a great story about the CIA.[17] An operative told him that the CIA believes that the ultimate operation would involve information gathered from everywhere; thus, *maximum data.* The analysis of all this far-reaching data would be kept ultimately secret; thus, *maximum control.* Ito then explained to the operative that this is exactly the opposite of what is true in the information world. The best analysis is ultimately public. The best ideas are those that can stand up to the public debate and survive. If an idea can be chewed up, spit out and still remain standing, then you have an idea with some legs.

Many companies still subscribe to the CIA's version of how to relate to their staff. They fear in-house rumblings. They would prefer that debate occur behind closed doors, so the larger base of employees doesn't get all stirred up. Companies want employees to have *maximum data* about what they need to do, but they still want to keep decisions under *maximum control.*

When a customer stops complaining, he or she is usually on his or her way *out the door.* Well, the same holds true for employee dissatisfaction. When people complain, they still care. You want that input. There are even consultants who specialize in these very issues—managing discontent in productive ways.

Most companies still make their official pronouncements as clean as possible, so no one can poke any holes. Information artists, like Ito and the gang behind the *Cluetrain Manifesto* recommend publishing drafts before you are ready and inviting rewrites. Tim Berners-Lee goes even farther, to suggest that you forge links between the final documents and the drafts that contain the tangents that often get lost when ideas get *perfected*. Proclamations should be starting points, not summaries. If white papers don't get dirty, no one is really reading them.

The tribal company strives for transparency, making its ideas, decisions and actions accessible, so everyone can become more intelligent. It no longer controls information in order to control decisions. It assumes that information is empowerment and that unrestricted input can make every action more intelligent. It allows rumblings to evolve into full-blown calls to action. It has its ear to the tribal drum and translates discontent into productivity.

B. When Power Lives Everywhere

John Patrick *lived* flattened power. He didn't wait for a formal budget. He never tried to own the innovation. He invited others to play along right from the start. Instead of asking for commitment, he went to that first Internet World conference in the spirit of trust. If people really believed in the same things he did, they would come.

The need for nimbleness has driven every company to empower its employees to make more immediate decisions. Top-down decision making—where the people on high make decisions about quickly moving events that they know less and less about—is far too slow, and far too divorced from the action. People at the periphery have their ears to the ground; they know things first. If they are not empowered, time is lost.

When someone makes a spur-of-the-moment decision this *is* the new direction, despite whatever plan might be on the books. Despite everyone's fears, the digital world is in fact making face-to-face, relationship-based skills even more imperative. There are no longer rules, policies, hierarchies or a lack of power separating you from others. As the lag time decreases between an idea and its implementation, or a purchase and its fulfillment, business policies move closer to being forged in real time. Real-time business means that face-to-face exchange is where the real decisions happen.

Westfield Hydroelectric was quickly expanding into foreign markets. It had two options: It could greatly expand its overhead in order to administrate complex projects in international markets, or it could use local talent and partner every step of the way. The company chose the latter. For Westfield Hydroelectric, a soft, warm, fuzzy quality called trust is an identified business strategy. It is at the heart of how the company defines its future. *If trust can't be established, the next generation idea, no matter how good it looks on paper, becomes irrelevant. Trust is the glue that holds these decentralized, real-time decision models together.*

It's amazing how often this simple word, *trust,* shows up in discussions of the new economy. In any alliance you have to trust your partners with very private information. To provide the best customer service, you have to trust outsiders to see your inner workings. To allow others to telecommute, you have to trust they are using their time wisely. To empower workers to act on what they see, you have got to give them a freer rein and trust they won't abuse the freedom. This small word could almost be considered the emotional motto of a tribal company.

In a tribal company, decisions and leadership flow every which way: top-down, bottom-up, side-to-side, inside-out and outside-in. Trust is the glue that allows everything to stick together. A tribal company knows it must build trust before it can build ideas. With a mutual trust that circles and builds and gains intelligence, all things are possible.

C. It's Not Who You Know, but How You Know Them
A professor at Babcock College participates in start-up companies

created by his past students. MIT knows its students' ideas are gold. It offers seed money, resources and coaching. Yale has become one of the best-funded colleges in the country, due in part to its early, early involvement in some great start-ups.

Most companies reluctantly accept that when their people get a really, really good idea they will tend to break away and start their own businesses. Yet some forward-thinking companies have begun to invest in these breakaway ventures. When an up-and-coming employee has the kind of hot idea that would cause him or her to go off on his or her own, these companies want to be the first to know, because they might want to invest. This strategy goes a step beyond *intrapreneurship*—the 3M-type model where originators of a new product idea get to share in the profits. In this case the host company is the venture capitalist, sharing in the ideas of the people that it has nurtured; it is practicing *extrapreneurship*.

In this case, a company views itself as an *incubator*. First you nurture and grow the talent of your employees, then you co-venture. When really cool people work for you, it is a natural process for them to grow. You have a choice of growing with them, or letting them go. As corporate boundaries become less and less defined, it will be far harder to manage how ideas unfold. Unless you build fluid, coparticipatory models of compensation, you will continually face losing your best people and the ideas they steward.

If the future of business rests on building relationships with every unique customer rather than just adding new ones, why not follow the same strategy with employees? Rather than continually seeking new talent, why not build your relationships with the people you have? SAS Institute is a tremendous example of this and has received a lot of press. The needs of its employees are so well served, from day care to support with mundane daily errands, that hardly anyone ever leaves even when they get very tempting financial offers. The millions the company estimates it saves on recruitment and training is turned back to the workers.

And if you are the employee, rather than focusing on seeking out the next company in your future, *why not love the one you're with?* Whenever someone relates his or her vision for an ideal work scenario, the first thing we always ask is, *"Have you tried asking your current employer if you could do this?"* Those who have chosen this path have had more success than you would ever expect.

Back in the days when it was still called Andersen, Accenture offered very few partnerships. *In fact, it wanted its new recruits to move on.* If an alumnus went on to become a key financial officer in a large corporation, then Andersen had yet another friend in a high place. Of course, with this kind of strategy you had better pay attention to whether your employees are having a good time when they do work for you, so they are inclined to remain your friends after they leave.

Tribal companies will consider paths for allowing employees to grow beyond the boundaries of the corporate walls. In the same way they seek out ways to participate more with every single customer, they will want to be involved with the creative dreams of every individual worker. They won't be afraid of breaking the barriers of acceptable risk and profit, sharing both with their employees.

D. Nimble Pods of Highly Committed People in Deep Relationship

They say that in Silicon Valley, no one works for companies anymore. These people are driving ideas in ways that transcend the particulars of which office space they happen to use that month.

The average person in The Valley stays in a job less than two years. People bump into the same colleagues in job after job, working under new corporate flags, focusing on fairly similar ideas. They live in idea communities, not corporate environments. These gangs of knowledge workers often travel together from company to company; they identify more with their shared visions of the future than with whoever happens to sign their paychecks. Thus, companies will have to radically redefine how they relate to the traveling nomads who pass through their doors. People will be attracted to creative styles of management far more than the specific tasks they are assigned. Although this attitude is more common to hot players in Silicon Valley, it could easily spread as everyone's tasks become more technical and their idea partners become far more vital.

Most companies are well on their way to becoming asynchronous. People can participate in meetings, contribute ideas to tasks or even manage others, all on their own time. Ninety-two percent of companies surveyed say they encourage their workers to work from home and not come to the office every day, and by 2010 it is estimated that 40 percent of all workers will telecommute. Some companies are pushing the envelope in terms of how far they can go in building virtual teams, questioning just how much face-to-face contact is really needed. An unintended result of an asynchronous work environment is that it is far easier to bring in part-timers, outsiders and wandering free agents to play along. *An asynchronous work environment where people contribute whenever they want and however they want further contributes to the sense that we work for idea communities far more than the entity bound by the corporate walls.*

Recently, one of the most groundbreaking discoveries in scientific history was announced: the mapping of the human genome. A fast-paced, nimble, deep-pocketed private research group that hoped to profit from its findings was racing against the more lumbering, egalitarian government-funded research group that was hoping to keep this knowledge in the public domain for all to use. It was a perfect laboratory for studying a race between a highly competitive setting versus a highly cooperative environment. It was a tie. It was a joint announcement. The researcher in the snazzy Armani and the scientist in his off-the-rack coat stood on the podium together.

Coopetition is the new jargon for harnessing the best of our personal ambition with our equally motivating desires to make a positive difference for others. Let's face it, we have both. Perhaps in slightly different personal proportions, we all want power and we all have the need to serve a greater good. One without the other is probably less efficient. Paul Newman founded a food company that is also a highly effective charity because it harnesses the skills of a highly competitive company that makes great profits. Denny's restaurant is reaching record new levels of profit because of its authentic response to charges of discrimination several years ago. Green companies are blossoming because this ideology feeds all the different bottom lines that companies need to care about—retention of employees, public relations, innovation, lower costs, etc. The newfound desire of companies to consider multiple bottom lines is a clear result of living in a more relationship-based environment, where it is far easier for people to see each other's true colors.

The authors of a book called *The Good Company* looked at the one hundred companies that were rated the best to work for because of their social responsibility, environmental concerns, family-friendly practices, etc. They found that these one hundred companies also made more money than one hundred peers who did not use these egalitarian standards.[18] The truth is out. The more bottom lines you feed, the more profits you catch.

Our super-solo system of rewarding individuals flies in the face of the highly collaborative ways ideas now need to happen. If only one person gets rewarded, he or she may unconsciously hold back in order to preserve a personal advantage. If genuine collaboration is not tangibly acknowledged, it may never fully surface.

Rob Rudin, CEO of Marshall Industries, threw out the commission model his company had used for twenty years—the same model everyone in that industry uses.[19] Instead of paying his six hundred salespeople and managers individual commissions and prizes, he put all the commissions into a pool to be shared. He made this decision based on a clear assessment of how people had related in the previous commission structure. In order to reach their sales quotas salespeople would push clients into purchases that were not necessarily in their long-term interests. Rudin knew that bonds were more important than brands, and he wanted lifelong customers.

He definitely had concerns that shared commissions would breed complacency because people would not get direct feedback for their efforts. Further, no one else in his field was doing this. It seemed almost un-American not to reward individual accomplishment. So it was with great trepidation that he took the leap.

Soon after the shift, his business doubled and profits increased. Serendipitously, one of his highest performers and most resistant converts suffered an unexpected setback with a key client and was saved by the new system. This once very vocal doubter became a leading advocate of the new system. Our understanding of compensation is only in its infancy; we may soon discover how motivating collective gain can be.

Most businesses barely acknowledge the power of the group. Individuals get most of the bonuses, not teams. Individuals get promoted, teams don't. Further, when a leading individual is promoted, the chemistry of a winning team is often lost. Yet most businesses pay almost no attention to the value of a winning team. Why not promote teams? Why not expand their scope and freedom as they demonstrate proficiency in working together? If you rewarded and promoted teams, you can bet everyone would help each other out a lot more than they do now. The new assembly lines are structured this way. Cars are assembled by teams; everyone is responsible for the quality. People love it. Quality improves. Even software designers who write code in pairs, although slower, make 30 percent fewer errors. But most compensation is still determined individually. Isn't it time to go one more step?

Some do offer financial incentives for people to recruit friends. In part, this can be a reflection of a tight job market, but businesses have also found that the friends of existing employees are more likely to stay with the company and in fact do better. Highly skilled workers do tend to move in packs. When one hears of a cool new venture, he or she brings his or her friends along. I can envision a time in the near future when people travel through their careers in pods. They will want to maintain their professional chemistry. Someday we may see traveling bands of bonded creatives conquering problems as they journey forward on a wild ride from company to company.

When Marc Andreesen, of Netscape fame, formed his new company, Loudcloud, he picked a stellar team of players he knew from past ventures.[20] For one year this group met together on a regular basis. But they had no clue what their business would be. Andreeson knew he didn't need a grand idea in order to start a business. If he got the right people together, the right idea would follow. New start-ups always raid their past employers for stellar players. It has been said that Cisco has even bought companies just to get their teams, caring less about the business than the players involved. Intellectual capital is a well-worn concept; you have to begin thinking of *collaborative capital,* the intelligence that is held in the chemistry of a stellar group. In fact, the future of business will be shaped by nimble pods of highly committed people in deep relationship.

Of course, the key to the above statement is the phrase *in deep relationship.* Anyone who has been on a really great winning team will tell you it becomes hard to settle for anything less.

Tribal companies will actively explore hiring, promotion and compensation that accelerates group processes. They will consider hiring, promoting and rewarding teams. They will explore the dimensions of motivation that get triggered only when we act in truly collaborative settings where rewards are shared.

3.3 THE POWER OF INTIMACY

This next archetypal story is much less sophisticated than Sue Brown's unintentional business empire or John Patrick's part in helping to turn around one of the larger corporate entities. It is a simple story about human potential.

A friend of ours taught with the Peace Corps for several years in an elementary school in rural Asia. Whenever she finished teaching a particular topic she would ask, "Who didn't understand?" To her amazement every hand would go up. Perplexed, she would look at everyone's pages of answers and discover that most kids had written the correct responses. What was going on?

She eventually realized that if even one kid didn't understand, somehow the whole class *knew* and they would all raise their hands until the very last child understood the lesson. The children were so bonded they could instinctively sense what was happening for each other without using words. More important, they didn't want to move forward without everyone on board.

This is another example of *tribalmind*. It holds powerful keys to skills we have forgotten and now desperately need. If we could access this depth of participation and investment in each other's ideas, the alchemy of collaboration would finally explode. I have seen average-performing players reach new heights due solely to shifts in the quality of their conversation.

If you want to think tribally, you must pay attention to the quality of communication that surrounds your new style of connected business. Ideas are structured in conversation. Radical, interesting, dynamic conversation breeds radical, interesting and dynamic ideas. When you deepen the quality of your actual conversations, you instantly elevate your entire business.

The last four dialogues concern how you relate to any one-on-one exchange. After you begin thinking customer-me, employee-me, you-me, then you must think about how you construct the level of shared identity that brings two people together in new ways and defines the potential of every conversation you have.

A. Rubbing Elbows to Create Sparks

Guy Kawasaki, lead player in the early days of Apple Computers, says:

The team should be tightly packed in a lousy building with lousy furniture. Tightly packed, because as MIT Sloan School of

Management professor Thomas J. Allen discovered, communication between people drops off drastically when they are more than thirty meters from each other.... A lousy building and lousy furniture are necessary, because suffering is good for revolutionaries.

He goes on to say that if you are promised a revolutionary work setting and you walk in and see Herman Miller furniture, run for the hills! [21]

The magic that happens when people rub elbows is often hard to maintain when the trappings of success make us comfortable again. There is no substitute for informal, down-and-dirty exchange. A business without a village square is losing ideas. A free agent that doesn't schedule frequent informal exchanges with peers and clients is losing valuable opportunities. A manager who doesn't *manage by walking around* (MBWA) is losing access to critical information that cannot be discovered any other way.

We were once visiting a friend who lived in a huge mansion with at least two or three sitting areas. Despite an abundance of comfortable chairs, we all ended up sitting on the steps of the large front entryway. The owner walked over and his comment was, "I guess you just can't get people off *the stoop.*" The trend toward open architecture and informal meeting spaces in corporate interior design is a direct result of companies valuing the informal exchange. The advertising firm Chiat/Day has created a village within the confines of a large, open industrial office space. Creatives hang out on cliff dwellings and there is a town square where everyone congregates. If formal meetings are the only time people see one another, then the magic of conversational jamming will never be discovered.

Bill Gross has launched over thirty companies through his business incubator idealab!. He purposely designed its physical space so that people would frequently bump into one another, and he actively supports the process of just hanging out. Bill Gross also says that the success of a new company is inversely proportional to the number of PowerPoint presentations it does! In other words, if you think you can plan it out, you just don't get it. You might almost refer to them as *disempowerpoint* presentations.

To seal the deal, those who have more meaningful connections with peers appear to be more likely to be innovative. A study of Nobel prize winners found that they were far more likely to have strong professional relationships than their less-stellar colleagues. Leading innovators reported having more social contacts. Contrary to popular stereotypes, geniuses are not social misfits; in fact, they are more likely to be the gabby types that hang out in the halls.[22]

How often have you been casually talking to someone and found yourself saying something great that you had no idea you had been thinking about? The mere presence of the other person is the catalyst for your newfound brilliance. How many times have you had an insight while engaging in a casual conversation, yet when you sat in a meeting the previous week trying to brainstorm about the very same problem, nothing came to you?

Recently, Philip and I were taping a radio interview. The moment the interviewer turned off the tape our conversation exploded in all sorts of interesting directions. We said to the interviewer, "It's too bad we couldn't have had this exchange on tape." He said, "I can't tell you how often that happens. I've even thought of pretending to turn off the tape, so that the exciting informal exchange that happens once the *show* is over would get recorded."

Real dialogue, in real-life settings, in casual time, with no agenda, and no pressure for take-away value is a vital source of genius. Something happens when the tape player is off that is hard to capture when formality is still in place. Yet in so many companies, particularly large ones, this kind of exchange is mostly untapped. Companies rarely access the dialogue that happens when people let down their guard.

Despite all this, many still consider social exchange non-value-adding. A consultant and anthropologist named Julian Orr conducted a telling analysis of Xerox's technical representatives.[23] Xerox provided representatives with a technical manual with every possible error code, assuming they had all the knowledge they needed. Yet the reps were continually confronted with how to go forward when the documentation left off.

Orr then noticed that the representatives were extraordinarily social, meeting for breakfast, lunch and even dinner at times. Over one particularly long cribbage game that Orr observed, the representatives slowly pulled apart and analyzed one of the most dramatic problems they had faced up to that point. These kinds of exchanges allowed them to identify who the experts were in certain kinds of knowledge and then build a body of information that went far beyond the technical manual. In these exchanges they discussed sharing expensive parts so that repairs could happen in a more timely fashion. As Orr states, "The reps' chatter stood out, however, because the process view assumed they worked alone and had adequate resources in their training, tools and documentation. Time spent together would, from the process perspective, be non-value-adding."

Tribal members know that unless people are rubbing elbows, there will be no sparks. They make times and places for informality to occur. They give space for the simple slip of the tongue or tangent of conversation to be taken seriously.

B. Randomness Rules/Size Matters

Once we showed up to lead a training and discovered that the entire team had almost identical backgrounds; most went to the same schools and had worked for the same handful of companies. They even appeared to have the same taste in clothes. It was hard to get any creative tension going since everyone had the same history.

Steve Jobs is known for putting an odd mix of people together on his technical teams—adding in a few artists, philosophers and general misfits just to keep things jumping on the Apple horizon. Homogenous teams may find it hard to create new connections; they just keep using the same social synapses over and over. You either have to mix up the players, or consciously provoke differences of opinion. This is the chemistry that drives breakthrough.

W. L. Gore, maker of Goretex, has long been one of the leaders in pioneering new employment forms. It has implemented a lattice-like structure that allows people to easily move around between projects and form internal idea communities that make sense in relation to what they are doing. The workers form associations based on the evolution of their interests, so motivation and commitment stay high. The more randomness that is tolerated and even provoked, the more unintended discoveries can surface.

W. L. Gore also limits the size of its intracompany, latticed groupings to about two hundred people. The CEO of Avid said that once the company grew past 150 people, his role became less about creativity and more about management. And as the numbers rose, he became less interested. Just an interesting footnote: The average tribe was less than two hundred people. Once it grew past that point, power plays would arise, people would jockey for position, and wisely the tribe would split apart. Some linguists feel that the human brain is wired to easily access and remember the names of just about two hundred people. After that you have to use prods like recalling the city where the person lives or trying to call up his or her face. In other words, it's natural to forget names; you're not wired to go beyond your tribe.

Nomadic tribes are even smaller and closely affiliated, since travel is too cumbersome with larger numbers. This is why highly technical teams have to be so much smaller. This is perhaps yet another sign of the tribal gene at work. We know in our bones how tribes work; we instinctively know how to reestablish this social form.

This is also why business leaders are studying groups like the Orpheus Chamber Orchestra. Unlike most orchestras they make decisions through consensus; there is no conductor leading the orchestra. Everyone takes a turn being in charge and making creative decisions, as well as serving the ideas of others. The result of this highly collaborative model is that this group has always stayed edgy. They also have a level of commercial success that is almost unprecedented for a group such as this.

A great article titled "How to Manage Geeks" advises managers to leave them alone.[24] Geeks know how to play together. They know what a job requires and they are often able to see things you can't. They actually have a keener eye for what makes a team click.

And what's good for a geek is also good for the more technologically meek. We all lean in the direction of tribal wisdom when given half a chance. Forward-thinking companies are not afraid to allow this tribal gene to surface, even if it means losing a bit of control. So when teams are assigned to a project, these companies let them create their own subcultures: decorating spaces, defining their own work rhythms, choosing their own leaders, managing themselves. Often the more these identities are formed, the higher the performance. There is an informal group wisdom that cuts in and allows groups to function far more successfully than they would with predetermined standards. These teams set their own directions and have their own identified results. So in effect, almost everyone is beginning to work in very small, clan-like settings.

Some companies persist in thinking that the more people you throw at a project, the faster it will go. They continue to throw numbers at a problem. When they want new product development, they figure more is better. But new-line companies know that increased numbers can actually slow down the process. Like nomadic groupings, the more complex a project is, the more the players need to be able to see each other and instantly know what everyone is doing. *Size does matter.* A law of diminishing returns sets in once a group has *more* people than it needs. Suddenly you need committees and rules, and unexpected surprises slip through the cracks because no one thinks to report them.

Some believe it is easier to start a new company than to change an old one. So, in-house start-ups often go to separate buildings, get cooler furniture and are given free rein. One group of in-house insurgents raised a pirate flag over their residence for the rest of the company to see. Of course, the day will come when every business has a pirate flag somewhere in its midst and then the true revolutionaries will have to find some new status symbol. But if you still have tight controls and entrenched habits, then pirate flags are a real good start.

Tribal companies know that innovation doesn't occur on schedule. They are also not afraid to have people follow pipe dreams, because sometimes it just makes good sense to start marketing pipes. They not only tolerate randomness, they provoke and pursue it. At every meeting they assign Ministers of the Irrelevant Comment and Meandering Sentence, to make sure that stray thoughts don't get lost in the thundering beat of a tight agenda.

C. There Is No Such Thing as a Secret

In the old *Star Trek* series, Dr. Spock would place his fingers on someone's temple and proceed to do a Vulcan mind meld. He would access every memory held in that person's brain and instantly know what he or she was about. Well, this may not be so far out from what happens in real life.

People think they can hide. They think they can play roles and that no one will sense what is underneath. But we all have that little kid inside us that can see through any pretense, and know exactly what is *really* going on. We all have that innocent little kid inside of us that instantly knows when the emperor has no clothes.

Empowered consumers, empowered employees, companies who have windows into your business, open books and transparent ways, mean it is harder and harder to hide secrets. In a collaborative world, there is a lot more truth. Brad Blanton has developed this into a corporate cosmology. He promotes the need for radical honesty and offers abundant examples of companies finding the creative freedom they seek merely because they start telling a deeper level of truth.[25]

We were once brought in to work with a group that was experiencing very flat sales. A few hours into the seminar we realized that everyone there knew a lot more about sales than we ever would. So what was the problem? Digging deeper, we found that there were a host of suppressed feelings that accompanied a recent expansion of the business. We not only surfaced these issues but provided a forum for them to be openly discussed. We didn't offer one scrap of useful sales training, but soon after our meeting, sales soared even beyond the previous stellar performance that had triggered the initial expansion of the business.

In the language of Alcoholics Anonymous, you are only as sick as your secrets. You are sick because you believe that you can pursue actions that do not affect everyone else. When a project is stuck, it is not always because people need to know more or get more training, it is often because they need to feel more. Any project is as sick as its secrets, or the emotions people feel they can't express. People can smell truth.

Truth matters even more in a sensitive, instinctual tribal company. Nothing happens behind closed doors. People are more opened up. They are invested and empowered. It is harder and harder to fake intimacy.

D. Getting Real

Max DePree, Chairman emeritus of Herman Miller, tells a story about the formative years of his company.[26] A new designer was about to come out with his first line of office furniture, which is always a very exciting time. One day this new designer came to him and in effect said, "You have to drop my line for next year and pick up this new guy I just saw at a student show held at the Museum of Modern Art."

DePree comforted this man, thinking that he was just having anxiety about having his first designs coming out in public. The designer persisted. DePree suggested that perhaps they pick him up for the next year. The designer said, "He won't be there next year." Finally DePree relented and picked up the student designer. His name was Charles Eames. The Eames chair went on to be the most successful chair in furniture history, and the relationship with the Eameses put Herman Miller on the map.

DePree uses this story and a few others to illustrate that the fate of his company rested on the *power of intimacy*. This is what allowed his designer to make choices that were far beyond what one would expect in a professional relationship. Without open-book management, long before intranets, with no clue about what a digital nervous system would some-day become, without Groove software and without receiving any formal training in team spirit, this young designer changed the fate of Herman Miller. He was able to reach this height of creative responsibility because that was how DePree ran his business.

Sometimes we get so caught up in the technical side of communication that we forget we don't have to do anything fancy. You merely need to go to the heart of how you talk to others. If you can't authentically connect with someone face-to-face, all the intranets and software in the world won't save you. No matter how hyperlinked a company is, real connection does not occur unless there is real feeling. It is a gutsy move that has to be genuine or you are just going through the motions. *You can't fake authenticity!*

Thus, making a company more transparent is less a tactical decision than an emotional choice. It will change how people relate to each other one-on-one. Choosing to implement a more dynamic compensation is not just the transfer of money; it requires a new kind of conversation with the people you work with. Building a relational business environment is essentially a psychological transition, more than a conceptual process. *You can't legislate intimacy!*

Most businesspeople still prefer to keep it *professional*. So-called touchy/feely behavior is still considered a waste of time. Then they wonder why most companies remain very isolating environments and why the people inside find it very hard to create meaningful personal connections. We want meaningful connection with our customers and peers, but we don't want to have to look at ourselves in order for that to happen. Few realize that deep relationship is possible without knowing a lot of personal history about another person. Deep relationship is possible well within the constraints of keeping things professional. It does not rest in more intimate content, but in closer process.

Mike Abrashoff was one of the youngest commanding officers in naval history. In the two years he captained the U.S.S. *Benfold,* it broke all records for coming in under budget, retention of recruits, battle readiness, etc. One day a young recruit suggested to him that they replace all the nuts and bolts on the ship with stainless steel so they wouldn't rust, and more important, so the new recruits wouldn't have to re-paint the ship every three months. Twenty-four hours and a thirty-thousand-dollar credit card charge to Home Depot later, the suggestion was implemented. It was a hundred small acts such as this that led to the extraordinarily large and measurable outcomes that made the *Benfold* the top ship in the fleet. Although he did come to know more about each of his crew, it was the vitality of the process and the quickness of response that changed the entire climate of his ship.

Tribal companies must do intimacy. They can't just give this idea lip service; they must dive into those dark scary waters. Every system that is put in place to increase communication must be matched by a sincere willingness to listen. When technology supports greater communication, then true intimacy must be awakened, or all the good-looking efforts will produce nothing new. In fact, connectivity without a real desire to listen will actually breed heightened frustration and more intense resistance because of the hopes and promises left unfufilled.

3.4 THE SECOND DAWN OF SOCIAL GENIUS

Tribal companies actively focus on twelve interrelated dialogues. Following are summary points taken from the discussions up to this point.

Actively evolve your dialogues with customers:

1. Bonds are more important then brands. Involved consumers are powerful collaborators in your future. You want them and need them. Thus, you must actively seek ways to bring their ideas into your business.

2. The new, improved customers are partners in your business. They want to help you do your work. The dialogues you forge with them are powerful sources of new products and services.

3. Ultimately, invested customers are the most involved customers. It's the closest bond you can forge. Business will begin to innovate in this area as much as the products you sell.

4. Consumer tribes are thriving on the noncommerce side of the tracks and may evolve in ways that further rewrite the rules of commerce. Forward thinkers are already planning for the day that customers will demand even more accountability.

Purposely evolve your dialogues with workers:

1. Organizations are more transparent, often making once-secret information widely accessible. Information will be designed to allow for empowerment at every level of the business.

2. Decisions are flattened. More policies are forged in the moment. Tribal companies trust people faster and trust them more, in order to grow rapidly.

3. Leaving becomes more rare when companies learn to participate with people as they grow, and develop strategies for co-venturing, intrapreneurship, and extrapreneurship.

4. Workers will live within idea communities that transcend the company walls. Forward thinkers will interface with this body of knowledge that is beyond the formal company boundaries. Asynchronous work environments will allow a broader level of participation. Nimble companies reward the performance of stellar teams and discover new ways of honoring collaborative efforts.

Don't rest so heavily on the technical side of connectivity, and truly deepen the process of every dialogue you have.

1. We are hardwired to be social. Informal proximity in and of itself creates sparks. Conversational jamming is more likely to occur when informal exchange is valued.
2. Appreciating randomness and giving it space to grow is one of the most fruitful paths to social genius. Wise companies will get excited when the unexpected begins to surface.
3. We are naturally telepathic. Secrets deny this and keep people from using their natural wisdom. Secrets force everyone to become less than who they really are. Eventually, people spend more energy in keeping the secret than in doing their work.
4. The future is structured in conversation. Deep relationship creates deep futures. A tribal company does not solve problems, as much as it solves relationships. A tribal company rests on its capacity for a great social life!

So what happens when the power of all this intimacy is really unleashed? What happens when thousands upon thousands of exchanges become more resonant, telepathic and dynamic?

I have always been fascinated by those rare periods in history when creative types seem to flock together. These moments in history offer clear evidence of our ability to go to new heights of creativity because of others. Thoreau, Emerson, Whitman, and Alcott all lived in the greater Boston area and were a close-knit artistic community that clearly spurred each other on. The early days of Esalen attracted a gathering of humanistic psychologists, which seeded the central concepts that still drive the personal growth movement. The South African activist Steven Biko surrounded himself with a group of equally spirited and brilliant players in his work to end apartheid. When he was killed, his compatriots were able to carry on his work, because he was not the sole leader. There have been many similar collective flowerings of creative thought: such as the Chicago School of Economics and the Abstract Expressionist movement in art. Today Xerox

Parc and MIT Media Lab are similar hotbeds of stellar contributions. Some even call Silicon Valley the Florence of the new Renaissance.

What would happen if all the separate learning communities that I just outlined were occurring all over the world, right now, multiplied by thousands?

Well, guess what? They are. Under the radar of most social observers, pockets of stellar genius are already forming. Neighborhoods may be gone, but there are more communities than ever before. Sometimes they live behind corporate walls, sometimes they are renegades on the edge of social acceptance and sometimes they are the rapidly growing estates of nonprofit groups that are rising to action all over the world and claiming the reins of political leadership. And they are all learning a new language that will allow them to leverage these gatherings into full-blown social genius.

The moment any group begins to form, the potential for tribal wisdom is triggered. New brain waves are provoked. A collective mind is born. Whenever we meet for a common goal, we have the potential to trigger entrained rhythms, cocreative experiences, heightened synchronicities and accelerated results.

We can deny this tribal potential and maintain formal, distant roles. We can meet and then choose to forget what really happened and walk off to do our own thing. Or we can consciously harness the potential for social genius. Out of necessity, a neotribalism is emerging that includes and transcends the original tribalmind. Much of the insatiable quest for power that still permeates the current economic environment may rest on our antiquated desire to be free from needing anyone. Once we *want* to need people, a new universe opens up.

Ultimately, the more any one player is empowered, the more every player along the way must also be empowered. A decentralized environment of savvy equals is the breeding ground of authenticity. Suddenly we are no longer customers, workers, managers or investors. When we are no longer just the roles we play, something far greater is freed.

If the next generation portends the future, then here is what is coming down the pike: Most polls taken of the new-millennium generation, now zero to eighteen years old, suggest that they are more altruistic, service oriented and care more about the planet and ecology than any other prior generation. They buy in packs, instant messaging as they make their purchases. They play complex collaborative games that cross international boundaries. They are far more tolerant and accepting of differences. Their relationships with peers are paramount. They expect a world beat. They saw their parents work hard, often sacrificing quality of life in order to get ahead. They say in polls that they don't want the same for themselves. It will be a few years before they seriously impact the workplace, but the word on the street is that they will want far more collaborative, fluid, balanced and noncompetitive environments.

Every year a professor at UCLA asks his MBA graduating class to write a personal vision of where they are headed. For years he had been used to receiving visions of some dot-com idea or new business that would lead to fame and fortune. In his most recent graduating class of 131 students, only five contributed this kind of vision. The other 126 described how they would help the world, give to others and use the digital environment to create social change and justice. He considered this a very significant turnabout.

Kids grow up steeping in a cultural soup, unconsciously absorbing the messages of their time. They offer the larger culture a mirror of what is bubbling up to correct the current misperceptions. Like a huge pendulum swinging through time, each generation balances out the one before. The new generation always chooses clear and specific attitudes that will break down an old world order and usher in something new. In this way they each leave their marks on the larger culture.

The Boomers built the early threads of the Web. The love and peace generation naturally jumped on board with the democratization of information. But much of the pace of this digital economy was the work of the X generation. They forged the explosiveness that has served to break

For over forty thousand years, the aborigines crossed a desert larger than the continental United States, never getting lost and surviving the harshest of conditions.

The desert has few obvious clues. One dune blends into the next in a way that could fool even the most highly trained eye. But these ancient nomads did not rely on visual clues. They traveled a far more interesting path.

When they reached a waterhole, they would tell a song/story. The song held the code that allowed them to intuitively know where to go next. This navigational tool was stored in their physical experience, an advanced form of instinctual knowledge. They were able to cross the forbidding terrain of the Central Australian desert by riding the songlines.

RIDING THE SONGLINES

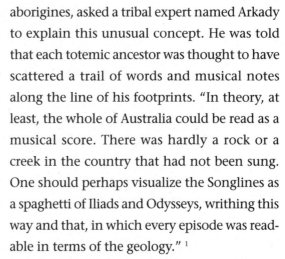

Bruce Chatwin, author of *The Songlines,* an extraordinary book about the aborigines, asked a tribal expert named Arkady to explain this unusual concept. He was told that each totemic ancestor was thought to have scattered a trail of words and musical notes along the line of his footprints. "In theory, at least, the whole of Australia could be read as a musical score. There was hardly a rock or a creek in the country that had not been sung. One should perhaps visualize the Songlines as a spaghetti of Iliads and Odysseys, writhing this way and that, in which every episode was readable in terms of the geology." [1]

It is not an easy concept for the western mind to grasp. Later Arkady explains to Chatwin the cause of all his troubles with the railroad people.

It was one thing to persuade a surveyor that a heap of boulders were the eggs of the Rainbow Snake or a lump of reddish sandstone was the liver of a speared kangaroo. It was something else to convince him that a particular stretch of gravel was the musical equivalent of Beethoven's Opus 111. [2]

The previous three chapters have described different facets of our journey into a world with fewer reference points. Perhaps you have already caught glimpses of this invisible realm. How do you then convince others that something quite intangible is so vitally important?

How Do You See the Future?

Two dear friends, Dan Hall and Deb Oakes, offered to consult with us about the future of our business. Dan is the owner of a small film and Web site production company with a handful of employees and Deb is the owner of a larger company with over one hundred employees that sells business furniture. We sat in Deb's stylish conference room, contemplating the road ahead.

At some point they asked us about our business plan. We responded, *"We don't have one."* They looked at each other and asked, *"Can you do that?"*

We were relieved to find out that we were actually in good company. *Inc. Magazine's* survey of the top five hundred small companies found that 65 percent began without a business plan and 35 percent operated without any financial projections. Also keep in mind that the *Inc.* five hundred is a list of the *fastest*-growing small businesses, so these are stellar companies, not just your average players.

In fact, even the highly reputable William Hewlett of Hewlett-Packard said of his occasional business school appearances:

> . . . the professor of Management is devastated when I say that we really didn't have any plans in place when we started—we were just opportunistic. We did anything that would bring a nickel. We had a bowling foul-line indicator, a clock drive for a telescope, a thing to make a urinal flush automatically and an electric shock machine to make people lose weight. Here we were with about $500 in capital, trying to make whatever someone thought we might be able to do.

Of course, it's easier to function without a formal plan when you have a two-person business, as we do. And it's even easier when the two people are married, therefore in close and continuous communication. Further, the nature of our business is more conducive to rapid changes in direction and spur-of-the-moment ventures. There are no factories to retool or major supplies to order.

But even with all that said, I still believe this more freewheeling, more impulsive way of working can be translated to larger and more formal business settings. ***More important, I believe this instinctive way of working has now become imperative given our economic acceleration and the driving demand for continuous innovation.***

AND WHERE DO GOOD IDEAS COME FROM?

Whether you are self-employed, a mom-and-pop store on the corner or with a multinational conglomerate, you all face growing pressure to stay ahead of the curve. Whether you are just starting out or have years of experience under your belt, you know that a big part of your upward climb rests on your ability to consistently show up with really good ideas. But, just where do good ideas come from?

1. Vance Patterson was CEO of the Patterson Group. One day a couple of workers were grilling their lunches on a device they had cobbled together from some spare parts of the industrial fans they made. The fan made for a more even, consistent cooking temperature. Patterson was so enamored of this device that the workers made him one as a birthday present. He loved it and couldn't get the concept out of his mind. Soon after, along with the two workers who had *invented* this product, Patterson patented the idea and began marketing a better mousetrap: a grill with even, steady heat. Hence, a new product, The Town and Country Grill was born.[3] In this case, his product development department was a couple of guys fooling around on a break, which he had taken the time to notice.

2. A woman who had just come out the other side of a difficult divorce opened a Web site with resources for others going through this process. The people who visited were buying a lot of the products she was recommending. One day, she approached a small but promising on-line retailer for a commission arrangement. She asked the retailer if she referred people to its site, could she get a cut on the books they purchased? Fortunately, this up-and-coming retailer called Amazon.com was still scrappy. Amazon.com said yes and the idea of associates programs was born. It did more for Amazon.com than the woman's Web site. It was a key reason Amazon.com skyrocketed to such quick visibility. As noted earlier, associate programs are projected to represent 24 percent of the on-line business. A rather ordinary customer looking for an angle happened to find an alert staffer who felt free enough to listen and leap. In doing so, these two individuals launched one of the critical marketing strategies of the on-line world.

3. Will Wright wrote what he describes as a "really, and I mean really, stupid video game" titled *Raid on Bungling Bay*.[4] In order to build the game, he designed utility programs that would allow him to build islands quickly or insert roads more rapidly. After he finished the shoot 'em up part, he noticed that he kept building more of these utility programs. He asked himself, *"What am I doing? The game is finished!"* But he was having more fun building the islands than destroying them. He became fascinated with the idea of bringing a city to life, adding layer upon layer. By following his bliss, he almost effortlessly developed a new game that allowed the player to follow his sequence of invention. The new game was called *SimCity*, one of the more popular and imaginative games now on the market.

4. In 1966, Dee Hock was working at the National Bank of Commerce in Seattle in charge of Bank of America's new credit card operations. At that time, its credit card system was filled with

problems. At a national meeting, Hock volunteered to be a good citizen and put in some extra time to help the company figure things out. Events rapidly escalated and he was hired by Bank of America, and essentially given a blank slate and told to *fix it.* In less than a year, at a speed no one could believe, the architecture for a business that would be owned by no one and run by everyone was set in place. The name of this budding venture was Visa. With 750 million customers and twenty-two thousand banks, it is a 1.25-trillion-dollar *nonstock-for–profit* organization. Hock didn't work his way up the ranks of power; he was catapulted to the edge of a large gaping hole and told to jump. With the help of many colleagues, Dee Hock filled this chasm with an organizational structure *that no one had ever seen before.*

5. Frederich Von Kulke had been wrestling with the structure of carbon and couldn't come up with a model that would explain its extraordinary behavior as the building block of all life. Spent and exhausted from beating his head against the proverbial conceptual wall, he took a nap. He then had a dream about a snake biting its tail. Upon waking he said, "That's it! Carbon is a ring!"

I am not saying that all great ideas come from unexpected sources, but you would be surprised how many do. We will sometimes ask participants in our seminars to make a quick list of the major turning points in their lives. These include events like meeting your partner, choosing your current profession or perhaps lucky breaks that took your career along faster than you expected. We then ask them to review the list to see how many of the events were the result of planning and foresight. Invariably, when they looked back at these turning points, a high percentage, if not all, turned out to be chance events—things that just could not have been predicted. And if this is so, what does it mean about how we structure the workplace for maximum innovation?

Of course, the above examples represent various degrees of surprise.

A grill cobbled together with spare parts is somewhat less startling to your belief system than suddenly being asked to fix a nationwide financial service, or perhaps deciphering the message of a dream that proposes to reveal the structure of matter. Unexpected events come in many disguises, from stray remarks to chance meetings to unusually provocative conversations, all the way up to events that seem like an answer to a prayer. Some say everything happens for a reason. You just have to look for it.

UNINTENDED MESSENGERS

One of the key features of a creative life is the ability to continually enjoy disequilibrium or turbulence. Children, great leaders and all adventurers naturally gravitate to the unpredictable. Children will purposely hang upside down on a swing, blood rushing to their heads, just for the fun of it. Adventurers will risk their lives for a slim chance to glimpse a spectacular view. They derive great joy from cognitive disruption, surprise and novelty.

Yet, as we grow older, or take on more responsibility, we often turn away from the very events that are most likely to provoke unintended consequences. We seek stability more than variety. We avoid cognitive dissonance in order to maintain efficiency. We strive for predictability, and then wonder where all the good ideas have gone. The price of experience is often the loss of wonder.

Henri Matisse is one of the greatest artists of all time. Considered by many to have almost perfect technique, he struggled on a daily basis to overcome his facility so that he could truly create something new, and not rest on his laurels. Sometimes he would even put his brushes on long poles before beginning to paint. It was the only way he knew how to escape the control that was locked in his exquisite draftsmanship. If you consider yourself experienced in what you do, perhaps you should also be considering your own version of long poles. Take a moment to evaluate if you are able to lose control or feel confused on a regular basis.

But entering the realm of the unpredictable may not be as hard as you think. In each of the previous five stories, there was one and only one behavior that triggered the eventual solution: *paying attention.*

Paying attention is not a glamorous leadership skill. We tend to focus on the more flashy traits like courage, boldness, risk, vision and charisma. *Just looking around* rarely makes it to the top-ten list of how to get ahead. Few spend time nurturing their talent to really observe, although it may be the most important tool we have. In each of the examples offered, the individual in question merely looked at what was just in front of his nose. The only difference is, these individuals were just a bit more alert than your average player.

Paying attention seems so simple, yet the implications are profound. Once you accept how much hinges on paying attention, without realizing it, you have also opened yourself up to a new world view. *What any unintended messenger shows us—whether it be a new person, an unanticipated idea or an unexpected opportunity—is that the road ahead is not quite so fixed and well organized as we would like to believe. When you begin to consistently pay attention, you begin walking the road less traveled.*

Here's the real fix on this new world view. Opportunity knocks constantly. It surrounds us on a daily basis. We swim in a sea of lucky breaks. Solutions are ever present, lying just below the surface of ordinary vision. Scratch the surface of business as usual, and infinity is bound to peek through. Paying attention is the portal that allows you to see beyond the world you already know. But alas, we are so busy getting the job done—tunnel visioned, with eyes trained fast on the target—that we miss the hidden potential that dwells around almost every corner.

- If Vance Patterson had been in a hurry to get back to important things, he never would have spotted the grill. This seemingly inconsequential chat with his workers may have been the most important thing Patterson did that year.
- If Will Wright hadn't paid attention to his seemingly silly fascination with building utilities, if he had chalked it up to lack of focus and gone back to his assigned task of building shoot 'em up games, he never would have envisioned SimCity.

■ If Dee Hock hadn't seen the gaping credit card hole as an opportunity to try out all his wild and crazy ideas about building systems that empowered people, he would have soon been back at his desk job, meeting deadlines. He would have let the people charged with the problem fix their own mess.

Fixed plans, rigid attitudes and blind determination often keep you from seeing the opportunities that lie smack dab in the center of your path. **To some degree, every plan is a self-fulfilling prophecy, guiding you to see only what you want to see. Despite its simplicity, the willingness to entertain the unexpected and engage the seemingly irrelevant is a highly courageous and creative act.**

Given our predisposition to stay on task and avoid unnecessary distractions or surprising tangents, some have had to hire others who can see through new filters. A symphony orchestra in Texas hired a rock promoter to be director—quite a bold move for what is normally a traditional, formal enterprise very dependent on hobnobbing with the cultural elite. This rock promoter's radical way of approaching the promotion of concerts blew a lot of well-established plans away. It also made the orchestra more profitable and led to interesting creative directions that someone schooled in the world of classical music would never have considered. A former rock promoter raising money from the country-club crowd is bound to blow apart business as usual.

A hospital CEO told us that the healthcare field is now looking very seriously at retailing in order to discover new ways of approaching *customers*. To keep up with an environment that no longer assures a fixed profit, it has to look through a new lens. However, when I asked this particular CEO if he had hired anyone from the retail field, the answer was no. Obviously, his hospital wasn't quite ready to take the same level of risk as the symphony. It was still using trained health professionals to develop this new marketing vision, and probably keeping the aggressive world of modern retailing at arm's length.

An inventor once told me that half of all inventions come from people outside the immediate industry in which the idea is discovered. In their ignorant bliss, these uninformed outsiders defy the prevailing wisdom, never having a clue that what they are planning can't be done. In fact, the friend who told me this was himself a resident from the other side of the tracks. He had just developed a way of transmitting data faster than the experts said was possible by using technology from another field.

It was this kind of thinking that led 3M to its famous 15 percent rule. Employees are authorized to spend 15 percent of every work day fooling around with ideas that might have nothing to do with their current job responsibilities. It is this thinking that also allows 3M to consistently meet its other very impressive goal: Thirty percent of its yearly income is derived from new products, invented within the last five years.

- Does this mean that if you want to raise the bar and have new products represent 60 percent of your yearly income, you have to follow the 3M ratio and give people nearly a third of the week off?
- Does this mean that if you want rule-defying innovation you need to hire half your people from outside the field?
- Does this mean if you want to play at the edge, you have to drop all plans whatsoever?

No. But it *is* interesting to consider how much daydreaming your particular industry or career would optimally require. If you are in a field experiencing a high rate of change, you might consider investing a higher percentage of your time bumping into the unplanned. *The knowledge economy will require a cognitive style that encompasses far more randomness than would have been acceptable in the past. It will require a profound ability to see past the obvious reasons we all offer for why and how events take place.*

Do You Draw Outside the Lines?
Radical language is now very popular. *Wired* magazine publishes

dictionaries of hip digital lingo that allow you to sound like you are an accomplished chaos rider. You learn to say *command Z*, meaning you have erased whatever has gone before. You use dozens of handy new phrases often pulled from the programmer's lexicon. Once you have a metaphor, you can slip almost any event into its rhythms. If it works for fibers and networks, why not apply it to people too?

But despite a more edgy linguistic milieu, many persist in the illusion that we can explain events in terms of flow charts and how tasks will move from one person to the next. No matter how much we have been exposed to *managing chaos*–type ideas, few walk the walk. We may pepper our conversations with phrases like *the learning organization* and claim to practice *creative deconstruction*, but actually *doing* these things is a far more challenging task.

You'll notice the moment a decision is made, people still fly to their posts. Charts are quickly tacked to the wall—everyone secretly hoping that if they are quick enough, they will finally be able to nail down an illusive, fleeting future. *If we can just get that plan up on the wall, maybe tomorrow will finally belong to us.*

Of course, we are shocked at how often things just don't go according to plan. Remember the Bill Gates maxim: The things you think will happen quickly seem to take forever, and the things that you think will take forever seem to happen overnight. This is because of the invisible, sticky fingers of turbulence. Linear plans develop all sort of unexpected quirks that make them far more complex than the rational mind ever expected. But the big surprises, like the Internet and wireless communication, seem to unfold in huge bold leaps of faith. They jump right over normal cause and effect and land in our collective lap almost fully formed.

Despite our managing chaos–type talk, we still believe our organizational charts accurately describe the chain of command and flow of communication. We believe that we have finally established some order in a very turbulent world. In fact, we even think that if we reorganize the lines on the chart, everyone will magically begin to report to new people and will have new and improved conversations and that decision-making will flow in entirely new ways.

Then Karen Stephenson comes along and tells us that organizational charts are mostly fantasy.[5] She has been asked by Steelcase and others to diagram the *real* path of communication within an organization. Her findings show that people don't follow the lines of the organizational chart when it comes to communicating information. Some individuals stand out as hubs, and almost everyone looks to these individuals for advice and guidance. Often these *hub people* have formal standings in the organization that bear little relationship to the real roles they play. The chart may propose entirely different people to be the locus of information gathering, yet no one seems to honor their roles except in the most superficial ways.

One Indianapolis Leader of the Year was a hospital CEO. Every year, she would ask her employees what they would really like to be doing and how they would like to grow. The organizational chart would then be reconfigured to reflect each of these visions. Thus, the organization was always a reflection of her people's dreams.

Can you imagine putting a real organizational chart on the wall, which shows a real map of who shares with whom and about what? Then imagine building teams and projects based on what people are really doing. Some are already experimenting with letting go of job titles and letting people move in and out of projects based on what interests them at the time and where they can best serve. There is a very delicate tension between accountability and trust that allows for maximum performance, and that tension should be flexible to each situation and adapted for different personality styles. If you haven't made some mistakes in this area, like trusting someone too much, then you are not really experimenting with this dynamic.

Most clever managers will admit to having designated truth tellers, *key individuals who will give them the straight talk, even if it's not what they want to hear.* Most often these bold messengers have no formal responsibility for the roles they discuss. In fact, they often inhabit rather inconsequential places on the totem pole; yet they seem to have a handle on everything that is going on.

A CEO recently told us that he has an informal board made up of people in direct contact with customers. Every time his designated board comes up with a decision, he immediately feeds it to his *real board*. He gets an immediate read on whether it will work and what changes need to be made. He saves a lot of heartache and a lot of time by operating this way. These days, unless they are practicing complete tunnel vision, almost everyone has participated in at least some form of MBWA, managing by walking around. *Most recognize that the only way to sense what is really happening is to venture into social territories that are not their usual habitat.*

But an even craftier level of invisible organization may be at work. Max DePree, chairman emeritus of Herman Miller, calls it roving leadership: "The indispensable people in our lives that are there when we need them."[6] These people don't just show up because they have job titles; they emerge because the group needs them.

If people show up because the group needs them, if heroes are created by the events that surround them, then progress may rest on a very unusual framework. It suggests that the very act of desiring a particular result may begin to invisibly elicit the path to it. It suggests a fabric of organization that is far larger and more interesting than the obvious action plan.

Of course, this is exactly what happens with any hot project. It feels like answers fall into our laps. Diverse players click in a way that leads to heightened efficiency and expanded brilliance. A sense of flow permeates what normally would be a stressful situation. I believe that we crave this flow, even more than we desire a particular result. When we hit the zone, the experience is its own reward. And without such sensations, life seems dull and obvious. We settle for ambition and motivation because the true spirit of creativity eludes us. A leader who can elicit that subtle experience of creative flow will always inspire performance that defies all expectations.

DILBERT CAME, HE SAW, HE CONQUERED

The Dilbert books didn't become best-sellers just because they were funny. They cast light on a shadow that was begging for an excuse to come out of the dark. They let the cat out of the bag. As a result, the author, Scott Adams, no longer draws just from his own personal experiences to create cartoons about irrelevant projects, pompous bosses and catch-22s. Crazy anecdotes pour in from around the world. The only problem Adams faces is that sometimes the stories are just so preposterous that if he put them in print, no one would believe they could really happen.

Dilbert is the personification of the employee who is starting to wake up. He suffers under the weight of organizational mindlessness and yet his own eyes have begun to clear. He clearly understands when tasks are purely for the purpose of creating an image, or as Dee Hock says, "Learning to retire while on the job." Dilbert represents a groundswell of sentiment that is brewing in every department across the land.

Here's a quick statistical profile of the U.S. population. These measures probably also reflect much of the industrial world. In fact, some Asian countries may be experiencing even higher percentages in some areas because of their even longer work week.

- Over 50 percent of all workers say they are dissatisfied with their current jobs.
- Twenty-five percent are actively considering changing their careers.
- Fifteen percent have tried Prozac and 10 percent are currently on some form of antidepressant.
- Twenty percent will experience a mental disorder. Half of those will be anxiety and panic disorders and the other half will be depressive disorders.
- Over half would consider a drop in pay if their jobs became more meaningful.
- Seventy-five percent would take a cut in pay in order to have more personal time.

- Fifty percent of all workers are experiencing symptoms of burnout. *Training* magazine estimates that treating corporate burnout has blossomed into a sixty-billion-dollar-a-year business.
- Seventy-five percent of the American public are actively looking for ways to simplify their lives.
- Between 15 and 25 percent have *voluntarily* accepted a cut in pay in order to downscale, simplify and engage in a less materialistic lifestyle. To some degree they have dropped out of the rat race. The Trends Research Institute calls this one of the top ten trends in the U.S.
- If you put this last percentage together with the previous one, it suggests that hardly anyone is still committed to all-out workaholism. Books with the words *balance* or *simplicity* in the title are all the rage. Companies offer sabbaticals to stressed executives and power-napping is being taught in corporations across the land.
- When asked what would make them happy, the top response from 66 percent of the public is to spend more time with their families. And 47 percent said they would be happier if they felt like they were making a difference in their communities.

Percentages have a curious way of making the trends seem like they are out there in the vast undefined general public. They're not.

The next time you sit around a conference table with about ten people, apply the following percentages. Half of the people sitting before you are dissatisfied or edgy enough to be considering other jobs. More than two are considering a new profession. Over half want more meaning in their work. One to two are anxious enough to be receiving medical support for their distress and more than one is probably on antidepressants. Half the table is exhibiting clear symptoms of burnout. One will probably experience panic attacks and one will probably experience depression. At least seven of those at the table are actively seeking ways to simplify their lives. Two-thirds want more time with their families and half would be a lot happier if their work were helping others. Also remember that two to three people are no longer even at the table because they have left their jobs to seek a less stressful way of life. And keep in mind that some of the people who are still at the table have kept in touch with these *freewheeling, courageous dropouts* and are regularly listening to their tales.

If you were about to climb Mt. Everest and were told that these percentages revealed the make-up of your ten-person crew, you might reconsider the venture. At the very least you would say to everyone, "We've got to straighten out a few things before we start climbing." You would never set out on such an adventure with this crew, and yet that's what you are working with on a daily basis.

The average workers are reaching the edge of what their nervous systems can handle; they just can't run any faster. They don't care quite as much about pursuing actions that don't hold much meaning. The average person is craving purpose and a sense that they are contributing to make the world a better place. Even if they present a brave face, these concerns are what they reveal in private.

THE RENAISSANCE

The number one reason people offer for why they leave the salaried world to live in Free Agent Nation is that they have to put on masks in order to go to work. They have to pretend to be something they are not in order to survive. And it is exhausting. It is the desire to bring their whole selves to work that is fueling much of this transition.

But remember, most of these free agents are turning right back around and working with the very same companies that they have left. And dialogue matters. More and more companies not only have to adapt to a more flexible workforce, they also have to regularly talk with people who have new kinds of beliefs—these discussions are insidiously infiltrating the tasks at hand.

The CEO of Monster.com suggests that one of the key workplace trends of the next decade will involve companies exploring ways to adapt to working with free agents. This will be the workforce of the future and they have values and workstyles that will require a lot more freedom and trust. More important, these nimble players will often be highly creative, therefore exactly who innovative companies need most.

Paul Ray, a social science researcher, suggests that a new wave of cultural values are emerging.[7] He calls this new breed *cultural creatives* and estimates that 25 percent of the current population falls into this category compared with 12 percent just a decade ago. The key characteristic of this group is that they welcome change and have a whole systems view of the world, which in turn results in new kinds of values about healthcare, ecology, education, politics, etc. The Harwood Group, funded by Merck, has come up with similar profiles and percentages as Ray, verifying that his thesis is probably on track.[8] The World Value Survey, drawn from forty-two nations representing 70 percent of the world's population, also showed a similar emergence of new attitudes and a drift toward more ecological, integrated views of the world. So this is a global event; it is not just confined to suburban burn-out.[9] In his book *The Post-Corporate World*, David Korten says:

> ... materialism is losing its grip on the popular psyche and we are witness to a sleeping giant—life reasserting itself in the form of an emerging shift in our cultural consciousness.... It is not only in people's personal lives that the emergence of the integral culture is finding expression. It is well being expressed in countless initiatives by ordinary people, doing extraordinary things to re-create livable communities, and a just, sustainable and compassionate world.

These trends cannot be divorced from how we think about business. If you were told that 25 percent of the population wanted bigger cars, plans would be well underway to meet this market. Twenty-five percent of the public are now embracing far more holistic, balanced views of the workplace and their place in the world, yet in most companies little is being done to address their concerns. And you are not just selling to these people; they are working for you. A cultural creative in the work-place is probably someone who considers a vast array of intangible forces that design what is possible at an organizational level.

The renaissance of the fifteenth century was triggered by a shift in employment patterns. The guilds collapsed. A steady paycheck evaporated. But the people who were let loose on the streets were not disenfranchised and powerless. They were a vast, creative middle class of people that were used to being valued and accustomed to making a difference. It was their personal searches that triggered the openness and experimentation of this first renaissance.

Similarly, in the dot-com crash, hundreds of thousands of creative types were let loose into the work force. Add that to the twenty-five-million plus members of Free Agent Nation and you have a cultural impact that dwarfs what was experienced six centuries ago. Add this to all the trends we have suggested up to this point: a breakdown of fixed, defendable product territories, merger mania, digital artists who can rewrite the commercial game, the rise of planet art, the power of dialogue to transform commercial relationships, the new values of the D generation, etc. Put all these factors together and you are walking through a vast terrain that has no map. You are going to *need* those songlines!

THE MIDAS FACTOR

We are in the curious predicament of the famed King Midas. Everything he touched turned to gold. He wasn't even able to eat due to the strange effect he had on his environment. He could not escape the world he had created through his own description of what was important to him. What he thought he wanted was killing him.

Every plan sets up a Midas effect. According to the new quantum science, if we observe only those outcomes we have designated in advance, we have also invisibly altered what will happen and will see only the questions we have asked. The observer and the observed cannot be separated. ***The goals, objectives, values and measures we continually estab-***

lish, which make us feel so in control, which allow us to feel that the future will unfold according to plan, which allow us to feel a sense of accomplishment, also set up the parameters of the culture we will allow.

Every group makes an invisible agreement about how much rebelliousness is allowed, how much confrontation will be tolerated or how much consensus is necessary before it can move forward. Every group sets limits on an infinite array of social behaviors. When a new person comes on board, the first day of work he or she is handed *The Very Large, Heavy, Ponderous, Invisible, Unavoidable Rule Book.* And he or she is also handed a script of the available roles. As excited as the person may feel and as many new ideas as he or she may have upon arriving, within days he or she is unconsciously conforming his or her opinions to what will be accepted.

But here's the clincher. If you decide to entertain these implicit, quantum, chaotic models of reality, it means that you have to live differently. You must begin reading the energy that underlies actions, the fields that organize behavior, and move toward models that can encompass far more indeterminacy than might at first feel comfortable. You have to develop your senses so you can perceive the deeper order that underlies all projects, all decisions and the very structure of any group behavior. *Using the Midas analogy, you have to make the decision that it is not gold that you want, but something far more precious.*

4.1 SEEING WITH NEW EYES

Greg Patterson buys struggling companies, builds them back up and turns them around for a profit. He makes these decisions for a large and very successful investment group, which he now heads. He has been doing this for over thirty years and says he has rarely made a mistake in his choices. He told us the secret to his success is his thirty-minute rule.

He walks into a prospective situation and makes an instinctive deci-

sion within the first thirty minutes. If his gut answer is yes, then the accountants and analysts will do months of assessment to verify that his initial hit is warranted. But he never begins the rational side of the process if his thirty-minute instinct is not positive.

By operating within this thirty-minute decision frame, he forces himself to sense those invisible dynamics that will determine whether the organization will be willing to change or whether it will cause a huge struggle. He can't ask too many questions. If he lets himself stay longer, his mind cuts in. He may start getting interested in the company's product, the nature of its business or become intrigued by the personalities involved. This intellectual seduction might make him override his gut feeling.

The information he would come to know could blind him from sensing the nature of the invisible field that shapes and defines the deeper behaviors of the organization. In our infocentric environment of continuous analysis of every input and output, we often divorce ourselves from our capacity to just *know* stuff. ***The world of implicit, distributed, cultural dynamics can only be sensed in this more immediate way; thus, we have to begin respecting instinct as a valid form of knowledge.***

We are fortunate to have worked with the Kaiser Institute's executive leadership program, which is boldly teaching intuition to senior executives as a critical management tool. As a result of his involvement in this program, a hospital CEO was able to pay attention in a new way. The hospital was well along in its plans to build an addition, but he kept having this nagging thought that it was not large enough. The size had been determined through careful forecasting and in connection with very experienced architects. Ordinarily, he would have trusted his experts and not given it a second thought. But armed with a new courage, instead he said to his board, "It makes no sense, but I think the facility needs to be far larger. Could we reexamine our projections?"

The projections were reexamined, and yes, there was a major flaw in the analysis, and yes, the new wing needed to be larger. Of course, people are more likely to indulge the whims of those at the top. But, if you want true brilliance, there must also be channels for those throughout the system to pipe up and say, *"I don't know why, but something is just bugging me about what we plan to do."* Or even, *"Since I started using this new system we've put in place something has not been right and I don't know what it is."* This is the *organizational gut*—the distributed instinct that lives in every exchange.

Normally, the moment someone says, "I don't know why, but..." the idea is suspect. Moving into a more instinctual world requires actions that are not yet accompanied by metrics and justifications. Often by the time you can justify a shift, it is already too late. I can't tell you how many times people have come up to us after a decision has been made and voiced their real thoughts. This is not just Monday morning quarterbacking; it reflects how consistently people sit on what they really feel.

But thanks to the hyperlinked company, intuition has become more acceptable. It will become more popular to voice what you really feel. The organizational gut has become more evident. The more that people can vent their real feelings on-line, often in a somewhat anonymous form, the more their X-ray vision will enter the public conversation.

I heard an interesting TV interview with Bob Woodward, *The Washington Post* reporter of Watergate fame. Woodward had just finished writing *Maestro,* a biography of Alan Greenspan and his rise and transformation as Federal Reserve Chairman. Greenspan had been born and bred as an inflation hawk, but he began to feel in his bones that his familiar ways of interpreting and curing inflation problems were just not adequate. It was an old mental model that no longer fit an information economy. According to Woodward, Greenspan believed the body could sometimes pick up information *before* the mind was ready to hear it. Long before his mind found reason to justify a new position, Greenspan trusted those edgy feelings.

I have just given several examples of quite successful intuitives, in part, to show that intuition is a reputable way of knowing. Some of the best folks in town use it. It requires paying attention to those edgy feelings and stray thoughts that the dominant part of your mind may not have yet considered.

A vice president of a midsize software company told us that he gets lots of great ideas. His problem is that he pauses. He waits. In a lightning-fast world, the moment is gone and someone else is already doing it. He came to us for help with, in his words, "dealing with the pause." The pause is mostly a fear of falling out of control. The pause is believing that what you know must have a justification or source in the world that you can see.

A more intuitive way of knowing is a direct result of the new economic landscape and the speed and density of information that we all must handle. Ordinary thought is just not fast or precise enough. The director of an innovation team told us, "We're not using as many focus groups, instead we're using the jaw-drop system. If my jaw doesn't drop, the idea doesn't fly!"

Early in his career, Greg Patterson was put in a situation where he had a clear choice. He was asked to evaluate a company, but did not yet have the requisite skills for attempting such an assessment. He had never done it before. He could have done more homework than anyone else in order to overcompensate for his lack of experience. This choice probably would have bred a lifetime of dwelling in facts and becoming a data-based overachiever.

His other option was to jump in and walk where angels fear to tread. He chose the latter. Early on he developed the habit of going with his gut and learned to rely on his intuition. He said that seeing this *vibrational world* is no more than that—building a habit. A lot of people are just in the habit of pausing, and looking for rational material. This is the razor's edge spoken about in many mystical traditions. It is a fine line that you have to walk in order to see both worlds, the visible and the invisible.

4.2 WE ARE HARDWIRED TO SENSE ENERGY

An aborigine crossing the desert doesn't look for visual clues. He sings a song learned from his ancestors and their ancestors before. The song triggers a muscle memory, a kinesthetic wisdom that contains the knowledge he needs for taking the next step.

There are a clump of nerve fibers just above the stomach that have the ability to independently process and interpret information. Author Michael Gershon calls this *the second brain*. This means when you experience a *gut feeling*, it is an accurate description. This second brain helps you create a response to an event that is somewhat independent of what the brain may have determined about the situation. The evolutionary purpose for this was for *fight or flight*. If a tiger was about to strike, you had to start running before the brain kicked in. Once solely for the purpose of survival, it is now an extension of our sensory faculties, if we choose to use it.

Researchers have identified a similar capacity in the heart, which allows it to interpret and create *thoughts* that are, again, independent of the brain's interpretations. The Institute of Heartmath has also been collecting a body of research in this area.[10] It has found that when you measure the electromagnetic field of the body, 90 percent of the energy seems to flow from the heart to the brain, and only 10 percent from the brain to the heart, suggesting that the heart informs the brain far more than vice versa. Of course, anyone who has been in a bad relationship, one they *knew* they shouldn't have gotten into, can confirm this flow of information. Thus, when one says, "Listen to your heart," there is an actual biochemical basis for this being a viable choice.

Neuroscientist Candace Pert's groundbreaking work has shown that molecules of feeling constantly flood the body, transmitting a particular emotional interpretation throughout the organism.[11] To put it simply, if you are feeling fear, every thought you think becomes steeped in the juices of fear. And psychologists have measured the impact of this. If you've just had a fight with someone, you will interpret the same set of facts differently than if you have just had an enjoyable experience and are feeling happy. So to some degree, feelings do define thoughts. We are never totally rational, even if we would like to think we are.

This was the kind of information Greenspan was tapping into when he felt that his body knew things before his mind was ready. In fact, a large body of medical research is demonstrating that the heart can think and that the body remembers and interprets information. *Thought* is not something that occurs just in the brain; it is a result of many fields of influence interacting.

These same fields of intelligence also seem to operate on an inter-personal level. For the first year or so of your life, you and your mother enter REM sleep at the exact same moment. In effect you dreamed togeth-er. This is why mothers can so easily hear their children crying at night; their brain waves are synchronized.

But this is only the beginning. Parents enter into a physiological dance with their children and the two seem to move to a common beat. In fact, if this invisible rhythm is not established, violence is far more likely. Early in my career I was associated with a research grant that used videotape to show that abusive mothers were out of rhythm with their children. They were then taught, through video feedback and coaching, to enter into a resonant rhythm with their children. No other training was offered about anger management or anything else. Incidents of abuse went way down. The children tended to cry less, and if they did, armed with this new sensory knowledge, the mothers were more quickly able to comfort them. Before the training, the children, who sensed the lack of rhythm, became more easily agitated. The unsynchronized mothers could not offer the invisible web that unconsciously allows a child to relax. Thus their actions were ineffectual and their frustration easily escalated.

The anthropologist Elliot Chapell also found a similar pattern.

Violent adolescents did not know how to mirror the conversational rhythms of their peers. They were *rhythmically isolated*, and deprived of a feeling of connection. Once again, when they were taught how to shift their rhythms to accommodate their listeners, all sorts of behavior improvements ensued with little or no additional counseling. Chapell also showed that the key to being popular is the ability to adapt your rhythms, depending on who you are with. Rhythms of conversation, head nodding and eye blinks that happen just outside of our conscious awareness send invisible messages to our listeners that we are with them.

If you are willing to go a little farther out in your thinking, Larry Dossey, M.D., has been on the forefront of proving that prayer affects healing.[12] When someone else prays for you, your T-Cell count really does go up. And this is not fringe stuff. Duke University and other major hospitals are now incorporating prayer into their strategies for rapid and effectual healing. Bottom line: It works. The supporting data is now vast. In a recent conference we attended it was reported that the head of the Texas Medical Association actually told a meeting of physicians that if they are not telling their patients about the power of prayer, they are opening themselves up to malpractice. How's that for an endorsement!

Obviously, the implications for team building and collaborative projects are quite interesting. A popular strategy for provoking creativity is what is called the boot-camp approach. Executives are taken on strenuous trips with activities such as rafting, climbing or ropes courses, and taken through a set of experiences that tests their physical and emotional limits. They are then asked to use these extreme states to catapult them into new ideas. Doug Hall, one of the leading creativity gurus on the scene, uses Nerf balls and laughter to generate hot ideas. Pool tables in the office or on-site gyms and athletic fields may work in a similar way. After a good sweaty game, you just might think differently.

This is almost identical to what happens in shamanic journeys. The shamanic traveler uses extreme physical states provoked by drumming, chanting, physical isolation, etc., to trigger new realizations. The chemistry of the body is altered in a way that leads to heightened awareness. All these ideas have one thing in common: If you change your physiology, you change your brain waves.

Larry Dossey interviewed a number of doctors who were making highly accurate diagnoses of their patients *before* they received any test results. When he asked them about it, they all mumbled something to the effect of: After years in the field, you have a lot of experience, so you tend to know how things will test out. You can imagine experienced leaders offering the same rationale for their quick assessments of situations or great salespeople attributing their quick client reads to years of experience.

Dossey makes the point that when doctors refuse to accept that their high degree of accuracy was intuition, they miss a lot of opportunities. By not treating their intuitive insights as a valid form of knowing, they preclude the opportunity of replicating their skills, training others and advancing the profession in some very powerful ways. The same can be said for business practices; by dismissing intuition as a valid tool, your options are far narrower.

In a similar vein, Abraham Maslow, a founder of humanistic psychology, began studying people who had peak experiences. He was attempting to outline the factors that would support people in expanding these moments of heightened awareness. These days it is also called *the zone* or *the flow*. One of the key discoveries was that *frequent peakers,* or those that entered the zone more often, also had a world view that encompassed the possibility of such events. They believed peak experiences were valid and therefore they occurred more often. Non-peakers had a negative opinion about such events and did not accept their existence. Daily life tended to confirm their belief just as consistently. So merely accepting new models of behavior may increase the frequency with which you see new sources of information. Merely knowing about the implicit world of kinesthetic knowing can, in and of itself, increase the frequency of this experience.

A senior vice president at L'Oréal told us a rather interesting story that confirms this point. For years the quality of scents in the perfume industry was limited. Despite many attempts, little improvement occurred. Then one day an employee from India suggested that they create a hood extending out many feet from the beaker holding the flower. He explained that in the Hindu tradition, the *aura* of a flower extends out many feet. If they could capture this invisible factor, the quality of the scent would improve. From the Western perspective there was no explanation, but it worked. See what an expanded worldview can offer.

4.3 EVERY ORGANIZATION IS HOLOGRAPHIC

The songlines that shape the aboriginal paintings, which make up their songs and are used for negotiating a vast desert, were first drawn as patterns in the sand. The wind soon blew those lines away, but the patterns were already imprinted upon the larger culture.

The founders of The Home Depot describe a scene from their early days, when they were trying to secure investments to open their first store.[13] One of their potential investors was Ross Perot of EDS fame, who was ready to write a check for one million dollars. This seemed like an astronomical amount at the time; they assumed their success was secured. At one of the final meetings where they were hashing out the details, Bernie Marcus said to Perot, "I have a two-year-old Cadillac on lease from my former employer. It would make sense for us to assume the lease, rather than go into a new car."

To which Ross Perot replied, "In my company, we drive Chevys."

Marcus again explained that it would be cheaper to lease the used Cadillac than to get a new Chevy. Ross Perot again replied quite simply, "In my company, we drive Chevys."

Marcus walked out of that meeting and said to his partner, "We can't take the money." Arthur Blank was shocked. He could hardly believe they were about to walk away from one million dollars in cold hard cash. But from that one exchange, Marcus knew that the corporate culture Perot expected would never work for him. It worked for Perot and EDS, but he would never be able to breathe in such an atmosphere. Much like Greg Patterson, in less than thirty minutes he knew the marriage would never work. One sentence spoke volumes.

A footnote The Home Depot partners add with glee is: Had Perot given the million, his share would be worth so much that it would have been the single best investment he ever made! For want of a Cadillac, a mighty kingdom was lost. Of course, if they had accepted the one million, they probably wouldn't have become The Home Depot that we know today—driven by extraordinary benefits for every employee, defined by a culture of freedom and built through the personal initiative that is constantly unleashed because the company gives its employees a lot of space to follow their instincts.

Philip once ordered a product from a mail order company. He got off the phone and said to me, "This company is in trouble." Again, it was nothing obvious; the clerk adequately took his order, but Philip read something between the lines. A week later in *The Wall Street Journal* we saw an article confirming that chapter 11 bankruptcy was imminent for this company. From time to time, Philip and I play the 800 number game; we each take a reading on the true dynamics of a company based on a very small encounter. And you would be amazed how often we get it right.

This is why many organizations are so stubborn. Consultants come in and introduce big bold strategies. Everyone learns what is expected, but over time little seems to change. Everyone slowly reverts to how things have always been done, because the small everyday behaviors that really run the show are never addressed. Everyday behaviors are the glue that keeps organizations stuck in their original form no matter how many big bold initiatives are introduced. Yet, hardly anyone focuses on the small stuff.

In their now classic book, *Built to Last,* James Collins and Jerry Porras suggest that the continual push for better results, better ideas, and new products, is not what will make a company great.[14] The HP way, like the Corning or the IBM way, is not a set of products. It is a set of attitudes that are reflected at every level of the organization. Given the right conditions, creativity, responsibility and vision are the natural state of every individual. These qualities don't need to be learned as much as remembered. They merely require the space where they can come forward.

4.4 STRANGE ATTRACTORS

Aborigine trackers are the best in the world, able to follow a man even years after he has walked through a dry desert terrain. An anthropologist asked one of these expert trackers how he did it. The tracker responded, "Oh it's easy. I walk with him." He does not look for clues; he enters the time and space where the journey occurred. He knows how to walk in the same world as the event he seeks.

The discovery of Post-it Notes was a pure accident. But as Collins and Porras point out, the conditions that supported this accident being recognized and translated into a viable product were *no accident.* Powerful organizational principles were in place to support this random stroke of luck.

Chaos theorists show how orderly systems break apart and how emergent dimensions of organization arise out of what seems to be pure chaos. Chaotic systems organize themselves around mathematical constructs called *strange attractors,* revealing a deeper order that lies beneath every layer of appearance. In a business, core principles serve this purpose. They reframe a vast series of seemingly random events of everyday behavior so that they reveal a deeper truth. They act in much the same way as strange attractors in chaotic systems.

In this next table, I combined three groups of ideas, paraphrasing them a bit.[15] I use 3M's guidelines for an innovative culture, a shortened version of Dee Hock's guidelines for building a nonowned organization like Visa and a shortened list of Peter Senge's principles for a learning organization.

3M	Visa	Learning Organization
Listen to any idea, no matter how absurd it seems	Equitably owned by all participants	You are not your job, position or role
Encourage, don't nitpick; let people run with an idea	Equitable rights and obligations	Avoid blame, focus on what you can do
Hire good people, leave them alone	Power, function and resources should be maximally distributed	Focus on patterns, not events
If you build fences, you get sheep; give people room	No participants should be left in a lesser position because of any new concept of organization	Any problem rests within the system; tell yourself the truth
Encourage experimental doodling	As much as possible, everything should be be voluntary	Choose a longer view to evaluate impacts
Give it a try and quick, or force change	It should not induce; it should compel	Ask for real collaboration
↓	↓	↓
Continuous Innovation	**Collaborative Network**	**Conditions for Learning**

For those who love tables, there are interesting observations that can be made by looking horizontally across the columns. But for the purposes of this next discussion, look down the columns, and see the flow of energy they each allow. I deliberately used three different systems so you could see that it is not the words that make for an outcome; it is the river of organization that allows a new direction to come forth.

Each case has described the very same behaviors that every company experiences, but mostly ignores. Each case has designed a set of principles that invisibly allows people to recognize and select certain behaviors as valuable. It makes order out of a vast sea of undifferentiated everyday behaviors.

We are still immersed in cause-and-effect thinking. Let's say we select a specific outcome, such as increasing collaboration. Then we throw a bunch of people together with a few seminars about teamwork and communication. We assume this desired outcome of increased collaboration can occur without a larger network of ideas that support it. No outcome can occur in isolation. No outcome is separate from the larger culture that surrounds it. With a larger behavioral system in place, a desired outcome is far more likely to occur. This is where the leaders of the future must refocus their attention—building the underlying foundation that allows their desired results to be continuously created.

4.5 SMALL RISKS TAKEN CONSISTENTLY CHANGE THE WORLD

We were at Coca-Cola the week its new CEO, Douglas Daft, was announced. A story quickly made the rounds. Here's the corporate myth that emerged, told and retold in conversations throughout its headquarters.

Coca-Cola had a system of employee badges that were color coded. Based on your job ranking, you received a particular color badge. You could walk in the halls or sit in the cafeteria and immediately know the job level of the person you just encountered. Everyone hated the badges.

At one of his first meetings, Daft said, "The color-coded badges have to go." Everyone nodded in agreement. It had been talked about for years. It was great to have someone at the very top voice concern. They waited for the next topic.

Daft said, "You don't understand, the badges have to go!" Everyone nodded again. *We agree. Now what should we talk about?*

Daft said once again, "The badges have to go. Now!" Someone was sent out to take care of it on the spot and non-color-coded badges were delivered before the end of the meeting.

Like Perot's "We drive Chevys," this was a holographic event. Volumes were said about the kind of CEO he would be and the new corporate culture he would represent. This story was told and retold with great excitement in those first days. It was a shot across the bow for those who were still feeding the old corporate myth that nothing would ever change.

A butterfly flaps his wings in a small garden in Japan. This small displacement of air is amplified by the empty space it encounters. It joins cross-oceanic currents and escalates into dramatic shifts in the upper atmosphere that in a few days will result in a tornado in Kansas. Deep organizational forces not apparent to the naked eye allow the flapping of a butterfly's wings to trigger mighty weather events on the other side of the globe. From the chaos theory we learn that when a butterfly flaps his wings in Japan, a tornado occurs in the Midwest.

This was the message reflected in the story about Douglas Daft. Everyone knew on some level that a small act of changing badges would echo across hallways, twist and turn through countless meetings and ultimately reshape larger corporate events to create a true climate of change.

Many still look for the killer application, the really big idea, the make-or-break contract or the invention that will make them famous. Yet, history tells us that very often small ideas go on to be huge in ways that just can't be predicted—like the idea for associates programs that began with a recently divorced woman who just wanted to get a few extra dollars for her efforts. Or the call-back system that has launched several mighty companies because one person noticed that it was cheaper to call Europe from the U.S. than the other way around. This small discrepancy could be parlayed into huge profits. Or the Post-it Notes story of a glue that wasn't effective for its intended task, but somehow found a mighty big purpose. Or the lone adventurer who launched a thousand Napster-like ships. In each case, a seemingly very simple act launched a mighty empire.

When things change slowly and events are not networked, it takes really big ideas to shift the course of history. In an accelerated, highly networked system, events affect each other far more profoundly. Small shifts can go a long way.

We call it the *one percent factor.* When sailing a boat, if you change course by just one degree, over the course of many miles that one percent difference results in a new destination. If you were driving a high-speed motorboat that one percent shift would show up even faster. If you were aboard a rocket that very same one percent shift would rapidly send you to a different planet. The faster you are moving the more impact small changes make. *In fact, small risks taken consistently can change the world.*

Continuing with our boating analogy, the trim tab is a tiny gear that allows a small steering wheel to turn a large boat around. Trim tab behaviors are the small choices that can have effects far beyond what would at first seem possible. My favorite part of our work is helping people to locate their behavioral trim tab—a very small behavioral shift that if consistently taken will change everything.

Now, let's go back to the example of the 3M core principles and see how they translated their general principles into knowledge that can be converted into action. On the left side are the same principles listed earlier, on the right are the actions that reflect the intent.[16]

3M Principles	Into Action
Listen to any idea, no matter how absurd it seems	Fifteen-percent rule allows individuals to explore self-chosen projects; 25 percent income from each division is derived from products invented in the last five years
Encourage, don't nitpick; let people run with an idea	Golden Step Award is presented to new business ventures; Genesis Grants Offer internal venture capital up to fifty thousand dollars
Hire good people, leave them alone	Technology Sharing awards are available for collaborative projects; Carlton Society honors original contributions
If you build fences, you get sheep; give people room	Intrapreneurship opportunities are available to run projects or divisions; dual ladder career track allows you to advance without giving up research interests
Encourage experimental doodling	New Product Forums and Technical Forums stimulate ideas and exchange; problem solving missions are sent out to customer sites
Give it a try and quick	High Impact Programs allow a few high-priority products out fast; product divisions are autonomous; 3M was also an early user of profit sharing

↓	↓
Continuous Innovation	**Holographic Beacons**

This is why the Post-it Notes story was no accident. Practices act as beacons. They encourage small behaviors that in turn reflect larger principles. If 3M had spelled out only the left side and not the right, it would not be what it is today. It would be like speaking without a listener. The right-hand list acts like a mirror, letting you see if your principles are being put into action. Most people don't ever spell out the left-hand side of the column. But even fewer take the next step to translate their principles into knowledge—observable actions that will ground these principles in behavior.

4.6 DISTRIBUTED INTELLIGENCE

A career accountant decided to build his lifelong dream and invest millions of his own money to create a high-end day spa. Halfway into the project he found himself in increasing amounts of turmoil. The accounting side of his brain had figured things out; all the choices had been worked out in advance. But as he dug the ditches and sculptured the building sites, the dream weaver part of his personality kicked in. He began seeing very different paths than what he had originally envisioned. Once he got his hands in the earth, very different messages came to him. He had to reconcile hard facts with unjustifiable leaps of vision that were triggered as he entered into the doing of his project.

This too is a common experience. As ideas are implemented they trigger a level of information that was just not there in the planning stage. Assigning people to carry out a plan without giving them some authority to question and revise the plan means that you lose a vital source of experiential wisdom. In many businesses a handful of people are designated as the creatives. The worker bees are supposed to implement the plan without too much discretion. As a result, all the wisdom that arises from *doing* is lost.

Of course, many know this and have devised ways to capture the knowledge that arises from moving an idea into action. For this reason, many companies now call on clients not only with a sales representative, but with someone from research and development, engineering, production, etc. A multidisciplinary team is more effective at seeing the real-life consequences.

Ultimately, the knowledge that is contained in doing is the heart of a learning organization. Great Harvest Bread Company is a franchise on paper, but it's a living university in practice.[17] Each of the twenty-four franchised stores uses the same recipes and standards, but every store is free to try out its own ideas about how to connect with customers and the community. This, in and of itself, is unusual within a business form that tends to make uniformity a religion.

Great Harvest has built a network of exchange that allows ideas to be freely swapped. A well-used Web site allows people to pose questions, share ideas and track the progress of new ventures. The twenty-four stores are really a learning community. They share at a level that has allowed them to begin to shape the future of the larger company.

- There is space to offer their real views about how the business is going. Sharing dissatisfaction is not taboo. This means people do not feel alone in their problems. It is the first step in problem solving. A communication space that does not allow for voicing concerns is not a true communication space.
- The home office is not supposed to be the brain of the organization; this leads to local experimentation and mutual evaluation.
- When something works, it is shared. Good ideas spread. Replication is validation. Less relevant ideas whither on the vine. The parent office does not have to play referee or act as official voice of what will be allowed.
- The parent office sets minimal agreements and then allows the collective spirit to find its way.
- Because this spirit of experimentation and distributed responsibility has been cultured over the course of years, the group has gotten smarter. They use their dialogue more productively and have learned *how to learn* from each other.

Great Harvest also offers an interesting window on the future of franchising. Franchising is one of the fastest-growing business forms in the U.S. and is poised to explode internationally. It is a curious mix of ownership and corporate control, with the small-business owner having most of the risks of ownership, yet few of the benefits. Franchisees have many obligations, such as kicking in for advertising and buying product from the central organization. They must pay yearly fees in addition to a share of their profits. Yet, they have few privileges and little say in how the larger business is run. Most often, they can't even sell their businesses without approval from above.

But it doesn't have to be this way, and it is a form that is not really suited to the new turbulent, customer-focused landscape. Interestingly, when Michael Jordan helped bring the first Starbucks into Harlem, for the first time in its history, Starbucks adapted its menu and music selections to the local neighborhood. Franchising could be a business form that offers both the advantages of name recognition and successful business formula as well as all the advantages of a learning community that amplifies the expertise of its local representatives. All franchises have to do is allow their representatives to be independent thinkers as well as obedient followers. With Visa, Dee Hock *invented* an organizational form that had never existed before. A lot of industries will be faced with inventing organizational models that never existed before if they want to capture the knowledge that is revealed by doing.

This is yet another line that must be crossed. Unless people have some freedom to act on their conversations, then true dialogue does not really exist. If a leader and follower are compelled to act in a particular way because of a contractual arrangement or because they are coerced into the exchange, then leading is not really happening. True leading exists only when people have choices. They come along because they want to and that makes all the difference in the world.

"A true leader cannot be bound to lead.
A true follower cannot be bound to follow.
Where behavior is compelled, there lies tyranny however benign.
Where behavior is induced, there lies leadership, however powerful."

DEE HOCK [18]

A great metaphor for the guidance that naturally occurs in distributed systems comes from the analysis of flock behavior in birds. A flock of birds maintains a tight flying formation over the course of many miles, yet no one bird is in charge. In fact, the lead bird may tire and move to the back, while another moves into the head position. Birds are able to flock because of small, consistent agreements between all the members. Leading is distributed.[19]

These agreements are so clear that programmers have been able to replicate computer-generated flocks that look just like real birds and yet are based on a series of mathematical agreements such as, *don't come closer than one foot* and *don't go farther away than three feet.* Guidance in distributed, adaptive learning organizations depends on small adjustments based on core values. Organizational flocking agreements might consist of rules like: *Don't move ahead unless others are with you, but if everyone is going in the same direction then someone must offer a contrary view.* Or perhaps: *No one should make really big decisions unless all voices are heard, but everyone should be able to make some decisions without having to ask anyone.*

4.7 AWAKENING THE FIELD

A nonprofit group I was working with was hopelessly mired in conflict. Months of conflict resolution techniques had made little impact. In desperation someone suggested that we *circle.*

This meant we would place our chairs in a circle and one person would speak until he or she was finished. Then the next person would take a turn, and so on. The only rule was you couldn't speak again until the entire circle had spoken and it had come back around to you. No one could stop a person who rambled on. No one could offer a brilliant analysis midway through the sharing. You couldn't even correct someone who had misinterpreted what you said. You just had to wait. The first hour was extremely painful for me. It tested the very boundaries of my patience.

Almost imperceptibly at first, the tension seemed to ease from the group. The people I had considered most irritating began to get a little more interesting. The people that I had judged to be seriously undermining the group process seemed to get a bit smarter. As the circling continued, much to my amazement, the conversation actually began to become quite interesting and vital.

It's fairly easy for me to talk in groups, probably because I am so opinionated and quick to form conclusions. Through this process, I began to see the value in not being able to share for long stretches. I began learning how much value there was in not saying something even when I thought my insight was particularly profound. I began sensing a deeper group wisdom that reached beyond any single person's input.

For almost four hours this group of fifteen or so people went round and round, stopping only briefly for short breaks. By the end, there was significant healing and insight. And no one had performed an elegant intervention; the solutions came from within the group.

Circling is the primary tool for problem solving in all indigenous cultures. The elders would form a circle and slowly consider a problem. They'd circle and circle. No one could dominate. The evolution of the group's understanding had to travel through the circle or it would not hold.

Many meetings begin with everyone having a position. Then there is a jockeying for influence and political territory. Then the meeting ends with everyone more solidly in their respective positions and aligned with the people who will serve their ends. Circling is such a powerful, and yet simple tool for dissolving much of the conditioned power play that passes for dialogue. Since that time I have used circling frequently for problem solving. It is particularly useful when some people or some views are consistently being ignored.

Back in the sixties, an organization in England was studying group behavior. Its strategy was elegant. Business leaders would arrive for a high-priced seminar lasting a weekend or more. At the first session a notice would be placed in the front of the room:

The task of this group is to observe itself. You have [x amount of time] to complete this task. The following people [short list of names] are consultants and available to assist you in this task.

That's it. That was the sum total of direction that was offered.

The so-called consultants would be dressed in black and would have the extraordinary ability to stay poker-faced no matter what was going on with the group. The group soon learned that these consultants would speak at rare moments and at best would offer cryptic comments like, "This group is covertly trying to create a leader." Or, "The ease the group is now feeling is really a form of denial." Depending on the mood of the group, they might use the comment constructively, rebel or just ignore it.

In this experience, participants no longer had identified roles or predetermined statuses. People wouldn't listen to you just because you were some important figure; in fact, they might not even know what you did. It was impossible to force the group to follow your direction for very long. Participants discovered that the only thing that worked was authenticity. The group develops a capacity to smell out any hidden agenda. Like a wild animal on the hunt, it would respond instantly to the faintest scent of control and rebel instantly. It is a fascinating process that shows people what true natural leadership looks like. It rapidly shows the veneers of civility and power we all use to cover or promote our underlying feelings. Although we love this process, we use it rarely, because the feelings it provokes are often so raw.

Once we were facilitating a team building session. We announced that for one hour we would do a Quaker meeting. One person actually said, "Oh, I've worked at Quaker Oats; their meetings aren't that interesting." Of course, the Quaker we were referring to is the religious group that holds its leaderless services without the role of a minister. Each member of the congregation stands up and speaks only when moved. In the interim, there may be long stretches of silence. It is yet another form of group process that gets to the kind of insights that are triggered in circling.

Any team that is truly committed to touching new levels of exchange must from time to time break up the traditional forms in which it communicates. We have all become so focused on staying on task, that we rarely allow space for people to drop their formal roles and habitual positions. Most books or courses on running a good meeting offer numerous strategies for stamping out the dreaded *tangents and off-task remarks*. I'm not saying a focused meeting isn't valuable, but if you really want depth you also have to allow time for *Blue Sky Meetings* (as a friend of ours calls them).

4.8 COYOTE BUSINESS

All the animals in the world got together and looked around.
They said, *"This world is a mess. Let's get rid of it and start over."*
The coyote says, *"Oh, I don't know. It's not such a big world.*
Let's clean it up."
NATIVE AMERICAN STORY

In Native American lore, the coyote is the trickster. It is the part of our psyche that turns things around in unexpected ways and creates unexpectedly large impacts. A few chapters ago, I shared the most depressing story I had come across in all my research. Now I'd like to tell the most inspiring one.

It was told by Paul Hawken, Amory Lovins and L. Hunter Lovins in their book, *Natural Capitalism*.[20] As you read along after each description, imagine twenty more equally interesting and brilliant solutions within that topic area that I did not take the space to describe.

Curitiba, Brazil, has a population the size of Houston, rapid rates of growth and, like many South American cities, 42 percent of the population is under the age of eighteen. Most Brazilian cities facing the same set of challenges have become centers of poverty, squalor, disease, illiteracy, congestion, pollution, corruption and despair. Curitiba has achieved just the opposite.

In 1971, Brazil was still under military dictatorship. The governor of the state was looking for someone politically nonthreatening to appoint as mayor of the town. He chose a mild-mannered thirty-three-year-old architect named Jaime Lerner, whom the authors describe as: "Informal, energetic and intensely practical, with the soul of a poet." But Jaime Lerner turned out to be a surprise. He served three terms as the most popular mayor in Brazilian history, has twice been elected governor of the state and has been spoken of as a plausible candidate for president of Brazil. Six mayors who have served after Lerner, although politically diverse, have respectively advanced his ideas while adding their own stamps.

Lerner merely wanted to restore the vibrancy and the diversity of the street life he enjoyed as a child. He had served as the president of the Curitiba Research and Urban Planning Institute and saw the city as a living laboratory to test the institute's ideas of a people-centered city. As you will soon discover, Jaime Lerner was definitely a coyote.

Inspired by Lerner's vision, the city began by addressing the overall city plan. Heretically, they chose to save almost all existing buildings, the ones with exquisite old architecture that most modern cities have lost. They established a series of interlinked radial streets and three parallel boulevards. These corridors shaped the evolution of the city, with mixed-income residences clustered around these central areas. They became the backbone of healthy neighborhoods, and thriving diversity.

Curitiba's transportation system has been called the best in the world, carrying twenty-thousand bus passengers an hour, about as much as a subway, but at a cost one hundred times less. Bus stations are designed around tubes that are fully wheelchair accessible and dramatically efficient at moving people on and off the buses. The system is completely self-financing from fares only. As a result, although Curitiba has one of the highest rates of auto ownership in Brazil—one car for every 2.6 people—there are no traffic problems. It has the lowest rates of driving in all of Brazil and the cleanest air.

The same efficiencies and stellar results describe almost all city services. Everything is recycled. A Garbage Purchase Program allows those in poor areas to make money collecting trash. A Green Exchange allows them to exchange bags of trash for food. Landfill has been reduced by one sixth.

The city protects seven square miles of parks, nine forests, a botanical garden, five environmental gardens, two environmentally protected areas totaling five miles along the river, 282 town squares, 259 pocket gardens and one thousand privately registered woodlands. You can't cut down a tree without city permission, and you must always plant two in its place. Everywhere your eye falls, there is green. Further, the Department of Health offers instruction in growing medicinal plants at home. A Community Orchards program supports people in growing food for their own use. And when adolescent kids get in trouble, involving them in gardening programs is often the treatment of choice.

Before developers could move in, the city bought sixteen square miles for its Industrial City. It used the same standards employed throughout the city: affordable housing, mixed use, neighborhood gathering places and ample green space. The city then recruited five hundred nonpolluting industries, which provide 20 percent of the total jobs.

The city built a cultural foundation, a publications center, a creativity center for children who make handicrafts for the tourist industry and a University of the Environment. Free universities for adults are run after-hours in every public school across the city and the classes are full. A forty-page directory of mostly free cultural events is published every month and distributed throughout the city.

Curitiba has the highest literacy rate in Brazil, 94 percent, and the lowest first grade failure rate. Environmental education begins in early childhood. Two hundred day care centers have eleven-hour days and are free for low-income families. Vouchers give companies tax waivers for sponsoring day care positions.

Sniffing glue is a huge problem among poor kids in South America. Curitiba addressed this problem by working directly with the largest glue manufacturer to add a foul smelling substance to all its glue, making it unsniffable. The city has sixty-four dropout centers dealing with problem kids and only a few hundred street children who are all registered and well known to local social workers. A call-in system handles thousands of calls a day, from people in need to reports of bandit tree cutting. Every call receives a response.

Obligatory free check-ups are offered to every child under the age of five and the results are recorded in their personal health book. Health programs have cut infant mortality by one-fifth in four years. Prevention is stressed throughout the public education system and eighty-eight health stations throughout the city distribute forty allopathic and traditional medicines for free.

As a result of all this there are: 96 percent basic vaccinations, 99.5 households with water and electricity, 83 percent of the people have a high school education and 75 percent of homes are owner occupied. The city has one-third of the national poverty rate, twenty theaters, thirty public libraries, seventy-four museums and cultural buildings, and 86 percent of the population receive weekly newspaper circulation.

The city government is mostly staffed by architects focused on solving problems, rather than typical bureaucrat types. Interestingly, these municipal departments are often headed by women. If there isn't a budget to launch a new program, something, however small, is started anyway, *so learning can begin as soon as possible.* The local government is an innovation machine. It launches recycling programs in days, new education program in weeks. Lerner says, "Credit cards give us goods quickly, the fax machine gives us the message quickly—the only thing left in the stone age is central government."

Let me share just a few more of my favorite nuggets. Graffiti is almost nonexistent. The residents do have a reputation for politely taping poems to utility poles. All the large bus terminals have what are called "Citizenship Streets." These corridors are lined with large, constantly updated bulletin boards that bring daily news from city hall directly to its constituents. The government is accountable, honest and transparent. Anyone who strays from these principles would be promptly skewered by the wags of the Boca Maldita, a picturesque public mall specifically dedicated to public grousing.

Remember, in every category just covered there are dozens more amazing solutions. When I first read the story it sounded like a fairy tale. It has been called one of the world's greatest cities. Over 99 percent of the residents say they wouldn't want to live anywhere else.

The results speak for themselves. But what is most magical to me about the story of Curitiba is the incredible creativity and aliveness that is unleashed for all its people. It is not just a city; it is a living, breathing web of creativity and humanity.

There are many ways to talk about Jaime Lerner. He was a great leader. He was a visionary. He was a good listener. He was a problem solver and a poetic soul. He certainly practiced coyote magic. And he exemplifies all the points we have just talked about:

- He looked through eyes that could see beneath the obvious and uncover deeper patterns.
- He realized that everyone is hardwired to sense energy and would instantly sense and respond to a new feeling in the city.

- He used small behaviors to target the whole. He understood that every small event revealed volumes about the big picture; therefore care was taken to make every discrete service reflect the larger vision.
- He was driven by core principles that never wavered.
- Principles were immediately and continuously translated into concrete actions that could refocus behavior.
- Small risks were taken consistently, in order to build larger impacts.
- He distributed intelligence throughout the system, so whoever had eyes to see could offer solutions.
- He awakened the field through active and continuous participation by all the people. *Circling* happened throughout the system; all voices were heard and all requests led to responses.

I wanted to tell this story for many reasons. In these times, when social problems sometimes seem insurmountable, it offers hope. It also shows how much one person can do, when he or she creates a space for others to come forward as well. It shows very vividly that the only way to solve problems is through a systems approach. There was not one solution. Solutions were everywhere, generated continuously. And each solution fed into the next. Everyone was empowered to solve problems. The system belonged to everyone.

One of the more interesting features of the new economy is that it has thrust all of us into a world of intangibles. You are not your organizational chart, your business plan or even the projects you are pursuing. You are not even the internalized series of goals, visions and dreams. In fact, your own body is not even solid. Fields of information continually wash through you to create the illusion of a stable persona. Once you allow this invisible, intangible world to emerge, your perspective on everything changes. But, here's the clincher:

Once you take a small step toward trusting your intuition, or viewing a project more holistically, you have fallen over the cliff into a new worldview. Those invisible lines of force will carry into a far deeper connection with the world. If you begin following the songlines, you will begin following the lines of energy that connect each and every one of us to a sacred contract with the land upon which we walk.

In ancient China you paid your doctor only when you were healthy. If you were sick, service was on his dime. Imagine that! Suppose you only paid for your computer when it worked without bugs. You paid consultants only when business improved. You only paid for your car as long as transport was error free, gas mileage was good and the ride was comfortable. You paid taxes only in proportion to the government's effectiveness in delivering worthwhile service.

Well, believe it or not, some companies have started to do this[21]:

- Carrier no longer sells air-conditioning equipment, although it is the largest provider in the world of such products. It now offers *comfort leases*. These leases give you good air, at the right temperature and you don't worry about a thing. As a result of this redefinition, Carrier has begun to offer lighting retrofits, install super-insulating windows and generally upgrade facilities so that they need less air-conditioning, yet can provide more comfort. Carrier has introduced highly ecological practices, because they save the company money.
- Ten million buildings in metropolitan France are served by heating companies called chauffagistes. You contract for a certain temperature range during certain hours at a certain cost. How that happens is up to them. They can convert your furnace, implement greater efficiency or even insulate your building. The less energy you use, the more money they make.
- The Swedish company Electrolux provides its customers with a guarantee of quality and reliability for its floor cleaning equipment, medical refrigeration and vending machines. Services are billed

monthly as long as the customer wants them, but they are never bound to the term of a lease or a period of ownership. Electrolux gains a competitive advantage because it focuses on providing better equipment, ensuring optimal maintenance, controlling costs and sharing a diverse fleet of equipment over many users.

At first these may seem like great marketing hooks. In practice, they lead to highly efficient, ecological attitudes. Each of the companies in question make the most money from right sizing, not selling you more than you need in order to make a profit or pushing some less effective model just to get rid of it. ***They make the most money for taking a wide, long, deep view.***

A company based on moving product makes the most money from selling the biggest thing as fast as possible. It profits from obsolescence. Its entire marketing strategy is built to make you feel that you need the next new thing. Despite talks of customer service, it can't afford to let you be so satisfied that you stay out of the market for very long. Most companies encourage you to consume constantly.

For Carrier, the biggest profits are realized when you buy the least. If it can give you a product that will last a really long time with excellent results, it makes the most money. It is a low-consumption model. Further, in this model any glitches or training costs are on Carrier's dime, so it thinks very differently about what you really need. If you think about it, you'll realize how many industries could be restructured along the lines of Carrier's model.

Companies operating from the high-consumption model tend to look at very narrow perspectives. If they can super-specialize and know something that you don't, then they will have the most power. This breeds closed-mindedness and a narrow frame of reference. It leads to sales representatives and consultants who speak in ways you can't understand in the hopes that you will give up your power to their expert opinion.

The beauty of metaphorically paying your doctor only when you are healthy is that it encourages open-mindedness, connectivity and a systems view. In ancient China, if someone was polluting the local village well, you can be sure the local doctor would be on the forefront of leading the resistance. His economic well-being is on the line. Further, he will not be afraid of entertaining psychological factors or considering folk-healing methods because his future depends on your well-being; he'll do whatever it takes. Everything matters. Similarly, Carrier, the French chauffagistes and Electrolux are motivated to consider as many contributing factors as they can. They strive for efficiency, less waste and will consider any avenue that seems to contribute to the health of their services. This breeds sensitivity to new ideas.

Paul Hawken, of Smith & Hawken fame and Amory and L. Hunter Lovins of the Rocky Mountain Institute have introduced an extraordinary model for the future of business. On the surface, it looks like getting more green is cost-effective, great for employee morale, heightens creativity, leads to new products, improves customer relations, etc. But once again, something far deeper is at work.[22]

- Lockheed Martin installed mechanisms for delivering natural daylight to conserve energy. It expected to recoup its investment in four years. Rather unexpectedly, there was a 15 percent drop in absenteeism and 15 percent gain in productivity. Lockheed's new lower overhead gave it the edge in a tough contract competition. This unexpected contract immediately paid for the whole building.
- A lighting retrofit was installed in the main mail-sorting facility in Reno for the purpose of saving energy. Unexpectedly, the new lighting also allowed workers to see better and reduced distractions and fatiguing noise. Productivity shot up, making this the best-performing facility in the West.
- Wal-Mart's experimental store in Lawrence, Kansas, installed a novel daylighting system in one half of the store and a fluorescent system in the other half. Cash registers were wired to detect differences and clearly

showed higher sales on the daylit side of the store. Workers preferred it too, so Wal-Mart is experimenting with this system in other stores.

These results are not unusual. Good working conditions such as daylight and the right temperature normally increase productivity from six to fifteen percent. Yet the typical business pays almost no attention to this. If corporate consultants could make this claim, *guaranteeing* an increase in productivity by six to fifteen percent, they would have all the business they ever wanted. They would be front-page news.

The authors ground their thesis in models drawn from indigenous cultures. When you assume resources are cheap, you tend to throw lots of money at a problem. You can afford to address one issue at a time. Native people can't afford this; they need to be thrifty. Every action must serve many purposes. Efficiency and low waste are hallmarks of the tribal way. Native people know resources are not cheap and therefore must be used with great wisdom to address multiple needs.

My own personal value system certainly leans in the direction proposed by Hawken and the Lovinses of greater corporate responsibility, ecological business practices and the need to consider multiple bottom lines. I highly encourage reading their book just for the number of constructive ideas it may trigger. I am definitely biased. *But although the efforts described above may have ethical, value-laden meanings, from what I can tell this direction also just makes good sense.*

It makes for a bigger world and thus adds depth to every problem you consider. With a bigger horizon and an expanded system, you also get a bigger toolbox. If you truly care about a learning organization, how can you construct a larger future if you continually leave out huge pieces of the puzzle? A systems view begins with how you think about yourself, your relationship to others and your place within a group. But once you start to build a systems view, suddenly there are no longer any walls. Social responsibility and ecological practices are the natural by-products of including more and more factors into your understanding of the whole.

Of course, this was the essence of the aboriginal worldview. It is impossible to fence off a small area and think that you have in some way separated one scrap of land from everything that surrounds it. In fact, for indigenous cultures the process of connecting with the land, nature and each other is the source of well-being.

Our mechanistic worldviews are collapsing. Infocentric worldviews that cause us to measure everything are having a difficult time staying relevant. There is a fundamental connection between accepting that you can access information in nonlinear ways and recognizing that an organization is inseparable from the quality of its relationships. When you learn to see with new eyes, then every action has impact throughout the system. You can't say, "We value collaboration and teamwork," and then perpetuate a behavior that, in fact, does not allow for collaboration. A principle you care about must be perpetuated everywhere or its true value is lost. This is the only path to authenticity.

Ultimately, once you begin to think and operate in terms of interconnected systems, you can't stop at any edge. You have to consider your relationship to the surrounding community and the land upon which you stand. It's just a natural result of following the songlines. First you ride your own songlines—the lines of energy that expand your own perception. Then you ride the songlines and begin considering the social, implicit side of the business equation. And before you know it, you've followed those very same lines of force into a far bigger arena.

In the native American tradition, Spider Woman is the creator of the world. She is also the big honcho storyteller. Her myths are the threads that hold our current reality in place.

But Spider Woman is also rumored to be a very reclusive sort. She rarely shows her face. Entire generations can come and go and she is nowhere to be seen.

In fact, she is so reticent, she emerges only at the end and beginning of new worlds.

She makes herself known when it is time for the old stories to be unraveled and new ones put in place. Legend says that whenever she does appear, look out! It's a sure sign that some big myths are unraveling and some giant, new, unexpected myths are about to come forth.

It doesn't take a genius to see that spider imagery is everywhere you turn in the digital world. We are told to build our web, make our businesses act like a spider and weave our networks. If the legend is true and Spider Woman is in fact showing her face, then you can be sure the really, really big mythmaking has only just begun.

CONCLUSION: WHEN THE SNAKE BITES ITS TAIL

The ancient symbol for the earth was a mythical snake biting its tail. Some called this snake Ourobourus.

A circle consuming itself implies that the future and the past have a common destiny. It suggests that the potential of one cannot be realized without the other.

This symbol foretold a time when that which was most new would turn back to its primordial roots. It prophesied a time when the most cutting-edge ideas would once again reflect the most ancient ways of knowing. The future would turn on the most ancient past and devour all that it had once been, in order to make it new once again.

So we gather around the warm embers of the flickering screen, trying to make sense of it all. When you are over the shock of this rude invasion of your comfortable life, the stress of all this change may actually take on a tinge of excitement. When you have peeled away a few layers of resistance, you will discover that the digital universe restores a sensory experience that, despite its high-tech trappings, is actually far closer to the world where our ancestors lived. Electronic information opens the door to our journey back, into a world where power lives everywhere. Intangible forces rule. Intimacy matters.

The first cognitive map we offered, *Who Owns the Wind,* showed that ownership as we have known it for tens of thousands of years has begun to break down. New avenues for peer-to-peer computing threaten our current channels of artistic distribution. The open-source movement is driven by designers who offer their software for free. Similarly, the developing capacity for distributed computing begins to further break down the need for sole proprietorship. The ease with which companies can blend their borders or outsource their business functions or build convergent products and services feed into an image of a far more fluid economic landscape.

We are also witnessing *The Return of the Storytellers.* The barrage of data that characterized the information age has caused the average person to withdraw, ignore and filter out much of what appears before them. The information era is being deconstructed and in its place is the rise of what we have called the experience economy. Almost every product and service must be reformulated as a relevant imaginary event that involves the participant. Traditional advertising will collapse in the face of real-life retailing and the desire of customers to play a part in everything they touch. In this new environment the ones who will win are those with the best multidimensional stories. Because digital artistry is now in the hands of the average person, creativity is becoming a planetary event.

We have become insatiable telepaths, needing to hear the constant buzz of the voice of the other in our own mind or we feel lonely. We sit by the tribal fire, clustered around our screens, sharing tales, enlisting partners in our petitions, forwarding our jokes. We freely network our intelligence, no longer caring quite so much if we get the credit for our bright ideas. Customers are organizing into consumer gangs with a newfound ability to direct markets. Many workers are fleeing to the creative fulfillment offered by Free Agent Nation. Others have learned to be workers without walls even within the confines of the corporate space. Thus the quality of the dialogue we are able to forge with both customers and employees is directly related to the innovation we are able to access. In this new erea, relationships are products. We are entering the realm of *Tribalmind,* that illusive field of intelligence that can be created only through interaction and is beyond the mind of any single individual.

The ancient songlines are once again being reconstructed along the threads of fiber-optics and wireless connections, and we discover that we must learn to think in similar ways. Our formerly fixed opinions collapse, not because of some deep philosophical transformation, but just so we can keep up. We run on instinct, because we can never absorb all the data necessary to form a response. We are freed to make irrational choices with fewer questions asked. No one has time to hear our justifications anyway, so we can drop the position statements. Those whom we answer to are just as crazed as we are. They are also working on hunches, so they are not about to challenge *your* sources. It is even fashionable to believe that experience and theories blind us from detecting the subtle clues about what lies ahead. We learn to speak in short, punchy sound bites. It is considered poor etiquette to write a long introspective e-mail. So we drop the analysis and just do it. We are strangely out of control, but then again so is everyone else. Chaos is once again driving our personal and collective future and we are learning to *Ride the Songlines.*

A unique convergence of economic and social factors has begun to break down the familiar order of our world. For the first time in tens of thousands of years, the cultural landscape is finally fluid enough for ancient ways of knowing to reemerge. ***An ancient hero with a thousand different faces is once again poking his wily, curious head into the realm of ordinary life.***

Being digital requires a perceptual transition very similar to the one that allowed the aborigines to see past the obvious features of their landscape and uncover the songlines of energy lurking beneath. The new economy requires seeing past the world of fixed appearances into a domain defined by imagination. It requires sensing the rivers of change that underlie our seemingly stable economic structures. It is a world driven by intangible values far more than by hard assets. Strategic plans have given way to unjustifiable leaps of faith. As a result, these primordial understandings of reality are reawakening and merging with the new freedoms forged by a super-accelerated economy into a rare blend of understandings we have called *Digital Aboriginal*.

The distinction between old and new economies has all but evaporated. *It's all new.* But it is far more than e-commerce, information technology and all the associated infrastructure and support systems that go with it. The new economy is all the freedom and varieties of creativity that are now possible. It is a way of being. Imagination is a daily ritual. It is business even faster than the speed of thought. It is the ever-approaching horizon of the new, new thing. It is a style of making things happen that no longer requires linear progression. We all get to skip steps. We all get to make quantum leaps.

The reason it is valuable to equate the digital psyche with the aboriginal mind is that both rest on understanding a similar dynamic, chaotic space. Since they were there first, the aborigines forged a lot of great behavioral solutions for coping with indeterminacy. Discovering how they were able to cope with an intangible reality can save us all a lot of time. We don't have to reinvent the behavioral wheel.

THE IDENTITY CRISIS

Here rests the heart of our resistance. Every new communication medium touches the user, tactilely shaping him or her into something new.

All technology is an extension of the human body. Get behind the wheel of a fast sports car and it doesn't matter if you are a bit out of shape. The moment you put your foot on the gas, you are transformed. You feel like a gazelle or a wild horse, the wind whistling through your flowing mane. Thus, the car becomes an extension of your foot, freeing all your senses to expand into your newfound speed. Or look through a telescope and suddenly your vision is superhuman, encompassing faroff galaxies. Look through a microscope and magically you can see patterns that are invisible to the naked eye.

It's fair to assume that the computer extends our brain. But what does the World Wide Web expand? It is surely an extension of our nervous system. It certainly stretches our senses. We can instantly tap into almost anything we might want to know. It definitely expands our social life. Our voices get louder as our documents gain the ability to span the entire globe. And with some increased bandwidth, we approach the ability to transport real-life events anywhere. We have stumbled upon the once-rare sensations of omnipotence and omnipresence.

In fact, we experience an extension of our sense of self. *Now wait just a minute.* Feeling like we have the speed of a wild animal or seeming to gain supernatural vision—that we can accept, even enjoy. But mess with this sense of self, the very boundaries of where I begin and end, and we are on dangerous turf. That's where the rubber meets the road.

We know we must adapt, but no one really wants to change. We know we are supposed to work collaboratively, but often we are curiously distant and removed from each other. We have been told it will build our emotional I.Q. if we bond with our team, but when the task is done, we often feel more alone and isolated than ever. We know we are supposed to be more innovative, yet sometimes this seems like a ploy to get us to run even faster. We know we are supposed to follow our passions, but often we just can't find anything that stirs those juices.

A strange restlessness is sweeping the land. Divine discontent— that provocative inner voice that says, "Is this all there is?"—seems to be so very much louder these days.

- Sometimes it takes the form of a blinding ambition that can be satisfied only by becoming a player on the edge, where new worlds are being born.

- Others are addicted to their own adrenaline—desperately afraid to stop, because the emptiness they have avoided for so very long may have finally become too huge to face.
- Sometimes it takes the form of frustration, the feeling that what you are doing just doesn't connect anymore and the most you can hope for is to carve out some small islands of meaning in a larger sea of futility.
- Others have given up, assuming the river of change has already passed them by and they are forever destined to merely go through the motions. Their only hope is that a lottery ticket or the right stock pick might free them from the desperation and powerlessness that lurks beneath the surface of their daily lives.

Whatever your personal variation of this restlessness may be, I'd like to suggest that part of the emptiness you may feel is a longing for a part of your being that was left behind many, many thousands of years ago.

"The discovery of the alphabet will create forgetfulness
in the learners' souls, because they will not use their memories;
they will trust to the external written characters and not
remember of themselves."

SOCRATES, *PHAEDRUS*

"Electronic circuitry is orientalizing the West. The contained, the
distinct, the separate—our Western legacy—are being replaced by
the flowing, the unified, the fused."

MARSHALL MCLUHAN AND QUENTIN FIORE[1]

"Cyberspace will shape humanity's consciousness like a magnet
shapes a pile of iron filings."

JEFF ZALESKI[2]

Culture precedes commerce. The transformation of the self precedes culture. It is not so much that cyberspace is changing us. Humanity has created cyberspace to express that which could come forward in no other way. Ultimately, the transformation of commerce rests on the unfoldment of the self.

Violence is a strong image for the change that now confronts us. Yet it is accurate. Unless an identity quest impacts us at that level, then lasting change is rarely realized. An identity quest requires that our familiar ways of being in the world begin to shatter. These are the chasms we must learn to cross.

- We hunger for a connection to our senses so that we can feel again.
- We search for an experience of ourselves that is not shattered into a million different roles that we play and people we need to please.
- We strive to feel our instinct and gain the courage to become bold again.
- We yearn for immediacy, so that we are no longer disconnected from our responses by an endless stream of analysis and opinions.
- We long for a tribe, so that we no longer have to seek out new landscapes without others to celebrate our discovery.
- We crave collaboration, mostly because we are tired of hearing only our own thoughts.
- We are starved for the feeling of generosity, so that we may once again have the desire to give.

We have become so very bored with ourselves that we are even willing to try on new understandings of how we define human potential. More than technology, it is these very natural and primordial hungers that are really changing the face of our world.

It is these longings that are reworking the shape of business from head to toe. They are revitalizing concerns about quality of life. They are driving us to seek out the corporate truth. Those whispering voices that urge us to begin listening again have now emerged into full-blown leadership models. Demands for innovation challenge us to truly pay attention to those around us; mindless role-playing no longer cuts it. Indulge in a moment of inauthenticity and the e-mails fly. A learning organization is a company that is changed by what happens around it. The good company is one where many bottom lines are fed and participation in the real world is restored. Many images for a fast company and the even faster entrepreneur rest on a return to a more diffuse, subtle world without boundaries and the kinds of unusual perceptions that arise from this stance.

THE CIRCLE'S PROMISE

It is said that when the snake bites its tail, a new way of knowing will be ushered in that encompasses and surpasses both that which is most ancient and that which is most new. It is said that when the snake bites its tail, a new world will be born.

With the emergence of the global village, we are returning to the fluidity and connectivity of our origins. We have taken a forty-thousand-year journey from our collective roots and tribal ways of being to a form of hyperindividuality, where every man is out for himself. But this cycle is reaching its nadir. The values of connectivity are returning. A neotribalism is emerging. A digital mysticism is forming. The depth, freedom and connectivity of the aboriginal mind are exactly what the knowledge economy requires.

Everything is falling into the present moment. Day trading. Instant mirrors. Immediate response. Constant feedback. Information on anything. Everything available. Twenty-four/seven. No attention span. Broad bandwidth. Instant gratification. Just-on-time delivery. Capital when you need it. Intimacy on demand. Everything needed yesterday. The speed of the market has become the speed of our own psyche.

As a result, speed will no longer be just a measure of time. It will no longer be a sensation of rapid pace. It will no longer be a measure of how fast you change. Rather, we will think of speed as a quickening of consciousness and the grounds for a new creativity. Acceleration will become a state of consciousness that paradoxically allows us to feel like we have slowed down yet makes us able to experience more in every present moment.

We are not turning back the clock; we are rediscovering our primordial roots in a far different way. We have an economic opportunity to bring these ancient mind-sets to an entirely new level of self-expression and social impact. The elders of almost any tribe tell us that the farther we go into the past, the farther we can see into the future. The more we mine the primal depths of human consciousness the more we can sense of what lies ahead. *We will all have to become more aboriginal in order to fully understand the potential that is contained in being digital.*

I firmly believe that we are entering the creative moment that was prophesied. We are witnessing a reemergence into Dreamtime, a place of pure potentiality. A million, million versions of creative variation are now possible, and viable and calling us. We are no longer doing business; we are doing creativity.

A great TV commercial for Agilent Technologies proudly proclaims that its lightning-fast technical solutions are possible because of *bubbles*. In the next scene you see huge, massive translucent bubbles floating through its office. Spaced-out workers sit at computers, gazing lovingly at the floating orbs passing by. Agilent's employees seem to adore the buoyant bounding bubbles.

Not many old-line companies would deliberately want to project such an ethereal image, yet the new-liners want to be viewed as artists of the abstract, masters of the invisible, travelers in worlds beyond ordinary vision. The new economy is based on floating wisps of concepts and bits, and bold new players who are free to announce their new attitudes.

We barely sell products anymore because information has defined how everything is exchanged. It puts almost every industry in the position of marketing its knowledge as much as its goods and services. And soon we will no longer be delivering knowledge; we will be marketing imaginary experiences. Again, business will cope by becoming even more ephemeral. In the same way that information has devoured products, experience will devour information, as commerce succumbs to ever more intangible influences and abstractions of how goods and services are defined.

Precisely because this new economy is so fluid, it more quickly and accurately reflects the human spirit. Rarely factored into the economic equations of the future are the evolution of personal intelligence and the transformation of the individual psyche. They are compelling forces, rarely discussed. *Ideas and imagination now drive this intangible economy, so it is far easier for the artistic and mystical dimensions of the human spirit to find their way in.*

The subtle, flowing, even bubbly nature of the new economy is perfectly suited to unfolding dimensions of pure consciousness. Our imagination will continue to soar in ever-new directions, not just because they are profitable, but merely because they look interesting. The human spirit has always driven social change. It is now just more obvious and rapid, because an information-based economy is so incredibly responsive to the flights and fancies of the human spirit.

The soul of the new economy will not necessarily rest on who makes the most dot-com millions, although that is often where change begins. I hope we have peeled back the covers on this incredible financial story to reveal a series of deeper trends that underlie this massive flow of money.

The real soul of this new era will arise from events that powerfully redesign our social landscape and the new personal freedoms that are triggered as a result. The soul of the new economy will emerge when we discover that corporations as we now think of them are often mirages; little is left except the meanings we are still willing to store there. The soul of this new economic paradigm will decentralize all forms of power until an equality is restored that has not been seen in recent history. It is in these kinds of social and personal impacts that the true power of this economic transformation will ultimately rest. *Revolutionary behavior* will become more central to the new economy than revolutionary technology. At that point you had better come to terms with your identity crisis.

When I look out on the vast and still-forming digital landscape, I see directions that are whimsical, mystical and just plain beautiful. We are witnessing an extraordinary interplay between information and imagination, between the rules of work and the pure play of the human psyche, between the sprit of commerce and the hand of the artist. These creative tensions will be impossible to stop!

The new economy is:

- *Nomadic*—Anything goes, because there are fewer fixed events and stable territories.
- *Imagination-driven*—It is fueled by our ability to tell great stories and drive new myths.
- *Collaborative*—It is driven by relationship and deep surrendered dialogue.
- *Discontinuous*—It moves by unpredictable leaps and bounds.
- *Learning*—It is shaped by the ability to absorb new directions and redefine how one knows one's self.

And yes, it is also a more mystical economy, structured by the evolution of consciousness.

A Mirror World

A powerful concept from the field of biology is called coevolution. It is a term popularized by Stewart Brand, Lynne Marguiles, Rupert Sheldrake and other systems-type thinkers. **Simply put, every organism and its surrounding environment evolve in tandem.**

The fur of an antelope is marked in patterns that echo the land where it grazes. But this is more than mere Darwinian survival—making a camouflage coat an effective strategy to avoid becoming dinner. Changes in the species trigger changes in the environment, and vice versa, until it is hard to separate the evolution of one from the evolution of the other.

Coevolution suggests that a discontinuous economy would engender more discontinuous organizations, which in turn would provoke more discontinuous talents in every individual. Then, in coevolutionary fashion, the more random creative process of the individual would echo through the organization, making it more dynamic, which would in turn become amplified in the larger environment, leading to even more turbulence. A creative spiral would be triggered, accelerating the forces of change and innovation at every level.

This is the thesis that has flowed through every single chapter.

- A nomadic economy causes organizations to become more nimble, outsourced and affiliated. The individuals who work in these organizations learn to travel more easily through its webs. In turn, as individuals gain access to greater flexibility, they will then want this freedom in their work settings, which in turn sets up a more nomadic economy.

- As marketing becomes less about persuasion and more about imagination, companies must reorganize themselves to encourage storytelling and create employees who are more interested in weaving tales. Because of our newfound ability to imagine new stories, in-house creativity and the larger spectrum of Planet Art will become one and the same, thus marketing will have to adapt.

- And yes, customers and sellers are all more tribal. And our deep human need for true intimacy is driving all this connectivity to become ever more authentic. So in turn, marketing, research and development and all forms of management will begin to rest on the quality of the dialogues we create. Innovation will rest on intimacy, which will in turn shape the direction of every new invention.

- The economy, organizations and markets are systems, channels for energy that can be perceived and followed. Our expanding sensory capacities and intuitive talents will in turn cause us to mold our organizations in new ways. As a result of this new vision the global economy will in turn become more personally relevant.

The economy is evolving in new and dramatic ways, and so are we. As individuals, we have become more nomadic, imaginative, tribal and intuitive. And you can't separate the player from the game.

It's a coevolutionary world, with every event mirroring, interacting and then changing every other event. We cannot know ourselves apart from the conditions that surround us. And we cannot fully understand the conditions that surround us—our businesses, our economy and our culture—without fully knowing ourselves.

Coevolution turns every noun into a verb, every fixed event into a process, every stable system into an unstoppable flow. Who we are and what we do become interacting fields of information that dynamically act on each other to create possibilities that have never been witnessed before. Who we are at the deepest levels of human potential and what we do in terms of shaping new economic possibilities have begun to echo and reverberate in one another.

The newest layers of the economy and the edges of the human psyche are inseparable. A new breed of digital aboriginals love the heart of business yet are tapping the depths of the human spirit, to generate new economic visions. There is little doubt the snake has begun to bite its tail.

ENDNOTES

CHAPTER 1: WHO OWNS THE WIND?

1. "Much was lost culturally when we transitioned to agriculture." Brody, Hugh. *The Other Side of Eden: Hunters, Farmers and the Shaping of the World.* New York: Farrar, Straus and Giroux, 2000. Also see Eisler, Rianne. *The Chalice and the Blade: Our History, Our Future.* San Francisco: Harper, 1988.

2. "Copyright is far more illusive in a digital world." Barlow, John Perry. "Selling Wine without Bottles." In *Clicking In: Hot Links to a Digital Culture,* edited by Lynn Leeson. Seattle: Bay Press, 1996, 148-172. For an overview of this issue from a more technical standpoint, also see Lessig, Lawrence. *Code and Other Laws of Cyberspace.* New York: Basic Books, 1999. For a review of the customer side of the equation, see Seybold, Patricia B., Ronni T. Marshak and Jeffrey M. Lewis. *The Customer Revolution.* New York: Crown, 2001.

3. "Laws can backfire." Goodwin, Mike. "Copywrong." Review of *Digital Coypright,* by Jessica Litman. *Reason* (July 2001): 57-61.

4. "Expanded bandwidth will further alter the solidity of products." Gilder, George. *Telecosm: How Infinite Bandwidth Will Revolutionize Our World.* New York: Free Press, 2000.

5. "The role of the artist will transition from static to dynamic." Fillmore, Laura. "Slaves of a New Machine." In *Internet Dreams: Archetypes, Myths, and Metaphors* by Mark Stefik. Boston: MIT Press, 1996.

6. "Art will become collage material for cocreative events with the audience." Gabriel, Peter. As quoted in *The Red Herring Guide to the Digital Universe.* New York: Warner Books, 1996, 31.

7. "When the standards of copyright are too low, intellectual progress is slowed." Berners-Lee, Tim, with Mark Fischetti. *Weaving the Web: The Original Design and Ultimate Destiny of the World Wide Web by Its Inventor.* San Francisco: Harper. 1999.

8. "The biggest shift is that digital artists will want to run the show." Drucker, Peter. "Beyond the Information Revolution." *Atlantic Monthly* (284) 4 (October 1999): 47.

9. "Open source puts an idea community face-to-face with profit-making entities." Moody, Glyn. *Rebel Code: Linux and the Open Source Movement.* New York: Perseus, 2001.

10. "Organizations can blend cooperative and competitive agendas." Hock, Dee. *Birth of a Chaordic Age.* San Francisco: Berret-Koehler, 1999.

11. "Small players can more easily aggregate their power; collectives are on the rise." Korten, David C. *The Post-Corporate World: Life After Capitalism.* San Francisco: Berret-Koehler, 1999.

12. "Hypertext is the foundation for a hyperlinked organization and culture." Rifkin, Jeremy. *The Age of Access: The New Culture of Hypercapitalism Where All of Life Is a Paid-For Experience.* New York: Putnam/Tarcher, 2000.

13. "Products will always tend toward becoming more free." Kelly, Kevin, *New Rules for the New Economy: 10 Radical Strategies for a Connected World.* New York: Viking, 1998.

14. "An open system runs on imagination." Negroponte, Nicholas. *Being Digital.* New York: Vintage, 1996. Another great article on this topic is by Rushkoff, Douglas. "The People's Net." *Yahoo! Internet Life* 7(7) (July 2001): 79-83.

15. "There is a worldwide acceleration of alliances, no one can go it alone." Andersen Consulting. *Dispelling the Myth of Successful Alliances, Special Edition of Outlook.* New York: Andersen Consulting, 1999.

16. "We will balance richness and depth of service with reach and critical mass." Evans, Philip, and Thomas S. Wurster. *Blown to Bits: How the New Economics of Information Transforms Strategy.* Boston: Harvard Business School Press, 2000.

17. "The center of a network is the most powerful place." Kelly, Kevin, *New Rules for the New Economy: 10 Radical Strategies for a Connected World.* New York: Viking, 1998, 12.

18. "Nimble electronic keiritsus allow idea communities to shape an industry." Oliver, Richard W. *The Shape of Things to Come: 7 Imperatives for Winning in the New World Business.* New York: McGraw-Hill, 1999.

19. "Creative deconstruction." Peters, Tom. *The Circle of Innovation.* New York: Vintage, 1999. Also see Foster, Richard, and Sarah Kaplan. *Creative Deconstruction: Why Companies That Are Built to Last Underperform the Mark—And How to Successfully Transform Them.* New York: Doubleday, 2001.

20. "Successful companies have always deconstructed their core businesses." Wacker, Watts, Jim Taylor and Howard Means. *The Visionary's Handbook: Nine Paradoxes That Will Shape the Future of Your Business.* San Francisco: HarperBusiness, 2000.

21. "When deconstruction doesn't go far enough." Newspaper alliance described in: Evans, Philip, and Thomas S. Wurster. *Blown to Bits: How the New Economics of Information Transforms Strategy.* Boston: Harvard Business School Press, 2000, 41–43

22. "A corollary to outsourcing is if you do own something, get maximum mileage." Davis, Stan, and Christopher Meyer. *Blur: The Speed of Change in the Connected Economy.* New York: Warner, 1998.

CHAPTER 2: RETURN OF THE STORYTELLERS

1. "Life is examined on the stage." Russian playwright Nicolas Evreinoff quoted in Rifkin, Jeremy. *The Age of Access: The New Culture of Hypercapitalism Where All of Life Is a Paid-For Experience.* New York: Putnam/Tarcher, 2000.

2. "We are drowning in information, therefore we are hearing less." Shenk, David. *Data Smog: Surviving the Information Glut.* San Francisco: Harper, 1997.

3. "The numbers behind data smog." Ibid, 30–31. Other numbers from Postman, Neil. *Technopoly: The Surrender of Culture to Technology.* New York: Vintage Books, 1993, 69.

4. "Attention deficit disorder is a cultural event." Schwartz, Evan, contributing writer for *Wired.* Quoted in Shenk, David. *Data Smog: Surviving the Information Glut.* San Francisco: Harper, 1997, 38.

5. "Adaptive responses to data smog." Ibid, 38.

6. "We can't slow down from sound bites to prose." Spretnak, Charlene. *The Resurgence of the Real.* Reading, Mass: Addison-Wesley, 1997.

7. "Vocabulary is declining, the written word is no longer central to communication." Ibid, 114.

8. "We are media grazers, we no longer give it our full attention." Smith, J. Walker, and Ann S. Clurman. *Rocking the Ages: The Yankelovich Report on Generation Marketing.* New York: HarperBusiness, 1997.

9. "We don't want to hear nowhere, nothing, no time unless they're really good." Negroponte, Nicholas. *Being Digital.* New York: Vintage, 1996.

10. "Access versus brand; we buy because it's there, not because we heard about it." Kuchinskas, Susan. "The End of Marketing." *Business2.0* (November 2000). Also, McKenna, Regis. *Relationship Marketing: Successful Strategies for the Age of the Customer.* New York: Perseus, 1993.

11. "Each successive generation will see the further decline of the brand." Smith, J. Walker, and Ann S. Clurman. *Rocking the Ages: The Yankelovich Report on Generational Marketing.* New York: HarperBusiness, 1997, 89–105.

12. "The digital generation is already out the door; they are masters of avoidance." Tapscott, Don. *Growing Up Digital: The Rise of the Net Generation.* New York: McGraw-Hill, 1998, 193–194.

13. "It's not a new broadcast opportunity, it's a vehicle for avoiding intrusion." Ibid, 185.

14. "'Give it to me straight' is what works in this new advertising climate." Smith, J. Walker, and Ann S. Clurman. *Rocking the Ages: The Yankelovich Report on Generational Marketing.* New York: HarperBusiness, 1997, 90, 94.

15. "Fake buzz is easy to detect; it's hard to plant false opinions." Shreve, Jenn. "Virtual Viral Marketing Virus." *Wired* (November 2000): 119.

16. "We can tie the impulse to buy with the capacity to buy—the ultimate marketing goal." Reid, Rob. "The Impulse Economy." *Business2.0* premier issue (1998): 93.

17. "Marketing From the inside out." Martin, Chuck. *The Digital Estate: Strategies for Competing and Thriving in a Networked World.* New York: McGraw-Hill, 1997.

18. "Too many bells and whistles slow down access and drive customers away." Newman, Michael. "Dotcom Inferno: Money to Burn." *eCompany Now* (November 2000).

19. Ibid.

20. "Associate programs will represent a quarter of all on-line purchase." Schwartz, Evan. *Digital Darwinism: Breakthrough Business Strategies for Surviving in the Cutthroat Web Economy.* New York: Broadway Books, 1999, 80.

21. "Cost-effectiveness of associate programs." Ibid, 81.

22. "Ads become like salespeople—paid on commission when they get results." Ibid, 71–92.

23. "When stealing is helpful—a description of ThingWorld technology." Ibid, 90.

24. "Telemarketing is so painful it may help trigger the end of selling." Petzinger, Tom. *The New Pioneers: The Men and Women Who Are Transforming the Workplace and MarketPlace.* NewYork: Simon & Schuster, 1999.

25. "The need for early involvement in a product story." Levine, Rick, Christopher Locke, Doc Searls and David Weinberger. *The Cluetrain Manifesto: The End of Business as Usual.* New York: Perseus, 2000.

26. "If they are willing to go outside the box, there are brave new roles for visual artists." Prendville Roux, Julie. "Imaginary Forces." *Communication Arts* (March/April 2001): 78.

27. "With smart clothes and body nets, distinctions between off- and on-line will fade." Dertouzos, Michael. *What Will Be: How the New World of Information Will Change Our Lives.* San Francisco: HarperEdge, 1997.

28. "The psychology of the D Generation rests on a new fluid sense of self." Turkle, Sherry. *Life on the Screen: Identity in the Age of the Internet.* New York: Simon & Schuster, 1995.

29. "It's a new sensory focus, tactile more than visual, oral rather than visual." Kogan, Robert K. *The Fifth Language: Learning a Living in the Computer Age.* Toronto: Stoddard, 1995.

30. "Our self-concept is adapting by becoming more transient and situational." Lifton, Robert. *The Protean Self: Human Resilience in the Age of Fragmentation.* New York: Basic Books, 1993.

31. "Even physical products will become fluid with printers that spit out objects." Mark Pesce interviewed in Zalenski, Jeff. *The Soul of Cyberspace: How New Technology Is Changing Our Spiritual Lives.* San Francisco: HarperEdge, 1997.

32. "Culturally, we will transition from valuing things to acquiring experience." Rifkin, Jeremy. *The Age of Access: The New Culture of Hypercapitalism Where All of Life Is a Paid-For Experience.* New York: Putnam/Tarcher, 2000, 211.

33. "Even art will become a clumsy, dripping service contract." Tom Sachs, artist in Mary Boone Gallery. Quoted in "Fahrenheit Future: The Next Frontier." *Gentleman's Quarterly.* (September 2000): 166.

34. "The military funded all the early players in the game industry." Herz, J. C. *Joystick Nation.* New York: Little, Brown, 1997, 205.

35. "Stores as fantasy wonderlands." Popcorn, Faith, and Lys Marigold. *Clicking: 17 Trends That Drive Your Business—And Your Life.* New York: HarperBusiness, 1997.

36. "Public projects crave art; entertainment is the center of commercial development." Malone, Maggie, and Malcolm Jones. "A True Urban Legend." *Newsweek* (October 27, 2000): 74.

37. "Ads will have to consider new fictive forms in order to capture the imagination." Critique of similar model used by Levi Strauss offered by Gilbert, Jennifer. "More Lost Than Ever?" *Business2.0* (January 2001): 70.

38. "The Web is the locus of a new social reality." Renan, Sheldon. "The Net and the Future of Being Fictive." In Leeson, Lynn, ed. *Clicking In: Hotlinks to a Digital Culture.* Seattle: Bay Press, 1996, 61–69.

39. "Characters will weave in and out of each other's plots." Ibid, 64.

40. "The rise of the personal brands: The bigger you are the smaller you must appear." Wacker, Watts, Jim Taylor, and Howard Means. *The Visionary's Handbook: Nine Paradoxes That Will Shape the Future of Your Business.* San Francisco: HarperBusiness, 2000.

41. "The public is primed for self-exposure" according to a CNN/*Newsweek* poll. Platt, Charles. "Steaming Video." *Wired* (November 2000): 154.

42. "We won't need products; we'll do it by ourselves." Deanna Perry. Quoted in Tapscott, Don. *Growing Up Digital: The Rise of the Net Generation.* New York: McGraw-Hill, 1998, 189.

43. "It's not science fiction, just fiction and creative vision that will define the future." Donatella Versace. Quoted in *Gentleman's Quarterly* (September 2000): 254.

44. "Planet art is on the rise as the arts become central to healthy communities." Kirschner, Scott. "Seattle Reboots Its Future." *Fast Company* 46 (May 2001): 142.

CHAPTER 3: TRIBALMIND

1. "Real opinions make themselves known in an open communication environment." Levine, Rick, Christopher Locke, Doc Searls and David Weinberger. *The Cluetrain Manifesto: The End of Business as Usual.* New York: Perseus, 2000.

2. "Command and control is dissolving into the adaptive organization." Davis, Stan and Christopher Meyer. *Blur: The Speed of Change in the Connected Economy*. New York: Warner, 1998.

3. "Decentralization is central to any description of the new economy." *The Circle of Innovation*. New York: Vintage, 1999.

4. "The Web is built by layer upon layer of open, decentralized architecture." Rheingold, Howard. *Tools for Thought: The History and Future of Mind-Expanding Technology*. Cambridge: MIT Press, 2000. See also Berners-Lee, Tim, with Mark Fischetti. *Weaving the Web: The Original Design and Ultimate Destiny of the World Wide Web by Its Inventor*. San Francisco: Harper, 1999.

5. "Swarm intelligence." Kelly, Kevin. *Out of Control: The New Biology of Machines, Social Systems and the Economic World*. Boston: Addison-Wesley, 1994.

6. "Technology will become seamless, disappearing behind the cyber curtain." Also of interest is Rheingold, Howard. *Virtual Reality*. New York: Simon & Schuster, 1991.

7. "Learning is based on the ability to encompass ever greater complexity." Senge, Peter M. *The Fifth Discipline: The Art and Practice of the Learning Organization*. New York: Currency, 1990.

8. "Organizational knowledge is most often implicit, invisible and social." Seely Brown, John, and Paul Duguid. *The Social Life of Information*. Boston: Harvard Business School Press, 2000.

9. "Demand/supply curve refers to a new dynamic where customers define markets." Berners-Lee, Tim with Mark Fischetti. *Weaving the Web: The Original Design and Ultimate Destiny of the World Wide Web by Its Inventor*. San Francisco: Harper. 1999.

10. Breaking the market share habit." Peppers, Don, and Martha Rogers. *The One to One Future: Building Relationships One Customer at a Time*. New York: Doubleday, 1997.

11. "Few companies redefine their customers at the level that is truly possible." Gates, Bill. *Business @ the Speed of Thought: Using a Digital Nervous System*. New York: Warner Books, 1999.

12. "Dialogues as products—who and how we need to talk to someone is product." Lewis, Michael. *The New, New Thing: A Silicon Valley Story*. New York: Norton, 1999.

13. Pink, Daniel. *Free Agent Nation: How America's Independent Workers Are Transforming the Way We Live*. New York: Warner, 2001. Also see Bailey Reinhold, Barbara. *Free to Succeed: Designing the Life You Want in the New Free Agent Economy*. New York: Plume, 2001.

14. "Workers without walls define the future through or around the corporate agenda." Randsdell, Eric. "IBM's Grassroots Revival." *Fast Company* (October/November 1997): 11:184.

15. "The transparent organization rests on allowing everyone to see the big picture." Case, John. *The Open-Book Experience: Lessons From Over 1000 Companies Who Successfully Transformed Themselves*. Reading, Mass.: Addison-Wesley, 1998.

16. "Knowledge is the Center." Gates, Bill. *Business @ the Speed of Thought: Using a Digital Nervous System.* New York: Warner Books, 1999.

17. "Managing information now rests on maximum data/minimum control." Ito, Joichi, and Mazuko Ito. Interviewed in *Clicking In: Hot Links to a Digital Culture,* edited by Lynn Leeson. Seattle: Bay Press, 1996, 95

18. "The more bottom lines you feed, the more profits you can catch." Rosenbluth, Hal F., and Diane McFerrin Peters. *Good Company: Caring As Fiercely As You Compete.* Reading, Mass.: Addison Wesley, 1998.

19. "When commissions cost customers." Hartman, Curtis. "Sales Force." *Fast Company* (June/July 1997): 6: 136–138.

20. "It's who you know." Shrage, Michael. "The Debriefing: John Seely Brown." *Wired* (August 2000): 205.

21. "Why we need to rub elbows to get creative sparks." Kawasaki, Guy, and Michele Moreno. *Rules for Revolutionaries: The Capitalist Manifesto for Creating and Marketing New Products and Services.* New York: HarperBusiness, 1998.

22. "Creative types tend to be profoundly social." Quinn, James Brian, Jordan J. Baruch, and Karen A. Zien. *Innovation Explosion: Using Intellect and Software to Revolutionize Growth Strategies.* New York: Free Press, 1997, 111.

23. "Knowledge lives in conversation." Julian Orr in Seely Brown, John, and Paul Duguid. *The Social Life of Information.* Boston: Harvard Business School Press, 2000, 100–111.

24. "Giving people space allows them to find their tribal gene." Mitchell, Russ. "How to Manage Geeks." *Fast Company* (June 1999): 25:174.

25. "There are no secrets." Blanton, Brad. *Radical Honesty: How To Transform Your Life By Telling The Truth.* New York: Dell, 1996.

26. "Intimacy as leadership." DePree, Max. *Leadership Jazz.* New York: Dell, 1993.

CHAPTER 4: SONGLINES

1. "The aboriginal songlines rest on a vision of reality unfamiliar to the Western mind." Chatwin, Bruce. *The Songlines.* New York: Penguin, 1988, 12.

2. Ibid, 14.

3. "Often the best ideas are right in front of your nose." Rosenwein, Rivka. "The Spin-off: Hiding in Plain Sight." *Inc Magazine* (January 20, 2001): 54.

4. "Follow Your Bliss." Will Wright's SimCity. Discussed in Kelly, Kevin. *Out of Control: The New Biology of Machines, Social Systems and the Economic World.* Boston: Addison-Wesley, 1994.

5. "The real organization chart." Karen Stephenson of Net Form, described in Gladwell, Malcolm. "Designs for Working." *New Yorker* (December 11, 2000): 60.

6. "When the student is ready the teacher appears; if the group is ready leaders appear." DePree, Max. In Wheatley, Margaret J. *Leadership and the New Science: Discovering Order in a Chaotic World.* San Francisco: Berret Kohler, 1992, 22.

7. "A value shift." Ray, Paul. "The Rise of Integral Culture." *Noetic Science Review.* (Spring 1996): 4–15. Also see Elgin, Duanne, and Colleen Davis. "Global Paradigm Report." *Yes: Journal of a Positive Future.* (1997): 17.

8. "More values shift." The Hardwood Group study cited in Korten, David C. *The Post-Corporate World: Life After Capitalism.* San Francisco: Bennet-Kohler, 1999, 218.

9. "It's a shift of global proportions." World Value survey cited in Korten, David C. *The Post-Corporate World: Life After Capitalism.* San Francisco: Bennet-Kohler, 1999, 219.

10. "The heart can think and the body remembers." Childre, Dr. Lew, Howard Martin, with Donna Beech. *The HeartMath Solution: The Institute of HeartMath's Revolutionary Program for Engaging the Power of the Heart's Intelligence.* San Francisco: HarperSan Francisco, 2000.

11. "Feelings are integral to our thoughts." Pert, Candace, with Deepak Chopra. *Molecules of Emotion: Why You Feel the Way You Feel.* New York: Simon & Schuster, 1999.

12. "Interpersonal resonance and the power of prayer." Dossey, Larry. 2001. Interviewed by Michael Tom. In *New Dimensions* radio show. February 5–11.

13. "Every statement is holographic." Marcus, Bernie, Arthur Blank and Bob Andelman. *Built From Scratch: How a Couple of Regular Guys Grew the Home Depot to $30 Billion.* New York: Random House, 1999.

14. "Discovery is not an accident; it rests on a culture that supports risks." Collins, James C., and Jerry I. Porras. *Built to Last: Successful Habits of Visionary Companies.* New York: HarperBusiness, 1994.

15. "Organizational songlines:" Table built from material in: Collins, James C., and Jerry I. Porras. *Built to Last: Successful Habits of Visionary Companies.* New York: HarperBusiness, 1994; Hock, Dee. *Birth of a Chaordic Age.* San Francisco: Berret-Koehler, 1999; and Senge, Peter M. *The Fifth Discipline: The Art and Practice of the Learning Organization.* New York: Currency, 1990.

16. "Creativity is no accident." Collins, James C., and Jerry I. Porras. *Built to Last: Successful Habits of Visionary Companies.* New York: HarperBusiness, 1994.

17. "A learning community." Hopkins, Michael S. "Zen and the Art of the Self-Managing Company." *Inc. Magazine* (November 2000): 54–63.

18. "Following must be voluntary or leading doesn't exist." Collins, James C., and Jerry I. Porras. *Built to Last: Successful Habits of Visionary Companies.* New York: HarperBusiness, 1994, 67.

19. "Flock behavior." Kevin Kelly shows how flocking applies to group behavior. Kelly, Kevin. *Out of Control: The New Biology of Machines, Social Systems and the Economic World.* Boston: Addison-Wesley, 1994, 10-11.

20. "A city that works, a web of solutions." Hawken, Paul, Amory B. Lovins, L. Hunter Lovins. *Natural Capitalism: Creating the Next Industrial Revolution.* New York: Little, Brown, 1999, 288-301.

INDEX

We would love to hear your comments.
You can reach us at:

tarlow@digitalaboriginal.com
The Praxis Group,
P.O. Box 353,
Crestone, Co 81131
719-256-4330

For more information go to
www.digitalaboriginal.com